Child
Protection

SECOND EDITION

Jennie Lindon

Orders: please contact Bookpoint Ltd, 130 Milton Park, Abingdon, Oxon OX14 4SB. Telephone: (44) 01235 827720. Fax: (44) 01235 400454. Lines are open from 9.00 – 6.00, Monday to Saturday, with a 24 hour message answering service. You can also order through our website www.hodderheadline.co.uk.

British Library Cataloguing in Publication Data
A catalogue record for this title is available from the British Library

ISBN 0 340 876069

Impression number   10 9 8 7 6 5 4 3 2 1
Year   2007 2006 2005 2004 2003

Copyright © 2003 Jennie Lindon

Typeset by Fakenham Photosetting Ltd, Fakenham, Norfolk.
Printed in Great Britain for Hodder & Stoughton Educational, a division of Hodder Headline Plc, 338 Euston Road, London NW1 3BH by J. W. Arrowsmith Ltd. Bristol.

Dedication

To my parents, from whom I experienced respect and such very good care.
To my son and daughter, who continue to teach me about being a parent.

Contents

Acknowledgements

I appreciate how much I have learned from conversations with children, early years, school and playwork practitioners, other fellow-professionals, and with parents. In particular, I would like to thank Fiona Becker from the NSPCC Training Unit in Leicester, Liz Cowley formerly Senior Development Officer at the Early Childhood Unit, Kathy Forbes of Buckinghamshire Social Services and Lisa Payne from the National Children's Bureau. I learned a great deal about court processes by running joint workshops on the Children Act 1989 with local authority solicitors – with special thanks to Croydon and Lewisham.

One of the tasks of this revised edition has been to extend across the UK. Many thanks to Kevin Kelman (Deputy Head and early years author) and to Alice Sharp (Early Years Executive Scottish Independent Nurseries Association). I appreciate all the information from team members of the Scottish Child Law Centre, Children in Scotland, Children in Wales, NIPPA and Childcare Northern Ireland.

Since the first edition of this book, I have undertaken a considerable amount of training with a wide range of practitioners. I have greatly appreciated comments, questions and insights into how the system works in detail in different localities. I would like to give particular thanks to the many residential social workers and foster carers for whom I have run a child protection training programme in Essex.

The photographs were taken at the Pen Green Centre for the Under 5s and Their Families, Corby; many thanks to Margy Whalley for granting permission to reproduce the images.

The examples and scenarios were developed from real people and places. In every case I have changed the names of children or adults and any other details that could break confidentiality. The only exceptions are a couple of personal examples, which are mine to choose to share.

Foreword 1

Child protection, as Lord Laming reminded us again in his recent report on the tragic death of Victoria Climbie, is everyone's business. Protecting children from harm is the responsibility of parents and professionals working with children right through to senior managers and politicians. And this is particularly so for early childhood workers, who are working with the youngest and most vulnerable children on a daily basis. Whilst social workers, the police, and health workers may take lead responsibility for formal child protection processes and procedures, it is teachers, nursery and preschool workers, childminders and play workers who know young children best. They work with them day by day, and they are best placed to pick up, through observation, when there are early concerns for a child's safety and well-being.

Knowing how important it is to detect early signs of physical, social or emotional abuse, can however make early years practitioners anxious. Is this behaviour or those preoccupations of a particular child 'normal' or is it something I should be concerned about? Has the relationship between a child and her father when he drops her off in the morning become very tense, and how can I discuss the child's anxieties with her father? How can we work together as a team within the nursery to share our concerns and to make sure that our policies are not just reports that sit on the shelf in the office and gather dust?

The second edition of this popular book has been revised and updated to provide practitioners with practical help to understand what they can and should do in their crucial role as front line workers. It provides a comprehensive account of child abuse and how practitioners can recognise signs of abuse; it covers the legal framework of child protection; it considers appropriate policies and procedures, such as proper supervision and support systems; and points to the centrality of observation and record keeping. There are a number of excellent scenarios covering the range of situations that early years workers might come across in the course of their work, and helpful notes at the back that give guidance on how such situations could be handled.

But above all, this book points to the centrality of good practice in everyday work with young children as the key to good practice in child protection. How we observe children, how we assess their progress and keep records of their interactions and their development, how we listen to and communicate with children, how we manage challenging behaviour, and how we relate to parents – all of these are the foundation of good practice in child protection. This practical and accessible book will provide early years practitioners with both reassurance in what they know already, as well as plenty of material for continuing to develop their skills, knowledge and expertise.

Dr Gillian Pugh OBE
Chief Executive
Coram Family

Foreword 2

When 13-year-old Karen told me her secret I was totally unprepared. It was 1970 and I was working as a psychologist helping children who had problems in school. Karen was a bright child, who had always done well, but over the past year she had become sullen and withdrawn, her work had deteriorated and she often missed school. Although she was wary of our meetings, she did tell me that she had three brothers and that her father had been killed in an accident at work when Karen was just a baby. Her mother also met with me and together we did our best to find out why Karen was going through this 'rough patch'. After all, she was a budding teenager and that explained a lot of her behaviour.

Or so I thought. The shock for her mother and for me was finding out that the 'lovely' man her mother was seeing had been sexually abusing Karen for over a year and she was terrified to tell anyone. Why didn't I even suspect abuse? Because the statistics at that time indicated that there was one case of child sexual abuse per million of the population. It seemed impossible that the one in a million had walked into my office.

Even in 1984, when I started Kidscape, there was no category for sexual abuse on the Child Protection Register (then known as the At Risk Register). Of course, we now know that physical, emotional, and sexual abuse, as well as neglect of children, are much more widespread than we ever envisaged. We have come a long way in our quest to keep children safe, but we still have a long way to go. That is why I am so pleased to welcome this new edition of *Child Protection*. Jennie Lindon has done an excellent job of bringing together the issues we need to understand and deal with all forms of child abuse. This second edition of *Child Protection* is easy to use and full of important, essential up-to-date information.

As for Karen, though her mother and I tried our best, we could not get anyone to believe her. The man in question, an upstanding member of the community, denied everything. He probably went on to abuse many more children. Karen has had a difficult time and is bitter about the way she was treated. I know she would be glad that Jennie has written this book which will help us keep children safe from all forms of abuse. I highly recommend *Child Protection* to anyone working with children.

Michele Elliott
Director, Kidscape

Foreword 3

In today's rich media world children can feel that the world is a dangerous place for everyone. Children need adults, whom they trust, to help them as they make sense of their world, come to terms with the likelihood of certain events and how to cope. All children and young people need support, but some are especially vulnerable because abuse is part of their daily experience. These children and young people need effective child protection through legislation and practice in line with government guidance.

Child protection is the responsibility of everyone: of parents and other family members and of professionals. Adults need to be empowered to keep children safe. They need to support children and young people as they take on appropriate responsibility for themselves and other children. With the expansion in childcare services, there is an increasing number of adults whose work involves daily interaction with children. They need to know what constitutes child abuse, how it can be recognised and what can be done to prevent and deal with risks to children. All have clear responsibility for child protection. So, what do they need to know and what can they do?

Jennie Lindon helps to answer some of these questions by identifying what constitutes physical abuse, neglect, emotional abuse and sexual abuse. Each area is examined and the vital part that practitioners play in supporting children and their families is made clear. This book is a vital resource for all settings and individuals offering children's services. It is recommended for initial training, for practitioners new to childcare, for health and education services as well as those with years of experience. *Child Protection* is for everyone concerned with children.

Diane Rich
National Professional Officer
Early Education
(The British Association for Early Childhood Education)
www.early-education.org.uk

EARLY EDUCATION
Celebrating 80 years
1923-2003

Introduction

Child protection is a crucial part of good practice in all early years, school and out-of-school services. Some practitioners will work in teams and some work largely alone, for instance as childminders, nannies or foster carers. Yet the vital contribution of these professionals has sometimes been overlooked in guidelines for child protection.

This book was written to support early years, school and playwork practitioners. It provides the knowledge and understanding to help you develop a positive role with children, parents and other professionals. The book explains how your responsibilities fit into the broader system of child protection and describes how awareness of possible child abuse can appropriately shape your work with individual children and groups.

This book was first published in 1998 as *Child protection and early years work*. This edition has been written to address a number of issues that needed to be updated or extended. This second edition now covers child protection legislation and practice across the UK – encompassing not only England and Wales, but also Scotland and Northern Ireland. Issues in good practice and statistics have been updated to recognise changes since the late 1990s.

The first edition stretched into the school years, but this edition more extensively considers child protection for later childhood and the first years of adolescence. There is also more detailed recognition of child protection relating to children with disabilities. The suggestions for resources of books and useful organisations have been extended and updated. The resources have also been extended to internet websites.

Practitioners in early years, school and out-of-school services all have an important role to play in protection and prevention. The chapters of this book cover information and advice that will help you establish good practice and increase your awareness of what you are already doing that supports effective child protection.

Chapter 1 places the current approach to child protection in context through some historical background. The chapter then moves on to explain the different kinds of child abuse and possible warning signs that should concern practitioners.

Chapter 2 explains how the child protection system works as a whole, including the legal framework within which all professionals must operate throughout the United Kingdom (UK), and some variations between the four nations that comprise the UK. It is important to understand the broader context so that you can place your own work in relationship to the responsibilities of other professionals.

Chapter 3 covers how child protection policy and procedures work in action for different group settings and the different situations that can arise if you are a practitioner working mainly alone. This chapter, and the following chapters of the book, explores in detail how you may become involved in child protection and how good practice can be established within all parts of the service.

Chapter 4 covers how child protection concerns can arise in early years, school and out-of-school services and the ways in which those issues need to be acknowledged and handled.

Chapter 5 covers appropriate practice with children, parents and within the team when child protection has become an issue in the practice of a setting or as it affects practitioners who work more alone.

Chapter 6 covers how general good practice with children and young people can make a difference to their welfare and increasingly support their ability to share in their own care and personal safety.

This book covers a range of services and professionals, so some decisions had to be made about terminology:

▶ *Practitioner* is used to cover all adults who are working with children or families in a face-to-face situation. Readers of this book will have a range of experience, qualifications and job titles.
▶ *Setting* is used to refer to any group situation and therefore includes the many different kinds of early years centres and nurseries, pre-schools or playgroups, primary schools, after school clubs and holiday play schemes.
▶ *Parent* is used to cover those adults who are significant carers of children in their own family. Sometimes the most involved family member may be a grandparent.
▶ Adults and children may be male or female. In order to avoid the clumsy s/he and him/her, I have mainly used the plural. It will be clear in the text, when it is relevant whether a child or adult is male or female.

1

Understanding child abuse

Child abuse in context

In broad terms, child abuse is:

▶ Doing something to a child that should not be done: anything that will injure them physically, distress them deeply emotionally or seriously disrupt their natural development.
▶ Failing to do something for a child that should be done, for the sake of their well-being, safety or continued positive development.

Within this broad framework there are different types of action, or inaction, that could be considered abusive in their consequences for children, and these are covered in this chapter.

Development of a child protection approach

Moves to establish effective child protection developed in the second half of the twentieth century. Since the 1960s the following developments have taken place.

▶ The acceptance of the reality of child abuse. An acknowledgement that child abuse happens and that it cannot be explained away as a few isolated incidents.
▶ A greater awareness of the reality of different types of child abuse.
▶ A growing acceptance that such ill-treatment is abusive and cannot be excused as falling within the bounds of parental or institutional discipline.
▶ The growing conviction that no civilised society should tolerate the abuse of its youngest and most vulnerable citizens. So, there have to be limits to family privacy and the right of parents to decide how to treat their children. In a similar way, the heads and staff of institutions should be accountable for how they treat children and young people.
▶ The accepted approach of listening to children and of accepting that what they say is as likely to be true as what an adult says. The previous approach was to believe the adult's version in any conflict.

PHYSICAL ABUSE AND ILL-TREATMENT

Child protection, as we know it now, is a relatively recent development. But it would be a mistake to assume that previous generations were unaware or uncaring about the ill-treatment of children. Even when physical punishment was far more socially acceptable, there was concern that children might be deliberately injured by their parents.

In 1868 Ambroise Tardieu, who was a professor of legal medicine in Paris, described the deaths of children from battering or burning. In the same year, Athol Johnson was noting that some children were arriving with repeated bone fractures at the Hospital for Sick Children in London. There was a strong resistance to believing that parents could deliberately and frequently injure their own children – the injuries could be plausibly explained by the effect of rickets, which was very common in children at that time.

The first English Prevention of Cruelty to Children Act was passed in 1889 and created the option of prosecution. Prior to this law, any actions on behalf of children were taken personally by relatives or neighbours. The National Society for the Prevention of Cruelty to Children (NSPCC) was also established in 1889 and developed a national network of centres and inspectors. The NSPCC's long tradition of protecting children is the reason that child protection procedures offer a direct role in leading the process to representatives of the NSPCC.

Children with repeated, hard to explain, injuries remained a medical puzzle until 1961, when Henry Kempe, in a presentation to the American Academy of Paediatrics, described the **battered child syndrome** and opened up a serious debate that adults, including parents, sometimes intentionally injured children. Tragically it took the non-accidental death of a child to bring the reality of physical abuse effectively into the public arena. In 1973 seven-year-old Maria Colwell was battered to death by her step-father. Maria was known to be at risk by the local authority and the inquiry in 1974 criticised the lack of communication between the various agencies involved with the family. The child protection register, first known as an 'At Risk Register', was established in 1975 as a national requirement for all local authorities to improve contact in such cases between social workers, the police and the medical profession.

Recognition of the physical ill-treatment of children was the first established base of child protection. By the 1980s it had became socially unacceptable to support physical punishment within schools and institutions. Successive legislation within the UK has made it illegal for adults to use any kind of corporal punishment on children in state and independent schools, the full range of early years group settings prior to school and residential children's homes. Some anomalies remain in some parts of the UK over practitioners outside groups, such as childminders, and the law still allows parents to hit their children. You will find a more detailed discussion of the situation, legal and good practice, from page 195.

NEGLECT

It was also hard for adults to acknowledge that some carers, parents or those with parental responsibility, could be so seriously neglectful of a child's well-being that the child could be very damaged or even die. As awareness of this aspect of child protection grew, it became clear that some carers neglected more out of ignorance, or being overcome by highly stressful circumstances. However, some carers deliberately neglected, and sometimes also physically abused, a child out of intentional cruelty, resentment and dislike of a child.

EMOTIONAL ABUSE

There has been a growing understanding that children's development and well-being can be undermined by continuous verbal attacks within the family. Their emotional and physical well-being can be destroyed by persistent verbal cruelty. Although recognised as a real possibility for some children, this kind of abuse can be the hardest to document.

THE EXISTENCE OF SEXUAL ABUSE

Through the 1960s and 1970s there was a growing acknowledgement of the possibility of physical abuse of children by the adults who were supposed to care for their well-being. Through the 1980s another realisation developed, that adults might abuse children sexually, either within the family as incest or by other adults trusted to take care of them.

In 1984, Kidscape was the first organisation to highlight the problem of sexual abuse for children in the UK, developing a helpline and programmes in schools. ChildLine, started in 1985, offered children and young people a chance to talk in confidence. Both Kidscape and ChildLine have extended their service for children who want to confide about bullying.

The events in Cleveland during 1987 brought sexual abuse into public awareness when 121 children were diagnosed by doctors as having been sexually abused. Most were separated from their parents, although the majority were later returned. Like many high profile cases of sexual abuse, the events of Cleveland are still discussed and there is certainly not agreement about who was in the right. The professional concerns that were raised over the situation were a major contribution to the pressure for a new piece of legislation, the Children Act 1989 (see page 46).

INSTITUTIONAL AND PROFESSIONAL ABUSE

Initially, the focus for abuse was on ill-treatment in children's own homes, but several cases emerged through the late 1980s and 1990s that showed how professionals could also be involved in systematic abuse. Scandals emerged from children's residential homes, educational and day care settings. Abuse could be physical, sexual or emotional and was sometimes perpetrated by single individuals, but in some cases by more than one member of staff.

Children and young people have been especially at risk when they are cared for or educated within closed systems, such as boarding schools or residential children's homes. Children may have very limited opportunities to tell about abuse or neglect and a realistic fear that telling will make matters worse, because they have to live with, or otherwise have very close contact, with their abusers.

Where those abusers have a professional or other status, then outsiders may be disinclined to believe the children. There have been a number of child abuse cases from within sport and leisure services. Parents and other adults have sometimes been loath to question someone who is so generous with their time and skills. Children have sometimes been unsure whether they are right to speak out, wondering if the verbal or physical abuse is a legitimate part of the training process in their sport. In different areas, other professionals within the same system have sometimes been far more concerned about the status and integrity of their school, profession or religious faith than the well-being of children.

Some of the scandals that broke towards the end of the twentieth and beginning of the twenty-first century were historical. The children who had been abused were now adults, sometimes well into their adulthood. Outside events, and sometimes another person who has spoken out, have then brought disclosures from adults, who have never told what happened to them in their own childhood.

A PERSONAL EXAMPLE

Recognition of sexual abuse has developed in the last couple of decades of the twentieth century, but this is not a new problem for children. Both my parents described to me incidents from their own childhood when a respected local adult was charged with child molestation and sent to prison.

This occurred with two very different communities during the 1930s: a Welsh mining town and a small Hampshire village. In the one case it was the local Scout troupe leader and in the other it was the choirmaster. Neither of my parents experienced direct problems with the people concerned, but they told me how the local children sensed something wrong about the behaviour of each of these men, even when they were not the children being molested. In the case of the scout master, boys had complained to their parents that they did not want to go away to camp with this man and his wife, but the children's concerns were usually dismissed. The choirmaster was known as a 'creep' and none of the girls wished to sit too close to him. In each case, local parents were shocked when the man was eventually arrested and imprisoned; the children were not at all surprised.

COMMENTS

▶ It would be inappropriate for you to ask anyone about such experiences out of the blue, but you may find that through conversation, reading or television programmes you will extend your understanding of how sexual abuse was part of the experience of some children in previous generations.
▶ Many children will not have been affected directly, but they have childhood memories of adults whom they sensed were not to be trusted, who overstepped unspoken boundaries in how adults should relate to children.
▶ A strong theme in teaching children self-protection is to support them in trusting their feelings of unease about any adult and to take them seriously if they express such concerns (see also page 205).

Who are the abusers?

Children are most likely to be abused or neglected by people who are well known to them: adults or young people who are family, friends or in a position of trust and responsibility for the child. The idea that children are at a great risk from strangers has arisen from media attention to the very few tragic cases of child abduction or unprovoked physical and/or sexual attack.

The most likely abuser is an adult, but young people (under 18s) have abused children who are known to them or for whom they are temporarily responsible. Actions between children that would be judged physically abusive, if done by an adult, will probably be dealt with through anti-bullying programmes in schools or other settings. Bullying has been taken with considerably more seriousness over the last decade or so. (See also the discussion on page 198).

Male abusers are far more common than female in the area of sexual abuse. However, sexual abuse is not exclusively by men. There are female sexual abusers and of course some women are capable of serious physical and emotional abuse and neglect. So it is very important for child protection to avoid the inaccurate view that somehow children are overall more at risk from men. Young people and even children have been involved in sexual abuse of peers or younger children and some vicious bullying has taken on a sexual element. When children and young teenagers are involved in abuse it is very likely that any action would include child protection concerns for the abusing children and young people themselves, as well as for those whom they have abused. It is very possible that children who abuse have themselves been on the receiving end of ill-treatment or some kind of abuse.

There is a great variety in the patterns of abusive behaviour and likely abusers. Abusers come from all social and ethnic groups. No predictions can be made with certainty that this 'kind of person' is very likely or unlikely to abuse on the basis of their group identity. Abusers have included members of professions that are based on trust, such as youth practitioners, social workers in residential homes, day care and educational staff and clergy from a range of world faiths.

There are a number of possible reasons why people abuse or neglect children and some of these are discussed within this chapter. Of course, explanations are neither excuses nor justification for allowing abuse to continue unchallenged. But useful work, that will help children and families, has to take some account of how the abusing situation may have arisen.

How common is child abuse?

One way of assessing the extent of child abuse is to look at the numbers of children on all the local child protection registers. The total numbers on the registers do not cover all the children and families involved in the child protection process. Some concerns about children and parents are judged to be best resolved through other measures such as family support (see page 154).

In the first edition of this book, I offered national statistics from 1994 for England. Statistics of this kind are gathered for the year completed at the end of March in each instance. In March 1994 there were 34,900 children on all the registers in England. The incidence of abuse is higher than the total number of children on all the registers because, however hard the social services and related professions work, some cases will not come to light. Additionally, it is not the same children on the registers year by year. For instance, in the year that ended in March 1995, 34,954 children were on the registers in England. But during that year the names of 30,225 children had been taken off the register and 30,444 added.

Figures for England from the end of March 2000, 2001 and 2002 offer a comparison of the earlier data and the following section also provides data from Wales and Scotland. Northern Ireland does not provide such national statistics at the time of writing (early 2003), but it is planned that they should be collected and published in the future.

▶ In England at the end of March 2000 there were 30,300 under 18s in total on the local child protection registers around the country. To put this figure in perspective, this total is 0.27 per cent of the population of children and young people aged 0–18 years in England. So there are a large number of children within the child protection system, but the overwhelming majority of children are not abused.

▶ As the statistical year ended in March 2001 for England there were 26,800 children (0–18s) on the registers. Over the twelve months of that year, about 27,000 names were added to the register and about 30,200 removed. These figures give you some idea of the changeover within a year and that the significant movement shown by the 1994 figures is still usual.

▶ At the end of March 2002, there were 25,700 0–18s on child protection registers. Over the year there had been 27,800 registrations and 28,800 de-registrations. 14 per cent of the children added to the registers had previously been on a child protection register. 10 per cent of the children de-registered had been on the register for over 2 years, so the majority had spent less than this time on the register.

The number of children and young people in total on the registers has been steadily declining over the 1990s and into the new century. The reduction does not necessarily suggest that less children are at risk. It is more likely that, in response to new guidelines in the mid- and late 1990s, professionals in the child protection system are more alert to protection through bringing in family support services, which may avoid the need for use of the register.

The child population is largest in England, compared with other countries within the UK. The figures from the rest of the UK are comparable in terms of the lower absolute numbers in the population of 0–18s:

▶ In Scotland, for instance, there were 2361 children on the child protection registers across the country in the year ending March 1999. Within the same period of time, just over 1900 children had been removed from the register. The figures for the end of 2001 were 2000 children and young people, and at the end of 2002 were 2018 under 18s. (The website does not give the end of 2000 figures.)
▶ In Wales in March 2000 there were 2416 children on the local registers, forming 0.36 per cent of the population under 18 years. The figures for the end of March 2001 were 2126 under 18s.

The child protection statistics quoted in this section are public information and the easiest way to access them, and other social care data, is via the government websites.

▶ The figures for England are available on the Department of Health website www.doh.gov.uk
▶ For Wales, go into www.wales.gov.uk
▶ For Scotland, access www.scotland.gov.uk
▶ Similar national statistics are not yet collected in Northern Ireland. There are plans to make such data available and new developments will be posted on the useful UK site of www.childpolicy.org.uk_

The pattern varies in each website and also changes over time. You usually track through areas of the site titled statistics or bulletins, and sometimes through social care or children's services. The search or index facility is sometimes useful, but not always.

Another way investigators have used to judge the extent of abuse is to ask adults to recall the events of their childhood and to classify bad experiences on whether they would be judged as abusive. This method has been used in trying to survey the extent of sexual abuse, but the approach has significant problems. For instance, David Finkelhor reviewed studies of sexual abuse in the United States. He reported that, depending on whose figures you took, you would predict prevalence rates in the general population of anything from 6–62 per cent for females and 3–31 per cent for males. The working definition of sexual abuse had varied from minor, though unwanted sexual attentions (which the study respondents themselves might not classify as abuse) through to increasing intrusive forms of physical contact. The percentages were highest when the definition of sexual abuse was made very wide.

Physical abuse

Physical abuse is defined as the actual, or likely physical injury, to a child or young person. Children may be physically abused through direct attack or by an adult's deliberate failure to protect them from injury or suffering. Physical abuse, with accompanying neglect, is the most common form of maltreatment of children. It is important to bear this fact in mind, since some discussion of child abuse and some media coverage imply that sexual abuse is the most prevalent risk to children.

Children and young people who are physically abused may be ill-treated in different ways:

▶ Children have been hit with hands, fists and with implements.
▶ They have been shoved or shaken hard, so that injury is almost inevitable.
▶ It is potentially dangerous to shake any child with violence, but babies are especially at risk from shaking. A child or young person will manage to brace their head and shoulders, at least against limited shaking. However, babies do not have the muscle strength to protect themselves and their heads are relatively heavy. Babies easily sustain neck damage and internal damage to their brain.
▶ Children have been bitten, burned or deliberately scalded, squeezed with violence or half-suffocated.
▶ Physical abuse has included deliberate poisoning of children with household substances, the inappropriate use of alcohol, drugs or prescription medicines.
▶ Abuse has also included ill-treatment of children that has frightened them,

for instance, shutting children in cupboards or other confined and dark spaces.

Signs that should concern you

The most likely warning signs of the physical abuse of children are injuries, perplexing illnesses, or a continuing pattern of accidents to a child for which the responsible adult(s) give no believable explanation.

The relevant carers will often be the child's parents, but some children are cared for by other relatives. The same pattern of concern should be triggered within early years, school and out-of-school services, when the child's injuries or unexplained symptoms are arising within the centre day or session. Cases of child abuse generally arise within the family but there have been instances when child care or education practitioners have been responsible for the abuse or neglect.

It is important to recall that young children collect a large number of bumps and bruises in the normal course of their play. Physically bold children, with a limited understanding or concern about risks, can have an early childhood full of minor, but understandable injuries. Even very responsible parents or practitioners can find that a child has sustained a more serious injury, such as fractured or broken bones, in a well-supervised setting that has been made as safe as possible. So, a consideration of possible physical abuse has to be *both* the visible injury to the child *and* the explanation of how this injury was caused.

This section continues with the signs that should concern you and be taken further. The steps you should take will be laid out in your setting's child protection procedures and your local guidelines. Details are discussed in Chapters 3 and 4.

ACCIDENTAL OR NON-ACCIDENTAL?

It will not be your job to make an assessment of whether a child or young person's injuries are definitely accidental or non-accidental. However, your knowledge of child development, and of this child or young person in particular, will be valuable. You would consider some of the following, initially to weigh up whether there is cause for concern:

▶ The age and mobility of a child — for instance a baby or a physically disabled older child is not going to manage the same kind of lively play and generally getting into 'playful mischief' that can be usual for an active three- or four-year-old.

▶ The explanation from the child and their openness about a bruise or bump. Many children are rather proud of their minor injuries from falls or understandable domestic accidents, and are only too keen to show you and tell their tale.

▶ The explanation from the relevant adult(s) who was responsible for the child at the time.

▶ The location and type of injury – some injuries may raise greater levels of concern than others.

▶ Whether this child has a sequence of accidents, each of which may come with an explanation, but which build to a serious catalogue of events.

You should be concerned about children who have injuries for which there is no obvious explanation. Be wary about improbable explanations or excuses, given by an adult or by the child, when the explanation keeps changing or if there is a refusal to discuss the reason for an injury. Initial unlikely explanations still cannot be seen as proof of abuse. Some children may, for instance, give a strange reason for their injury, but further conversation with the child and parent reveals that children have produced this story because they were doing something they should not. Under these circumstances, the children, even young teenagers, are most worried about getting into trouble themselves. They cannot foresee that their unlikely version of events could bring suspicion on their parent or other carer.

A continuing pattern of odd accidents, even if each individual explanation seems possible, may be a warning sign of abuse or a neglectful lack of supervision. Again, a worrying pattern cannot be taken as proof without further exploration. Children may be abused or so poorly supervised that they get hurt too easily. But some children have problems of physical co-ordination or may be found to have failing eyesight. A few children have brittle bone disease, which means that very minor accidents can create fractures and breaks. Anyone involved has to keep an open mind when the worries first emerge.

You will find further discussion about possible accidental and non–accidental injury on page 124.

VISIBLE INJURIES

Injuries may include bruising, black eyes, fractured or broken limbs, burn or bite marks. Bruises to the bony parts of children's bodies, such as elbows and knees, are more usually the result of normal childhood bumps and scrapes. Whereas bruising to the softer parts, such as upper arms, thighs and cheeks may result from pinching, biting or beating. Do bear in mind, of course, that you must avoid leaping to assumptions about who has inflicted the injuries. Sometimes a careful exploration with a child will highlight that the injuries are the result of bullying by other children.

Many children have slight differences of colouration in their skin, but this variation can look like bruising on dark-skinned children, especially of African-Caribbean, Mediterranean and Asian origin. These naturally occurring patches are called mongolian blue spots. They have a defined edge and are a consistent slate blue in colour, unlike genuine bruising that tends to vary in shade and changes over a period of days.

Children may sometimes tell you that someone is hurting them. But sometimes they are as concerned to hide their ill-treatment as the adults who are inflicting it. So, you should be alert to a child who is very reluctant to undress for games or for a routine medical check or to uncover their limbs in the hotter weather – **unless** there is an alternative explanation for their unease. Some children have family reasons of culture or religion why they do not want to undress and these should be respected. Other children are very self-conscious about their bodies because other children have been rude about their size, shape or skin problems like eczema.

THE BEHAVIOUR OF A CHILD OR YOUNG PERSON

There may be behavioural signs that all is not well with a child or young person, and the underlying reason may sometimes, but not always, be that there is a pattern of abuse.

- ▶ You should be concerned about children who are very reluctant to go home at the end of the day or session, or resistant to going with a particular family member.
- ▶ Self-destructive tendencies in children are a warning sign of emotional disturbance, although not necessarily abuse. You should not ignore evidence of self-harm; it is in no way a normal phase of development. Young children may show worrying patterns such as pulling out their own hair or head banging. Older children and young people may show self harm by cutting themselves or such risky patterns of behaviour that they are almost certain to be injured.
- ▶ Children who are persistently aggressive towards other children will need clear adult guidance away from this pattern of behaviour. Actions from

children, that would be called physically abusive from adults, are likely to be dealt with in the context of bullying. A positive approach to behaviour in any setting should avoid a punitive focus and give opportunities that help children and young people to redirect (see page 192). However, supportive adults need to notice children and young people who have developed strong habits of cruelty and physical attack. You have to question how they have learned this pattern of behaviour and there is a possibility that they are imitating what has been done to them.

▶ Young children need to learn how to be careful with animals and understand that pets can be hurt. You should be concerned about older children who are cruel to animals, especially if they are unresponsive to clear adult boundaries. Joint work between the RSPCA and NSPCC has shown that some children who abuse animals have themselves been physically abused and are working out their anger and pain on a more vulnerable creature than themselves. In violent households, cruelty to animals may be part of the more general abusive pattern led by adults' behaviour.

In all these situations, you will begin to make sense of your concerns in the light of your knowledge of the usual range of behaviour for this age group, as well as any factors such as learning disability that affect realistic expectations.

ACTIVITIES AND QUESTIONS

The majority of parents whose children sustain minor or more major injuries are not abusing their children and it is important to bear this point well in mind. You will find more on positive ways to communicate with parents in Chapter 5. You can use this activity now to develop your insight into the parent's perspective when someone is questioning an injury to their child.

All group settings and individual practitioners, such as childminders, should keep an accident book. You need to log any injuries that children experience while they are under your responsibility. Take a considered look at all the incidents over the last few months.

1 Do one or two children appear much more often than others in the records?
2 Are there some incidents when the children's injuries seem surprisingly serious, given the situation in which they occurred?
3 Are there some areas of the setting or pieces of equipment that seem to be the focus of more minor accidents than others?

A careful review of the accident book can often point to improvements in practice, or tell you that one or two children seem to be especially vulnerable. But imagine that someone used these incidents to challenge you, with comments like:

▶ 'You're clearly not taking proper care of Sam. Otherwise how come he keeps having all these accidents?'
▶ 'You can't be telling me the whole truth. Erin couldn't have got this badly hurt just playing about on a grassy slope!'

How might you feel, or how have you felt, when you have been put firmly on the spot by parents who were not satisfied with your explanation of how their child was injured in the centre? Discuss these issues with your colleagues and use the insights to help you to see both sides of this kind of difficult conversation.

Possible reasons underlying physical abuse

Children are physically abused by adults, or by young people, for a number of reasons. It is important to understand the possible reasons because work with families and individuals has to take account of circumstances. But reasons are not, of course, excuses or justifications for abusing children.

▶ Family stresses are sometimes taken out on the child(ren). Financial and other worries may make parents less patient or they may focus their anger on the person close at hand, the child.
▶ Young parents or carers who are unsupported may become overwhelmed with the responsibility for babies or young children. Their frustration or panic may combine with a genuine ignorance of how their actions can injure children.
▶ Physical discipline may get seriously out of hand as a parent's frustration or temper leads to fiercer attempts to control a child's perceived misbehaviour.
▶ Some adults, for a variety of reasons in their own background, relish inflicting cruelty on others, and children are an easy target. Powerless adults may enjoy wielding a sense of power over the young and vulnerable.
▶ Within families, one child may be abused, when another is left unharmed. The twisted thinking in the family may be that this child is the bad one or the unwanted child.
▶ The abuse of children may be part of a broader pattern of domestic violence in this home.

▶ A small minority of adults who deliberately injure children are seeking attention for themselves through the apparent medical emergencies in their children. This pattern is called Munchausen Syndrome by Proxy — see below.

Risks from domestic violence

The term **domestic violence** is sometimes used only to mean male violence towards their female partners or ex-partners. Statistics indicate that men are most often the perpetrators of violence in the home, but it has to be recognised that in a small minority of cases it is the woman who is violent, towards her partner or their children. Domestic violence or domestic abuse is not only linked with poverty or stressful living conditions; the situation can arise in any social class or ethnic group.

Children are adversely affected by living in a home where there are regular violent disputes. Their emotional well-being and psychological development is poorly affected even if they do not suffer any physical abuse themselves. The likely risks are that:

▶ Children are distressed by continuing arguments in their home and by the threat of possible violence. They may be torn by conflicting loyalties between their parents and can also be pulled into the damaging secret that nobody outside the family is to know how bad matters have become.
▶ Children may fail to be protected in a home full of violence. Conflicts between the adults may erupt into physical attack and the children are caught in the middle. The adults may not intend that the children are injured and they do not directly attack them, but the adults' violent behaviour injures children as bystanders.
▶ Men prone to violence sometimes also attack children or threaten to do so in order to control their partners. Children in violent homes are sometimes physically or sexually abused by the father or stepfather.
▶ Parents under extreme stress are not in a position to offer their children the kind of support that is necessary for healthy development and some mothers or fathers may divert their frustration and anger onto the children. Children in their turn may become aggressive to other children, or may turn in on themselves to become distressed and withdrawn.

Munchausen Syndrome by Proxy

Munchausen Syndrome was first described in 1951 by psychiatrist Richard Asher who was seeing adult patients who deliberately made themselves ill or claimed to have a variety of serious symptoms in order to gain medical attention. These people often sought very intrusive medical procedures, such as unnecessary operations, at a whole series of different hospitals. The name derives from the highly unlikely tales told by Baron von Munchausen, a traveller and writer.

In 1977 the term was extended by Roy Meadow to describe the behaviour of adults who claimed that a child in their care was seriously ill when this was not the case. Adult carers, in most cases the mother, reported a series of imaginary symptoms for the child or interfered with medical investigations to make the claims appear supported. In a few cases adults were actually causing injury to the child which led to dramatic symptoms. Meadow called this pattern of disturbed adult behaviour **Munchausen Syndrome by Proxy**, and it has also been known as **Meadow's Syndrome**, fabricated illness syndrome or illness induction. This situation is specifically included as a form of physical abuse of children.

It is important for you to realise that this syndrome is rare. So you should not swiftly assume this is a likely explanation when a parent is persistently concerned about the health of a child when there is no easy or immediate explanation of what is the matter. There is plenty of anecdotal evidence that concerned parents have been proved to be right in their worries, although medical or other professionals could not initially find an explanation or diagnosis.

Parents and other carers who claim healthy children are ill or who deliberately harm children to create a medical emergency seem to feed off the drama of the situation. They seek the reflected attention onto themselves of having a dramatically or frequently ill child. Some seem to like the kudos of being seen as an important and self-sacrificing carer for the child. The end result for children is unnecessary illness and medical intervention and confusion over their own health and well-being. A few children have died as a result.

Female circumcision/female genital mutiliation

In the 1996 revision of *Working together*, the Department of Health specifically included female circumcision as a form of physical abuse. Female circumcision, in any of its forms, has been illegal since the Abolition of Female Circumcision Act of 1985. The recognition that this practice is a form of abuse has led to its being described as female genital mutilation (FGM).

FGM is practised by some Muslim communities in North African countries such as Somalia and the Sudan (and also some Christian communities) and Middle Eastern countries such as the Yemen and also parts of Indonesia. Muslims who reject the practice argue that there is no basis in the Qur'an for what is a cultural, not a religious, tradition. However, communities and families who promote FGM regard it as a crucial part of how girls become women and a means to ensure that daughters are marriageable. Families living in the UK have been able to find some doctors who are prepared to circumcise their daughters and some traditional circumcisers operate illegally in this country. Otherwise mothers or grandmothers take the girls back to the family's country of origin in order to obtain the operation.

The practice has been made illegal in the UK because the procedure results in considerably greater mutilation of the private parts of females than the usual circumcision procedure for males. Girls either have the clitoris cut or suffer the removal of all the external labia and almost complete sewing up of the vaginal opening (infibulation). The circumcision itself can be very painful, since traditional circumcisers do not necessarily use pain relief. Girls can bleed dangerously and be left with pelvic infections, gynaecological problems and later difficulties with childbirth.

The issue of FGM is one in which child protection concerns are in inevitable conflict with the wish to respect the usual practices of some religious or cultural groups. It is an important reminder that respect for any cultural practices should never override concern for children's well-being. The most important guiding principle is that a cultural practice should not lead to the injury or any other ill-treatment of a child. Child protection teams who face this issue have to be ready to justify their stance from the legal perspective and the well-being of the girls involved. The team will also need to offer support for those families and girls who wish to break with the practice, since they are likely to face hostility from their community. You are unlikely to encounter the practice unless you work in a school or after-school club, since girls from these communities tend to be circumcised from between four to twelve years of age.

There is not an equivalent stance about male circumcision, although many people feel strongly that this is an inappropriate practice, unless there are very clear medical indications for the removal of a boy's foreskin. In previous generations the circumcision of baby boys was more common in the UK on the grounds of easier personal hygiene, but this practice has now been discredited. Some Jewish and Muslim groups regard male circumcision as an important religious and cultural rite.

Children who are HIV-positive

In their booklet, *Children and HIV – guidance for local authorities* the Department of Health made it clear that a child's being HIV-positive is **not** in itself sufficient reason to place the child on the child protection register. Services should be provided to the children on the same basis as their peers.

Certainly some families whose children are HIV-positive may have been afraid of seeking help because of their wariness of local child protection procedures. The way through which a child has become infected might, on the other hand, give rise to child protection issues. For instance, if there was evidence that the HIV infection had been transmitted through sexual abuse or gross neglect of the child such that they had come into contact with infected needles.

Practitioners will not necessarily know if a child is HIV-positive, since it is not required that carers are informed of this health condition. Normal good practice for hygiene and first aid in the centre should provide adequate protection. The main issues will be about care in dealing with cuts, abrasions, nose bleeds and other bodily fluids.

Neglect

Abuse through neglect is a continuing pattern in the treatment of a child or dependent young person. Persistent and severe neglect can include different kinds of failure to care properly for a child. Neglect can be difficult to assess in practice and this form of abuse has received rather less attention from the media than physical or sexual abuse. Neglectful treatment could arise in the following ways:

▶ Children may be given inadequate food so that they are malnourished or actually starving. Neglected children have sometimes been found going through dustbins for food.
▶ Very young children, and some older children with disabilities, need considerable support with feeding. Neglectful adult carers may unrealistically expect children to feed themselves or rush to feed a baby or child in such a careless way that the food will almost inevitably come back up again.
▶ To date, neglect of children's nutritional needs has been focussed on insufficient food and malnutrition. However, there is the strong possibility that parents, and other carers, will be regarded as neglectful if they allow children to eat excessive amounts of food and seriously imbalanced diets.

Obesity is a growing problem in the UK, with serious health implications. Adults are responsible for guiding children in healthy eating habits.

▶ Children are not given warm enough clothes for the time of year, so are cold and ill throughout the winter months. Children may be in unheated bedrooms with insufficient bedclothes for the temperature. Children, especially very young ones who are unable to climb out of their cot and find more layers, have died of hypothermia and related neglect, even in households where the adults are warm and healthy.

▶ Sometimes, parents or other carers have grossly neglected a child's basic physical needs so that they are dirty, remain for ages in unchanged nappies or have infections that would have improved with basic medical attention.

▶ Leaving young children home alone or with inappropriate carers would be regarded as neglectful, although the legal situation in England is rather odd (see below).

It is important not to underestimate the risks of severe neglect to babies and children. Some children have died as the direct consequence of neglect, and others have been in a very poor state of health and general development when the seriousness of their situation has been realised. Various inquiries into child abuse have raised awareness that families who are neglectful of their children have sometimes drifted for a long time, perhaps years, even with social work support. But nobody had made a comprehensive assessment that the family has gone beyond the bounds of 'acceptable parenting'. The input of practitioners who see the child regularly can be crucial in this kind of situation. You notice what is happening with children and can observe and record their health and general well-being.

A concern that parents are doing what appears to be their best under difficult circumstances has to be balanced by an objective view of what is happening to the children. Some local child protection guidelines have explicitly recognised that support work focussed on adults, for instance over drug or alcohol addiction, must never be allowed to mask the importance of assessing children's well-being when these adults are parents.

Home alone and young carers

Young children, or older children with disabilities, are not able to take care of themselves without adult support. So parents, or other carers, who leave them alone will be judged neglectful, because of the high risk that children could come to harm. In England, unlike Scotland, there is no legislation that determines how old a child must be before they are left alone at home (12 years in the Scottish legislation). However, English adults can be prosecuted for neglect and cruelty because of actual injury or the high likelihood that a child or young person could come to harm under the circumstances, including the length of time they were left on their own. In England, it is not possible to hand over responsibility for a child to anybody younger than 16 years of age. So parents remain responsible for the actions of younger day or evening sitters. The teenage sitters can themselves also be held accountable for abusive or neglectful actions that they can be expected to have understood.

Practitioners in school and out–of–school services need to take care over different family patterns. School age children and young people can be competent and able to manage some, or much, of their own care, and to be responsible members of the family. Within some social and cultural groups it is much more usual that children help with domestic tasks and with the care of younger children. So, it would be important to avoid criticism of a family pattern only because it does not fit your own cultural experience. However, practitioners still need to be alert to inappropriate or heavy responsibilities on a child and the well-being of young siblings, if an older brother or sister takes on much of their care. There would also be cause for concern if young carers' responsibilities meant that they missed school or were unable to complete homework on a regular basis.

In the UK there is a hidden group of young carers who take over family responsibilities as a result of the physical or mental illness of a parent. The children and young people are often very concerned to hide the level of their domestic responsibility for the fear that their family will be disrupted by the intervention of social services. Legitimate concerns about the well-being of the young carers have to be pursued within the possibilities of family support, as well as respect for what the children and young people have managed. Precipitate action otherwise brings about the family breakdown that the young carers have struggled so hard to avoid.

Signs that should concern you

Children who are neglected will show a pattern of the results of their poor care, for instance:

▶ They may be thin (health records show that they fail to put on weight). A malnourished child can be tired and lethargic.
▶ If you feed children in your setting, you may find that a child arrives desperate for food and eats a large amount when it is available. Their state of hunger may be noticeably greater after the weekend.

▶ Children may be regularly dressed inappropriately for the weather, for instance, thin summer clothes and sandals on a cold winter day. They may show the signs of being cold on a regular basis, for instance, chapped hands, chilblains or unnaturally reddened skin in a white child.

▶ Children and their clothes may not be kept clean so that they are dirty and/or smelly. Soiled clothes, such as underwear, may be put back on a child rather than removed for washing.

▶ Parents may be unreliable in bringing the child to the setting on a regular basis or in picking the child up at the end of the day or session. The parents themselves may be in an unsafe state to care for children: drunk or showing the effects of drugs.

▶ Children may have untreated medical conditions or infections that are left to worsen rather than improved with basic home care or seeking medical treatment.

▶ Sometimes all the children within a family are neglected, but it can happen that one child is singled out and is visibly treated worse than the other children.

Children who are neglected sometimes fall into the group described as showing faltering growth or a **failure to thrive**. However, babies and children certainly should not be classified as at risk in this way, unless there has been a careful assessment, over a period of time. The experience and records of all the professionals involved with the child and the family have to be taken into consideration. Faltering growth cannot be diagnosed just by plotting a baby or child on the average growth charts; these charts are based on variations around the average and some babies and children will always be on the 'light' side, just as some are on the 'heavy' side. Height and weight has a genetic component and small parents are likely to produce children who are smaller and lighter than the average. Some babies and children have digestion or allergy problems that affect their ability to keep food down or to digest it properly. Other children have eating problems and parents' understandable concern over mealtimes may inadvertently worsen the difficulties. Such families may appreciate advice from a practitioner, but they are not neglecting their children.

So, a number of possibilities has to be explored when concerns are raised about a child. Records of a child's physical and general development can be crucial in making sense of whether a child is being neglected. For instance, neglected children may be in considerably better health and energy after spending time away from their family.

Possible factors leading to neglect

By definition, neglect occurs in families that are functioning poorly but there may be different reasons for the difficulties. The distinction is made between primary parental incompetence, when parents have very little idea how to take care of a child and secondary parental incompetence, when circumstances are weighing down a parent who would otherwise be able to manage. Neither situation can be allowed to continue at the cost of the child's well-being, but some understanding of what is going wrong, and why, is important for decisions about how best to help.

In the case of primary parental incompetence, neglect may arise mainly from parents' lack of basic knowledge or understanding. For instance:

▶ Some parents may not know what to do because of their own childhood has given no useful experience of how adults care for children. They may themselves have been abused or neglected as children and have no positive model to help them.
▶ Parents with severe learning disabilities may not understand what a baby or young child needs and the consequences of poor care.
▶ Teenage parents who are still very young and without family support may also have little idea of what baby and child care involves. They may feel overwhelmed by the responsibilities and the change brought about in their life. Young mothers may also be stunned that a baby whom they hoped would satisfy their own emotional needs is a very needy individual.

These are all possibilities but, of course, there is no absolute link between these circumstances and child neglect, or abuse. Some adults who have experienced very unhappy or disrupted childhoods are able to be good parents to their own children. They have looked for positive models outside their own childhood or been guided by a supportive partner whose childhood was much happier. Parents with learning disabilities or very young mothers can often cope with appropriate support.

In the case of secondary parental incompetence, families would normally cope under favourable circumstances. However, adverse events have overwhelmed the ability of one or both parents to cope and the well-being of the children suffers. For instance:

▶ Parents may be experiencing extreme financial hardship, debts and all the worries that come in their wake. It is important to realise, however, that some families with serious money worries do not neglect their children and some families with no financial problems do neglect one or more of their children.

▶ Physical or mental illness in the family may have incapacitated the main carer of the children. Psychological disturbance in the main carer may also lead this adult deliberately to neglect one child in a family, who is seen as a problem, unwanted, the 'wrong' sex. Alternatively the parent's energy may be diverted to caring for a very sick or elderly family member. The children are being overlooked, effectively forgotten or expected unrealistically to take care of themselves.

▶ Parents who have continuing problems of alcoholism, substance abuse and other addictions, like gambling, are likely to lose sight of the needs of their children. Time, attention and family money may be diverted away from the children's needs and towards the addiction.

▶ In some families deeply held religious or philosophical views may lead to what is judged to be neglect from outside the family. Parents may refuse conventional medicines even when their preferred alternative methods are failing to help a very sick child. Parents may also refuse life-giving interventions such as blood transfusions; Jehovah's Witnesses are opposed to this treatment. These situations are very difficult since an outside authority has to judge the limits to any parent's right to decide. Parental preference is sometimes over-ruled legally in these circumstances.

Emotional abuse

All children who are abused are affected emotionally, to a greater or lesser extent. Therefore, it is reasonable to say that emotional abuse plays a part in all types of abuse, as these experiences will affect children's sense of security or trust, their belief in themselves as worthwhile individuals who deserve care and their likely feelings in the future towards other children and adults. However, for some children, a pattern of emotional abuse is the main or only form of abuse in their lives.

Emotional abuse is a persistent pattern of deliberate uncaring or emotionally cruel treatment of a child. It can be hard to detect and it is important neither to overreact nor to underestimate what appears to be happening to the child. A judgement of emotional abuse has to take account of patterns and a continuing experience for a child or children in a family or in a setting or a school in which a child is regularly targeted for emotional abuse. Persistent or severe emotional ill-treatment or rejection of a child has a negative effect on their all-round development and their behaviour. Children need to experience affection, security and encouragement. If these experiences are denied to them, the children can doubt their own worth, their ability to make relationships or their capacity to learn and deal with life. Children may be physically unharmed but so badly affected by emotional abuse that they are in poor health or react by harming themselves. Children and young teenagers can be seriously depressed by this experience. The emotional and psychological scars can last well into adulthood.

Emotional abuse might take the following forms:

▶ Children are verbally abused, told they are 'stupid', 'useless', 'ugly' or 'should never have been born'.
▶ They may be subjected to continuous criticism or faced with unrealistically high adult expectations, which no child could ever meet.
▶ Their interests and achievements are ridiculed or compared unfavourably with someone else, perhaps a favoured sibling.
▶ Any apparent affection felt by the parent is made dependent on the child's behaviour or achievements. Children may never feel sure of their parents' love nor can easily predict what will make them withdraw their affection.
▶ Children may be overprotected to a unrealistic extent so that they cannot gain any sense of confidence or appropriate self-reliance. The continuous message is that they are incompetent or unable to deal with circumstances outside the home. Parental overprotection can be hard to assess, especially where a child or young person's disability or health condition means that a higher level of care is necessary.
▶ Communication with the child may be distorted so that adults use their maturity inappropriately to make a child feel guilty for family situations that are not and cannot be the child's responsibility.
▶ Children may also be emotionally damaged by experiences of domestic violence (see also page 15) or family conflict. Children may feel torn between two disputing parents and the adults may deliberately use the children to vent their own feelings or verbally to attack their partner.
▶ Some children and young people face such a barrage of verbal threats and personal attack, even without physical abuse, that they describe their experience as a kind of emotional terrorising.

Children and young people can on occasion be emotionally cruel to each other. An effective bullying policy and practice in school and out-of-school settings needs to recognise that verbal cruelty can be as devastating to a child's well-being as physical attack (see page 198). However, rather like physical aggression, you should be increasingly concerned about children and young people who have a pressing need to be emotionally cruel to others. Again, you should wonder to what extent they were recycling verbal abuse and threats that formed their own daily experience.

Families can go through difficult times and parents try their utmost not to take out their stress on their children. Some parents respond well to help from relatives, friends or trusted practitioners who are involved with children and the family. Parents acknowledge the difficult situation that has developed and are prepared to work towards changing it. Other parents, and some carers, are resistant to acknowledging what is happening or to change the situation. They persist in believing that the child deserves the emotional abuse, the fault and responsibility all lie with the child.

Signs that should concern you

No adult, however caring, manages to be patient and considerate with children all the time. Parents are not perfect and sometimes they get cross or their own concerns temporarily overwhelm them. Normally considerate practitioners may look back and feel that they did not give children the attention they needed or the adults jumped to an unfair conclusion over the behaviour of another child. But kind and reflective adults who treat children well and with respect, will admit their mistakes and make the effort to put right their oversights. They will listen to another adult, fellow-parent or colleague who points out that a child is being treated too severely or that their expectations of the child are unrealistic. An adult who is emotionally abusing a child carries on with this treatment regardless of the obvious distress of the child.

Any of the following patterns of behaviour in children should concern you, although none of these alone is proof of emotional abuse.

▶ When your observations and records show that a child is developmentally delayed – especially if your usual efforts to help a child are not creating much progress. There are many different reasons for developmental delay, but persistent emotional abuse can stunt children's motivation to learn.
▶ When children indicate, through words and body language, that they think they are worthless, stupid or unattractive.
▶ When children persistently blame themselves or seem to expect you to blame them or punish them. Be aware of children who are very distressed by their mistakes. Some children are by temperament, as well as experience, hard on themselves, or set themselves tough standards. So, you cannot afford to jump to easy conclusions.
▶ When children harm themselves with persistent hair pulling, picking at their

skin or head banging or have compulsive rituals such as very regular and lengthy hand washing.

▶ When children find it difficult to make friends and the reason seems to be that they do not see themselves as worthy of being liked.

▶ When children are either mistrusting of adults and appear to expect them to be unpredictable and unpleasant, or are prone to cling in an undiscriminating way to any adult who is kind to them.

Possible reasons for emotional abuse

There may be different factors that cause adults to abuse children emotionally:

▶ Some adults may be reliving their own childhood experiences of cruel words and relentless criticism. It may not occur to some adults that there are better ways to treat children. Parents may really believe that they are unaffected by the treatment they received, and so they cannot possibly be harming their child(ren).

▶ Adults' own troubles may be projected onto the children. In a life plagued by worries and doubts about their own competence, adults may feel better by bullying and abusing children. Sometimes parents explicitly blame one or more of their children for causing their problems or 'ruining my life by being born!'

▶ Some emotional abuse seems to arise from an adult dislike of a child. The abuse is excused on the grounds that the child is persistently naughty, awkward or insolent. In group situations, adults who abuse one child sometimes seem to be motivated by the thought that picking on this child will keep the rest of the group in line. Such adult behaviour is seriously unacceptable.

▶ Emotional cruelty from adults seemed to arise through an abuse of their authority. The adult feels powerful by ridiculing a child or always finding something to criticise.

▶ Some adults believe that children will not learn without being hit, or the threat of such punishment. In a similar way, other adults believe children should learn by being criticised and punished for their mistakes, but that encouraging words will make them proud and bigheaded.

Sexual abuse

Sexual abuse is defined as the actual or likely sexual exploitation of a child or adolescent, who is dependent or developmentally immature (because of age in years or the impact of learning disabilities). The point about sexual abuse is that the younger, more dependent or vulnerable individual is not in the position to give consent to acts that would be acceptable between genuinely consenting adults. Some sexual abuse involves acts of force that would constitute a crime even if adults were the only people involved.

▶ Sexual abuse of children sometimes involves full sexual intercourse, or abusers work their way towards this goal.
▶ But abusive use of children in a sexual way also includes intimate fondling and masturbation – either using a child in this way or requiring that they perform such acts on the abuser.
▶ Children and dependent young people have been coerced into tolerating oral or anal sex.
▶ It is also regarded as abusive for adults to engage in sexual activity in front of children. Sex between consenting adults is a private activity and trying to involve children as watchers is regarded as an abusive form of sexual exhibitionism.
▶ It is also regarded as abusive to coerce children into looking at pornographic photographs or films or to make them take part in such filming. Child pornography is not a new problem by any means; it has a long history. However, the technological possibilities of the internet have opened up new directions in possible abuse.
▶ Some sexual abusers coerce older children and young people into some form of prostitution, either by forcing them onto the streets or by 'selling' the children within the abuser's own home.

Available statistics indicate that more girls than boys have experienced some form of sexual abuse. However, both sexes are definitely at risk and it seems very probable that boys, especially from middle childhood and into early adolescence, may under-report sexually abusive experiences. Some children are sexually abused only once, or for a very short period of time, but for some children the experience carries on for years.

Signs that should concern you

As with any kind of child abuse, there is no neat checklist of certain signs of sexual abuse. Any of the following observations should concern you but are not in themselves absolute evidence of sexual abuse.

Within normal development children are very physical in their contact with one another and often like to be close to adults whom they trust and like. Children often show curiosity about their own and others' bodies and are sometimes relatively uninhibited in their behaviour. Any concerns must be placed within an understanding of the normal range of children's development and their current grasp of socially accepted behaviour for private and public situations.

THE CHILD'S BEHAVIOUR

▶ Highly sexual behaviour from young children, rather than affectionate physical contact should concern you. It is not within normal development for children to persist in trying to make physically intimate contact with other children or with adults, especially once another child or adult has said 'No'. Such behaviour is outside the boundaries of children's usual wish for touch and cuddles. (See also the discussion on page 182 about the differences between the physicality of young children and sexuality.)

▶ Children who are being sexually abused may express their worries and experiences in their play with dolls or small figures. They may produce sexually explicit paintings or drawings, showing unusual knowledge for their age of sexual activity. Older children may write or tell stories and poems that disclose or hint at their distress.

▶ Any sense you make of the concern must allow for the fact that many young children are interested in bottoms and 'willies'. So you must consider how far this child's play is out of the ordinary. Young children are often interested in these body parts in relation to going to the toilet, which is a direct part of their daily experience. The detailed sexual function of those same body parts should not be part of their knowledge.

▶ Young children often fiddle with their private parts, but you should be concerned if a child seems to masturbate a considerable amount. Even if careful checking does not arouse child protection concerns, a child who needs to self-comfort a great deal through masturbation is showing their need for significant emotional support.

▶ Some children with learning disabilities will behave like much younger children, and that situation may mean they are less aware of the boundaries between public and private behaviours. Practitioners, and parents, need to focus on supporting children and young people as they learn, but should not easily dismiss worrying behaviour patterns as an inevitable consequence of a disability. You need to explore the loop of 'would we be concerned if this child was not disabled? So what makes us so sure that the actions can be explained away by the disability?'

▶ What children say may concern you if it shows a sexual knowledge or curiosity unlikely for their age. Again, it is important to have a broad framework in which to make sense of any concern. Some parents are honest in answering children's questions and so a four- or five-year-old may be interested and well-informed about 'where babies come from'.

▶ Readers who work in schools and out-of-school services will know that the playground language of some children can be robust. Even when some families are careful about their own language and conversations in front of their children, those same boys and girls may hear some of the adult, and occasionally offensive lyrics, of some forms of music. Practitioners need to track the origin of some phrases that children say or sing. The words may need attention in terms of 'we don't sing that song here, because ...', but there may be no further concerns about a child's direct experiences.

Children and young people may show language or behaviour that raises concerns in different ways:

▶ Sometimes distressed children will tell you about unhappy secrets or games about which they are uneasy. When children disclose sexual, or any other, abuse it is important to carry on the conversation with care (see page 107).

▶ Some abused children react to their experience by regressing in development, for instance, toilet training, by having nightmares and many daytime fears. A formerly calm child may become unexpectedly aggressive or a confident child very withdrawn.

▶ You should never ignore any form of self-harm from children or talk that suggests they feel they are unworthy or that life is not worth living. This kind of behaviour is not just a phase and should be addressed, but you cannot be sure that abuse is the reason.

▶ Children do not like everyone equally and sometimes they dislike or are uncomfortable with someone for reasons that have nothing to do with abuse. However, you should wonder why a child does not want to be taken home by a particular person or has talked about not liking a particular evening sitter. You cannot jump to conclusions but it would be appropriate to talk with the parent. It would also be essential to follow up indications that a child sees very wary about being in the charge of a particular member of staff or the arrival of a frequent visitor to your setting.

PHYSICAL CONDITIONS

Some physical symptoms should concern you in children. But, again, few of these are clear evidence of abuse, rather than some other physical condition that needs attention.

▶ Pain, itching or redness in the genital or anal area needs medical attention but the condition could be the result of thrush or threadworms. Both of these conditions cause very uncomfortable itching and can lead to broken skin if the child has scratched vigorously. Persistent constipation can cause redness and anal fissures or bleeding from the strain.

▶ Bruising or bleeding in the genital or anal area again needs a medical check as does any child's clear discomfort in walking or sitting down. But you have to keep an open mind, as does the doctor who examines the child, because children do sometimes slip or fall and land heavily on their crotch area.

▶ A vaginal discharge or apparent infection in a girl should be checked. Again, be aware that children sometimes stick small objects into their bodily orifices and fail to retrieve them. An otherwise harmless object creates an infection if left.

▶ A doctor would assume sexual abuse if a medical examination showed evidence of a sexually transmitted disease in a child. STDs are caught from very close, intimate contact with an infected person, not from toilet seats.

▶ STDs in older children and young teenagers, as well as pregnancy in under-age young women, raise the possibility of sexual abuse. An alternative is that young people have developed very risky patterns of behaviour, and that prospect would also be cause for serious concern.

▶ If you work with older children and young teenagers, you need to keep a perspective on usual levels of flirtatious behaviour and physical contact. You would be right to feel concern about behaviour from this age range that made you think they could be sexually active.

Sexual abusers

The vast majority of identified sexual abusers are male and are known to the children whom they abuse – either because they are a relative, a family friend or a trusted person who has access to children through their work or voluntary activities. Abduction and abuse by strangers are very rare and it is because such incidents are so unusual that they receive significant media coverage. Some women have been found to sexually abuse children, so this possibility cannot be discounted.

Adult sexual abusers are now frequently called paedophiles. The word 'paedophile' comes from two Greek words: 'paedo' meaning boy or child and 'phile' meaning a strong or excessive liking. Sexual abusers used to be called child molesters and, although this term is now rarely used, it does raise awareness that there are some different patterns in sexual abuse.

Paedophiles

A paedophile is, by definition, an adult who is specifically sexually attracted to children and very young people, below the age of sexual consent. Paedophiles lose sexual interest in children as they grow out of childhood into adulthood.

Children are their preferred objects for sexual activity and fantasy. Paedophiles may be heterosexual or homosexual. A common misapprehension is that all gay men are potential paedophiles, but this is untrue.

Paedophiles can spend a great deal of time gaining a position of trust with children, in a paid job or through voluntary activity. Some target particular children and spend time getting to know the child and gaining the trust of the family, before moving in on the child. This process is called grooming and paedophiles may be targeting several children at any one time. Paedophiles can feel sexually excited by steadily increasing their contact with a child and their plans fuel their sexual fantasies. Some paedophiles become known to older children and young teenagers as the person who runs 'open house', where young people are welcome with no questions asked. Under these circumstances paedophiles may have contact with many children, some of whom they do not abuse.

Sexual attraction to children and very young people is a compulsive pattern of behaviour. Paedophiles do not inhibit their actions unless they have been pressed to acknowledge the genuine damage done to their victims. Paedophiles may be attracted by child pornography and in some cases this activity is part of their system of abuse. (See also the discussion about the internet on page 32.)

OTHER SEXUAL ABUSERS

Some adult sexual abusers do not show the classic paedophile pattern, in that they have, or have in the past had, sexual relationships with other adults. These abusers seem to home in on children and young teenagers because they are available or easier to intimidate. What seems to happen is that such abusers, mainly men, turn to children or under-age young people when they feel under stress or rejected in their adult relationship. They find children – their own, step-children or children of friends – less threatening and justify their abuse on the grounds that they are not harming the child or that the child sought and welcomed their form of affection.

Some sexual abusers have themselves been abused as children. As a child or young person, they developed a distorted understanding of how to form affectionate relationships. As an adult, they may be exercising a sense of power over children, because they feel incompetent in relations with adults. However, by no means all children who have been sexually abused go on to abuse as an adult.

Organised groups

The majority of sexual abusers appear to act on their own. However, there have been cases of groups of adults engaging in systematic sexual abuse of children. Such cases are rare, but when they have happened there have been different patterns.

Organised sexual, or physical abuse, has become established in a professional setting such as a day care centre or residential children's home. Children are coerced into secrecy or told, with tragic justification in some children's homes' scandals that nobody will believe them if they tell, because they are bad children with a track record of misbehaviour and absconding.

Rare instances of systematic abuse in families have involved either several generations of the same family or a linked group of local families. The organised abuse groups of family and friends have involved men, women, boys and girls, although there are still proportionately more men involved than women.

During the 1980s and early 1990s a few cases of groups abusing children gave rise to claims of satanic sexual abuse. The claims of some writers in America were extraordinary and ignored all normal rules of evidence. Considered research in America and the UK does not support the claims of extensive satanic abuse in either society. However, some abusers have used bizarre rituals and props to intimidate and silence children. These activities do not seem to have been genuine satanic activities, but the children have believed that the adults had strange powers over them. Groups of abusers have also used systematic cruelty and ill-treatment of children (such as shutting children in cupboards for long periods of time) in order to disorientate them and make them more compliant through fear to tolerate perverted sexual practices.

Use of the internet

Organised paedophile rings have been uncovered. Such networks more usually involve abusing men and boys, although women and girls have sometimes been involved. Such rings pass children between adults and are often linked with child pornography. In recent years paedophiles have increasingly used the internet to access and exchange child pornography and to groom children and young people.

In recent years international police operations have uncovered some significant internet websites. The ring called the 'Wonderland Club' was exposed in 2001 and during 2002 a huge subscriber website was discovered that operated out of Texas in the United States. Such cases have shown the extent to which paedophiles exchange abusive images within well-hidden websites. Some participants in such websites claim not to be sexual abusers because they only download the images. But of course children have to be abused in order to create the pornography and possession of such images is now a crime.

It can be a profound shock for children and young people, who have been sexually abused, to discover their traumatic experiences have become public property for paedophiles through the internet. This realisation can bring new levels of distress and a sense of powerlessness to children and young people who are already damaged by their abuse.

In their email communications with each other, paedophiles also support the stance that their behaviour is acceptable, just another sexual orientation. Some paedophiles make contact with children and young people through the many ordinary internet chatrooms. Their aim is to identify personal concerns or needs that will enable them to entice this child or young person into a meeting without the knowledge of their family.

Young abusers

Sometimes children or young people who are being sexually abused start to abuse others while they are themselves still young. The inappropriate or abusive behaviour of children or young teenagers may be the first warning sign that they are, or have been, sexually abused.

Adults have to make sense of sexual activity and experimentation between children and young people in the light of developmental norms and the ability and experience of these individuals. Unwary adults, or those who would rather ignore the whole issue, may dismiss activity as normal childhood experimentation or as 'boys will be boys' (either for youthful heterosexual or homosexual activity).

It is often not straightforward to reach a judgement about whether an activity is sexually abusive between older children and young people. Considered judgement and careful discussion with colleagues has to weigh up:

▶ the age of all the children and young people involved and what is within normal range for close physical contact or possibly sexual activity for this age group. You would interpret differently the same behaviour for seven-year-olds than for thirteen-year-olds.

▶ any factors that suggest one participant is putting high levels of pressure, coercion or threat on another participant in even low level sexual activity. This situation would remove the possibility of informed consent between peers.

▶ other relevant factors such as the learning or physical disabilities of individuals, which could make them less able to understand or refuse approaches of their peers.

An NCH Action for Children project, undertaken in the mid–1990s, identified underlying themes in how children start to abuse others in a sexual way:

▶ An adult sexual abuser may coerce one child or young person into inflicting abuse in their turn. This activity may be part of sexual satisfaction for the adult.

▶ An abused child has become very sexualised in his or her behaviour. Children may seek sexual encounters with peers because this is the only way they have learned to make close contact.

▶ A child may act in a sexual way to a younger or weaker child more as an exercise of power. The abused child has been made to feel powerless and he or she may be trying to feel powerful in their turn.

▶ A young abuser may not have been directly sexually abused in a physical sense, but may have been exposed to pornographic material or to exhibitionist adult sexual activity. The child's judgement of normal behaviour has been distorted.

Young abusers can experience a mix of emotions when they abuse others. The NCH project reported that young abusers do not necessarily experience sexual satisfaction. They may feel:

▶ very angry at the time they sexually abuse others
▶ excited by the sense of power and secrecy
▶ temporarily relieved of their feelings of worthlessness through sexual contact with younger children
▶ guilt and fear that they are becoming like the person who abused them.

Whatever the exact reason for the child or young person's own abusive activity, their experience has been abusive and has distorted their development. For this reason, the professional approach has to include support for the young abuser as victim, as well as a child protection investigation following all the usual steps for the child or young person on the receiving end of the abuse.

The harm of sexual abuse

Unless the sexual practices are very intrusive or violent, children are less likely to suffer physical injury than to be psychologically damaged by the experience. Sexual abuse matters because of the short- and long-term impact that the abuse can have on children and young people:

▶ It is the responsibility of adults, especially those in a position of trust and close relationships with children to help children and young people to establish the boundaries of appropriate physical contact and respect for others. Sexual abusers are crossing and disrupting the very boundaries that they should be helping to create.

▶ Sexual abusers confuse and distort children's' growing understanding of relationships because they have replaced proper affection with sexual contact. The emotional upheaval, especially within the atmosphere of coercion and secrecy, disrupts children's legitimate wish for attention and care because these needs are met with an inappropriate sexual reaction.

▶ Children can experience, and be left with, painful feelings of guilt that somehow they brought the experience on themselves, or are to blame because they accepted gifts or treats from the abuser. Children's natural wish for physical contact, cuddling and affection is manipulated through sexual abuse and children can feel responsible. Yet it was entirely the adult's responsibility to offer appropriate intimacy to a child or young person.

▶ When children's disclosures of sexual abuse lead to the break-up of their family, they may feel, or be made to feel by some members of the family, that this crisis is their fault.

▶ Children may not be believed or felt to be at least partly responsible when the abuser is a respected member of the community and 'not the kind of person who would do this'.

▶ Depending on the reactions children experience when the abuse is disclosed, they may feel dirty, as if they are unpleasant and unworthy. The abuser may also have threatened children that they will be disliked and rejected if they break the secret.

▶ Children should be able to trust adults to protect them and not to violate

them. The experience of sexual abuse can leave children feeling powerless and betrayed. The abuser can have shaken their trust in adults in general.

▶ The sense of betrayal and powerlessness can be heightened for those children and young people who discover their abuser has used visual records of the abuse through pornography or posting on paedophile websites on the internet.

▶ Children's emotional and sexual development can be disrupted. They may have later doubts about their sexuality and how healthy relationships should operate. Adults who experienced sexual abuse may fear, with some justification, that their later adult partners would be disturbed or reject them if they knew what had happened. Boys abused by men can sometimes experience confusion about their sexual identity. For instance, a boy whose orientation would be heterosexual wonders if he might be homosexual.

Adults, or young people, who sexually abuse children are using those children to satisfy their own sexual desires and impulses. Abusers often claim that the younger, or less mature, individual was a willing partner. However, abusers twist the idea of informed consent. Genuine consent means an agreement within an equal relationship and abusing relationships are unequal. Abusers are in a greater position of power because they are older, larger or stronger and may have a position of authority or trust over the child. Anyone who abuses a child often builds a web of coercion to try to prevent discovery and reduce the likelihood that a child will be believed. But sexual abusers are especially keen to force apparent cooperation and secrecy since adult abusers know they are breaking an important social taboo.

A child's compliance and silence about the sexual abuse may be coerced through various means by the adult or young person who abuses.

▶ Abusers may threaten to hurt the child or someone they care about.

▶ Abusers may claim that nobody will believe the child if they tell or that others will blame and despise the child if the abuse is revealed. This threat can be especially effective if the abusing adult is in a position of authority over the child (through family or professional position) or is a respected member of the local community.

▶ Some abusers attempt to bribe children with presents or treats and then induce a sense of guilt because the child accepted the gifts or outings.

▶ Some abusers work to convince children that what they are doing is normal or acceptable, as an activity within the family or between people who supposedly care for each other.

The abuse of disabled children

Any child or young person can be vulnerable to abuse, but many people hoped that somehow disabled children would be relatively safe, because they were in a protected environment or that nobody would be that cruel and exploitative. Unfortunately, disabled children can be even more vulnerable to abuse and neglect than their peers. Some of the main issues include:

▶ Children may need more personal physical care because of physical disabilities or they need help at an older age because of severe learning disabilities. Such care can, of course, be offered with respect and consideration. Yet disabled children may be vulnerable to anything from poor standards in their care to a direct abuse of their need for help.

▶ Unsupported and exhausted parents, or other carers, may snap under the relentless pressure of a very high demand for care – twenty-four hours a day, seven days a week in some circumstances.

▶ Continued intrusive medical procedures necessary for some children's conditions may leave them with an underdeveloped sense of their own privacy or bodily dignity. Abusive behaviour by adults or young people may not seem so out of the ordinary or unacceptable.

▶ Children and young people with learning and/or communication disabilities may have difficulty in telling a trusted parent or carer that something wrong is happening to them.

▶ A high level of physical disability may make it hard for a child to resist an abuser.

▶ Adults may overlook the need to talk with children about appropriate physical touch and sexuality with young people. The mistaken assumption may be that children are within a protected environment or that sexual awareness and behaviour is irrelevant to disabled young people.

▶ Children may have a relatively high number of carers because of their condition or because they attend a number of different specialist facilities. Children may learn that intrusive attention by relative strangers is normal. There may also be no key adult who is keeping a close eye on the child's overall care.

▶ Carers may feel (inappropriately) that abuse or maltreatment matters less when it involves disabled children.

Good practice with all children is to offer respectful and appropriate physical care (see page 178) but the importance can be especially sharp in this vulnerable group:

▶ Children should be asked about their preferences for their personal care and adults should listen in whatever way these wishes are expressed.

▶ Children should be enabled to partake in their own care as much as possible by adult time and attention and support for children as they learn, even if the learning is very slow.

▶ Care routines should not be rushed and children should be treated as individuals, so they develop a sense of appropriate respectful treatment. They should know the people who care for them so that children and young people do not start to believe that anyone might appear and deal with their intimate needs.

▶ Staff groups, in partnership with children's parents, need to discuss ways of working to provide consistency and good practice and for ensuring that disabled children are not vulnerable to abuse.

The consequences of abuse

Each of these four broad types of abusive experience matter for children and young people:

▶ Some children are injured or die as a result of physical abuse or severe and persistent neglect. For some, their health and development may be seriously endangered.

▶ Children who are abused have also experienced a vital breakdown of trust. Often it is the very adults who should be caring for the children and protecting them that are abusing them.

▶ Children who have been abused may be left with doubts about themselves as individuals worthy of affection and care. A great deal depends on how other responsible adults have been able to help a child who has been abused.

▶ Children may be distressed, emotionally confused about what has happened and frightened or wary for the future. They may doubt their own ability to take care of themselves or of trusted adults to protect them.

▶ There is a risk of setting off a cycle of continued abuse. Some abused children react by abusing others in their turn – through anger and distress, as the result of coercion by the abusing adult or in emotional confusion over how you should conduct relationships and handle either affection or conflict.

Caring adults who work with children can help them, and support non-abusing parents, in ways that will enable children or young people to emerge from their experience. You cannot make the experience not have happened but you can make a difference to children in rebuilding their life and trust in others. Most children who were abused do not go on to abuse (physically, sexually or emotionally) as adults, or parents themselves. It is estimated that about 30 per cent of abused children become abusers in their turn. So, a continuing cycle is a risk but is definitely not inevitable. Although they may bear the emotional scars, many adults who experienced childhood abuse are very clear that they will never behave, or allow anyone else, to behave in that way to their children.

Scenarios

A number of scenarios now follow. These examples are for you to consider, and ideally to discuss with colleagues or in your student group with a supervisor.

For each of the scenarios, please consider the following questions:

▶ Should this situation concern you? If so, in what way does it concern you?
▶ Given what you have read in this chapter, do you think that the child in this situation could be experiencing abuse? If so, what type(s) of abuse?

Please note that you might be still be concerned, but not feel that the situation was abusive as such. There could still be issues that you judge should be addressed in good practice.

You can return to one or more of these scenarios when you have read more of the book, especially Chapters 3 and 4. At that point you could consider the following questions:

▶ Should you talk with the parent in this situation? What will you say? Practise some real phrases, or explore the situation in a role play with a colleague or fellow-student.
▶ What further information might you, or a more senior colleague, seek?

You will find a short commentary on each scenario from page 221.

Clement

You work in a local authority children's centre. Clement, who is two years old, has started at your centre this week. Clement seems happy and he talks with words and a few two-word phrases. But he has very little idea what to do with the play materials that you would usually give to his age group and is keener to handle the baby toys. He cannot walk but stands steadily holding onto a firm surface and cruises along by hand holds.

The health visitor has told you that Clement was found a place in the centre because she realised that the boy's mother and grandmother did not let him out of his cot. They both expressed great worries about the potential dangers to Clement if they let him roam around their flat, or if they took him out into the local neighbourhood. Both women seem caring towards Clement but the settling-in time at the centre has been hard, as his grandmother has been especially concerned about Clement's safety in the playroom and the centre garden.

Heather

You have recently joined the staff of a small private nursery school. Heather is nearly four years old and has been attending the school for six months. She is an articulate girl and has started to talk with you about what she has done at the weekend or the previous evening. In a conversation with you yesterday, Heather was describing a film she had watched on television that you know did not start until 11-00. You said to her, 'You were up very late, Heather. Did Mummy know you were watching that film?' Heather replied, 'Oh, Mummy was with John. They were in the bedroom, doing . . . Well, you know what.'

Today, you notice that Heather is playing with Jack in the home corner. When you look more closely you realise that Heather is sitting astride Jack and bouncing up and down. She is making grunting noises that sound very like orgasm. At that moment a colleague goes into the home corner and pulls Heather off Jack, saying, 'None of that, Heather. Don't be silly.' In a coffee break later, the other member of staff explains, 'I should have told you. We have to watch Heather. She tries that sort of stuff with the little boys. Poor kid, it's not her fault. Goodness knows what she sees at home. But we can't have it here.'

Danny

Danny is the youngest of five boys in the Sanders family. Danny attends the nursery class where you work and three of the other boys are in the primary school. Danny is frequently dressed in clothes that are torn, dirty and smelly. His shoes and socks appear to be too small for him and are affecting how he walks. You have spoken with teachers in the classes of the other Sanders boys, who say that these children are usually in clean clothes and sometimes in trainers or sweatshirts that are fashionable. When you mentioned Danny's shoes to his mother, Mrs Sanders told you firmly that she does not have money to burn and Danny should be grateful that he has a choice of clothes that his brothers have not ruined.

You continue to be concerned about Danny. Something he says to you makes you suspicious that he is shut in the cellar but, when asked, Mrs Sanders says that Danny was shut in by one of his brothers as a joke and then the boy forgot. A singed area of hair and what looks like a burn on Danny's scalp is explained as, 'I got the hair dryer a bit close to him last night. Kid wouldn't sit still!'

One afternoon you overhear Mrs Sanders talking to another mother, who is expecting her second child and says she is hoping for a girl this time. Mrs Sanders says that Danny should have been a girl. 'I wanted a daughter. Do you think I wanted all these boys! But Danny fixed that for me. It ruined my insides having him and he was such a sickly little runt. They had to change all his blood when he was born, so it's not like he's really mine, anyway.'

Janice

Janice is three years old and has attended the pre-school for several months. She started when her mother had not long given birth to a baby boy, Sachin. Janice's brother is very unwell. Sachin has been in hospital several times, but as yet with no definite diagnosis of what is wrong. Her mother is distraught over Sachin's illness and has told you that she is getting very little sleep, what with Sachin screaming and Janice wanting to get into bed with her and her husband.

When she started pre-school, Janice was a relatively quiet child but made friends and joined in the play activities. But over the last few weeks you have noticed a significant change in the child. Janice spends a lot of time rocking and hugging herself. She has complained to you of stomach aches and one day says that her bottom is 'so sore'. You tried to speak with Mrs Matthews but she rushed off. The next morning Janice comes to pre-school with a long scratch mark over one cheek. Her mother asks to speak with you in private and as soon as you are alone together, she bursts into tears.

Janice's mother admits that she hit her daughter the previous afternoon. She had found Janice trying to put Sachin in the dustbin – 'I just snapped. I hit out at her and my ring scratched her cheek. It's terrible. I said I would never, ever hit one of my children. My father used to hit us; I can't believe I did it.' You take the opportunity to ask about Janice's remark of having a sore bottom. Mrs Matthews replies straightaway, 'It's the constipation. Janice won't go to the loo for days, then of course she's in terrible pain when she finally does go. And then she has stomach aches as well. We've taken her to the doctor and he just says it's all about Sachin and Janice'll get over it. I'm at my wits' end!'

Cameron

Cameron is six years old and was born when his mother, Becky, was in her late teens. Becky has tried to continue her own life and, although there have been no concrete worries about Cameron, neither his nursery nor his primary school feel that they have been able to get Becky to understand the perspective of her son. This summer she went on holiday to Greece with a new boyfriend and left Cameron for three weeks with some friends of hers. Cameron was very distressed while Becky was gone and has been loath to let her out of his sight ever since. Becky finds this very irritating and continues to say that she explained everything to her son and it was not a suitable holiday for a child – 'So what was I supposed to do?'

Cameron does not seem to like his mother's new boyfriend but Becky says that her son is only jealous and does not like sharing her. The teachers have noticed that Cameron is quieter than he used to be. Recently he said to the one male teacher in the school, 'I hold my willy, don't I? Nobody else should hold my willy?' Cameron was unwilling to say any more but he was later overheard saying to one of the other boys, 'Does your Daddy hold your willy?' Sometimes the new boyfriend comes with Becky to pick up Cameron from school and Cameron refuses to take his hand. This afternoon it is just the boyfriend, without Becky, and Cameron has refused point blank to leave.

Sajida

Sajida is seven years old and attends your after-school club which is linked with her primary school. Sajida has Downs syndrome and her development is closer to that of a four-year-old. She has a helper, Amy, who stays with her during school time but does not attend the club. Your impression is that Sajida's mother still has difficulty in reconciling herself to having a disabled child and speaks with much more enthusiasm about her son, who is nearly five years old. You have never met the father.

Sajida seems to have a lot of accidents, both at school and at home. Within the last year, she has had a badly twisted ankle, a fractured arm and numerous bruises. Each time there has been a reasonable explanation and Sajida's mother and Amy agree that the child is very clumsy. You have seen Sajida bump into tables and sometimes other children, but she has never sustained more than a very mild bruise at the after-school club.

Today Sajida arrived at the club with Amy, who said that the child had slipped in the school toilets and hit her head on the taps. Sajida has a large swelling and bruise over one eye and a reddened area on one arm, where Amy says she tried to grab the child to prevent her fall. Later this afternoon, you are sympathising with Sajida, saying, 'You have a lot of bangs, don't you? How did you slip?' Sajida looks puzzled and you say, 'Amy says you slipped over in the toilet.' Sajida shakes her head and says, 'No, didn't slip. Amy banged me.'

Abbas

Abbas is ten years old and attends your primary school, with his sister Nneka, who is seven years old. Both children appear happy, well cared for and attend school regularly. You and your colleagues have become aware that Abbas seems to carry a great deal of responsibility for Nneka. He accompanies her to school and home each day and deals with any messages for her class teacher. Abbas stays if his sister has an after school activity, but has declined chess club for himself, with the explanation that he has to get Nneka home and organise the evening meal. You have also heard from the parent grapevine that children who invite Abbas round to tea always have Nneka as well, since there seems to be no other option, even at the weekends.

You and your colleagues are concerned not to appear to criticise Abbas' family organisation just because you feel he is carrying undue responsibility for a ten-year-old. There is no direct cause for concern about either child, although a few comments from Nneka have made you wonder if Abbas has sole responsibility well into the evening sometimes. This year Abbas will move on to secondary school and the transition will involve a much longer daily trip for him, if he is still to bring Nneka to primary school, a walk that involves crossing two main roads. You wonder whether to raise the issues with his parents and in what way you could show respect as well as some concern.

Selena

Today in your secondary school you have intervened in a shouting match in the corridor between several fifteen-year-olds. Once you had calmed the group down somewhat, it became clear that there was much more going on than a temporary disagreement. Selena had been screaming at Ian to 'leave me alone, you pervert-stalker!' and had called her peer several other offensive names. However, when it was obvious that you were willing to listen, two other teenagers in the group had started to explain the events of the last few weeks, and a tearful Selena confirmed what they said.

Ian has been following Selena home, calling her on the telephone despite being told to stop many times by Selena and most recently by her father. Selena had confided in her close friend, Jake, who had tried to talk some sense into Ian, but only succeeded in reducing the activity for a short while. Ian also follows Selena at school, stands very close and stares at her 'all the time', so Selena had tried to engage the help of her class teacher. Selena's view is that this teacher 'just didn't want to know' and commented, 'If you stop encouraging him, then he'll lose interest'. Selena is now angry, distressed and beginning to be scared, because in the last few days she has received text messages bordering on obscene, and believes they are sent by Ian too.

You are faced with a situation that needs proper attention and checking out for reliable information, including whether your colleague was as unhelpful as Selena describes. Your school is strong on the principle that students speak up about any kind of bullying or harassment.

2

How child protection works

The legal framework

The changes in child protection over several decades are due in part to how children are now perceived. Child care is no longer seen to be a completely private issue that remains the business of families. The view that parents, or any other relatives, cannot simply deal with children as they please has become well established. Society, backed by legislation, leaves parents a considerable amount of flexibility in how they care for and raise children, but does place boundaries to family choices.

Four nations comprise the UK: England, Wales, Scotland and Northern Ireland. Central government in London continues to make some decisions that affect everyone and some legislation applies to all four countries. However, the process of devolution over the last decade of the twentieth century has meant that many aspects of government are now the responsibility of the National Assembly of Wales, the Northern Ireland Assembly and the Scottish Parliament. In particular, each nation determines most of the legislation and guidance that affect early years services, statutory education, child protection and social services. There is a great deal of common ground over principles and good practice, but the details can vary.

Over the 1980s and 1990s new legislation was passed in the UK to provide a more effective framework for the care and protection of children. The relevant laws are the Children Act 1989, which applies to England and Wales, the Children (Scotland) Act 1995 and the Children (Northern Ireland) Order 1996. Each of these laws are primary legislation; they lay out the details of the law in legal language but do not fully describe or explain how child protection works in daily practice. Legislation is supported further by guidance issued by national government departments. Local child protection committees, who bring together key professionals, are expected to draft specific local guidance documents. In this and other chapters, I explain how the child protection system works in general. However, all readers need to consult their local procedures and guidance for more detail, as well as useful information about people and organisations in their area.

The Children Act 1989, Children (Scotland) Act 1995 and Children (Northern Ireland) 1996 Order are all laws that cover child care and family support in the broadest sense and the sections covering child protection are part of more wide-ranging legislation, also encompassing services for children in need. The Children (Scotland) Act 1995 stands out as the legislation that most took account of the United Nations Convention on the Rights of the Child. Each Act or Order also covers the registration and inspection of early years services that fall outside the education system.

These laws have each established some key principles that should underpin all practice with children:

▶ The welfare of the child must be paramount in any work with a family, known as the paramountcy principle.
▶ Work must be conducted in partnership. Professionals are expected to work together in a spirit of inter-agency co-operation and to work in a co-operative way with parents.
▶ Children are not the possessions of their parents. Parents have responsibilities for their children, not absolute rights.
▶ The principle underlying each law is that children should preferably be raised within their own family, but that the welfare of children requires that there are limits to family privacy and decision making.

ACTIVITY

All practitioners need to know how their work could fit into the big picture for child protection and how the system operates in the local area. Local authorities have to organise the steps in the whole process in the way required by national guidance, but there are minor local differences. You need to know, and have easily to hand, the names and contact addresses of all the professionals who form your local child protection system.

1 Ideally your local authority should provide a straightforward summary leaflet that describes your role in the whole area of child protection. Find the material in your setting and read it. Use the information to start your own folder on child protection in your area. Note down any questions that you would like to explore.
2 You may not have easy access to such a leaflet. Perhaps you are working in a private nursery that is not fully integrated into the local network. You could see if any other settings, for instance a local family centre or school, have such material. Alternatively, local child protection guidelines

are a public document. You may be able to consult a copy in the reference section of your local library.

3 If no such material exists locally, then arrange to visit a member of the local child protection team or a duty social worker. You could use the material in this chapter to guide your questions as you fill in the local details.

Steps in child protection

These steps are not negotiable depending on local authorities' preferences; the procedures are laid down by the national guidance and local authorities have to follow them. The guidance also lays out time limits on the steps in the process; it is not allowed to drag on indefinitely. Appendix 2 has a flow chart that summarises these steps.

The description in this section applies to child protection procedures, as they usually operate throughout the UK. The steps are very similar, including the key role of social workers, the use of case conferences and the child protection register. The steps operate within some national variations.

In Scotland a unique system of Children's Hearings deals with juvenile and family matters, including some aspects of child protection. Concerns about a child are dealt with by local social work departments through a similar process described in this section, including the use of case conferences. Any concerned person can also refer a child to the Children's Reporter. The Reporter will work in partnership with social workers to decide whether the case should be dealt with by the Children's Hearing, comprised of volunteer lay people drawn from the local Children's Panel. As regards child protection, the Children's Hearing would probably be involved if there was a need for emergency legal action by application for court orders. The Children's Hearing can deal with emergency orders, but the Procurator Fiscal would be the person to decide if a child protection case would go on to court within the criminal system.

Children and young people have not only a right to attend their own Children's Hearing, but also an obligation to do so, with few exceptions. A safeguarder can be appointed to support individual children and young people to enable them to express their views and to speak on their behalf.

In Northern Ireland, the responsibilities within child protection rest with the four local Health and Social Services Boards or Trusts, who are in turn responsible for setting up the Area Child Protection Committee. Social workers operate within these four areas.

Step 1: Initial concern and referral

The child protection process is started when someone expresses concern about the welfare of a child. This concern may be expressed from one or more of the following sources:

▶ Professionals within the health services such as a family's GP, the health visitor, a school nurse or some other specialist health professional involved with a child and family.
▶ For younger children, practitioners in early years care and education services may be the first people to voice worries about the health, development or safety of a child. In the case of older children, concerns may be expressed by staff in the child's school, after-school club or other facilities that a child attends regularly.
▶ Child protection concerns may be raised by social workers themselves.
▶ It is not always professionals who first voice worries about a child. Some child protection inquiries are started as the result of fears for a child communicated by members of the child's own immediate family, other relatives, friends or neighbours. Child protection is viewed as a community responsibility, not one limited to professionals.

Child protection concerns might then be communicated to the local social services department, the police or the local NSPCC. The local police will probably have a special unit for child protection. It may be called the Family Protection Unit (FPU) or the Child Protection Unit or Team. The NSPCC are more active in some local child protection systems than others, but the organisation has a legal right to take proceedings under the Children Act.

Step 2: Initial inquiries and strategy

Any concern regarding the possible abuse of a child has to be considered and an initial investigation made. The steps in the child protection process are intended to be steady as well as timely. The aim is that any concerns are checked carefully but that no further measures are taken unless it is judged necessary. At the start of any investigation, a decision has to be made whether the inquiries will be made by the social services on their own or whether the investigation will be a joint one, also involving the police and possibly an NSPCC social worker.

There has to be an initial strategy meeting to plan any future investigation and at this point there are three main possibilities:

1 On the basis of the information available, it is decided not to go further with the child protection process for this child. This decision does not mean that the child and any concerns are ignored. Other possible work with the child and family may be discussed but the judgement is that there are no current child protection concerns. Not all enquiries by any means lead to a case protection conference.

2 It is decided that the case requires investigation on the basis of child protection concerns. Initial plans will then be made for an investigation and assessment.

3 The third possibility is that the risk to the child(ren) is judged to be so great that steps must be taken immediately. The investigation and other steps in the process will also be undertaken, but the child is judged to be in danger of serious and immediate risk and action cannot be delayed.

IMMEDIATE MEASURES OF PROTECTION

The principles guiding child protection stress that professionals must act in the best interests of the child, but not take more action than is necessary. If the child cannot be protected given all the facts of the nature of the risk (who, what, where, when, how) then the child is judged to be at risk of significant harm. Action can then be taken under each of the Children Acts in different parts of the UK to protect children from immediate danger. Such steps are not taken lightly and are not used in many child protection cases. The general principles of legal process are that:

▶ The welfare of the child must be the prime concern.
▶ The aim is to avoid and reduce delay that would leave children in a seriously unsafe situation.
▶ There is to be no court order (emergency or other kinds) unless making an order is clearly better for the child. Court orders are not to be used as a matter of routine.

If a court order is necessary, then there are two choices with child protection legislation:

▶ In England and Wales, an **Emergency Protection Order** can be taken out by social services or by the NSPCC. This order is only allowed when there is an immediate risk to the child and social workers have to make a case to the court when they apply for the order. The order will be granted if the child is not safe at home, the parent(s) will not permit the voluntary removal of the child and there is nowhere for the child to be kept safe with the parents' consent. The effect of an Emergency Protection Order is to compel a parent, or other relevant person, to produce the child and allow the local authority to remove him or her to a place of safety. The order can also be used to prevent the removal of a child by parents or other persons from a place that is judged to be safe for the child. The court can additionally issue a warrant authorising a police officer to assist in the removal of children, or in preventing their removal by the family.

▶ Alternatively, the police have the powers to remove the child to suitable alternative accommodation or to prevent the child being removed from a specific place.

In Scotland, when it is judged that children are at risk of significant harm, there are two options:

▶ A Child Protection Order enables a child to be removed from an identified risk and to a place of safety.
▶ An Exclusion Order enables the removal of the person alleged to have abused a child. This order is regarded as important, so that children are not removed unless there is no other way to keep them safe.

In Northern Ireland, the options are:

▶ A Care Order makes a child the responsibility of the local Health and Social Services Board.
▶ A Supervision Order places the child under the supervision of the Board but without assigning parental responsibility.
▶ An Emergency Protection Order enables a child to be made safe.

DEVELOPING A PLAN FOR INVESTIGATION

The initial strategy meeting must plan the investigation if the decision is to proceed with a child protection enquiry. The details have to be decided, on the basis of the information available so far, the strands that have to be followed and the other professionals involved with the family. It has to be clear who will be responsible for conducting the investigation and making contact with the child, family and other involved agencies. The strategy meeting basically assesses the evidence so far. It is possible that, at this point, the police representative might say that there is insufficient evidence to suggest a possible criminal prosecution in the future. Then the police will not be involved further in the process for this child.

Understanding the role of the police

The work of the police in the child protection process is rather different from that of other professionals. They can only justify their continuing involvement with a child protection case on two related grounds:

▶ That if the abuse is proven, then the abuser(s) will be proven to have committed a crime. The alleged actions have to fall within one of the possible categories that define a crime under law.
▶ There has to be sufficient evidence that a prosecution is likely to succeed. In England the police who have investigated a case then pass on the evidence to the Crown Prosecution Service (CPS) who make the final decision whether to go ahead with criminal proceedings. In Scotland this decision rests with the office of the Procurator Fiscal and in Northern Ireland with the Department of Public Prosecutions (DPP).

If the police withdraw from the child protection process, it does not mean that they believe the abuse of this child does not matter, nor that they think someone is mistaken or lying. It means that either there is no identifiable crime, however powerful the information collected, or that the evidence collected is judged as too weak to stand up in court. Of course, some cases do go to trial and, for various reasons, do not result in a prosecution. It is important that you understand the limits placed on the police force, since you may be supporting both parents and children who have unrealistic hopes that a recognised abuser will definitely be punished in law.

Generally speaking, the police are only involved in a child protection case when there is possible physical or sexual abuse or neglect, since the actions of the abuser may, but will not definitely, constitute a crime. Emotional abuse, even when well supported by a child protection investigation, cannot produce evidence that falls into a category of a crime. So police involvement continuing through the child protection process is very unlikely if emotional abuse is the only strand in the investigation. But it is important to realise, for yourself and in supporting parents and children, that very serious steps can be taken on behalf of a child at risk whether there is an identifiable crime or not. The possibilities for child protection under each of the Children Acts do not require proof that a crime has taken place. (More on page 56.)

In Scotland, the police have a general duty to investigate on behalf of the Procurator Fiscal, when they have reason to believe that a criminal offence has been committed. Each Procurator Fiscal is the local representative of the Lord Advocate, and can interview witnesses.

Step 3: Investigation and assessment

A full investigation has to be carried out after the strategy meeting and before the child protection conference. This investigation is carried out as part of the requirements under child protection legislation and is a necessary part of the later decision at the case conference (Step 4) whether, or not, to place the child's name on the child protection register. A child cannot be registered without this prior investigation.

Guidance has established that the prime tasks of an child protection investigation are to:

▶ Establish the facts about the circumstances giving rise to the concern.
▶ Identify whether there are grounds to consider that the child is or is not likely to suffer significant harm.
▶ Identify the sources and level of risks.
▶ Decide on the necessary protective and other actions in relation to children.
▶ Secure by interview or medical examination the evidence from which a decision can be made regarding civil or criminal proceedings (the difference between these is explained on page 167.)

The principles of an investigation are that it should:

▶ Always be child-centred and any procedures should be undertaken with the child's feelings and experiences in mind. Interviews or examinations should be explained and undertaken with consideration, avoiding further distress to an already hurt or confused child.
▶ Have due regard to the legal requirements. However concerned professionals may be about a child, they must act within the law.
▶ Involve parents and carers in the whole process unless it can be clearly justified as prejudicial to the investigation. For instance, parents might be excluded if they continually disrupt meetings or intimidate the children. In that case the parents' views should still be sought and they should be given information. If parents refuse to cooperate in the investigation, a Child Assessment Order can be obtained (in England and Wales) to compel some co-operation and allow assessment of the child.
▶ The legislation in Scotland and Northern Ireland also allows for court orders to require parents to allow an assessment to be made of a child at risk, when parents' co-operation is being withheld unreasonably.
▶ Fully assess the child's circumstances before any action is taken.
▶ Undertake interviews with an open mind, having regard to different child care practices but with the welfare of the child as central.

Step 4: The child protection conference

Not all child protection concerns reach this stage. The whole point of initial inquiries and the investigation is that further steps are not taken unless there is genuine cause for concern. Some children are best helped by organising different kinds of family support services.

The child protection conference, sometimes known just as a case conference, brings together any professionals with relevant information to share and the family itself. The conference has to be called no more than 10 days after the concern has first been lodged. A child protection conference is attended by some but not necessarily all, of the following people (representatives from different professions are not invited unless they are involved with the family or have a direct contribution to make):

▶ A social worker will definitely be present.
▶ The parent(s) will be invited.
▶ A residential social worker, foster carer or family centre worker.
▶ In Scotland, the Children's Reporter.
▶ The police, represented by the liaison officer from the Family Protection Unit or the investigating officer. In Scotland the police would usually represent the Procurator Fiscal.
▶ A medical professional such as the family's GP or the school nurse.
▶ A representative from education or day care – teacher, head teacher, early years practitioner or an educational psychologist.
▶ If relevant, someone from the Probation department.
▶ A local NSPCC social worker.
▶ A representative of the local authority legal department.

Studies of the child protection process have suggested that co-operation between different professionals is most likely at the beginnings of the process and at the investigation stage. Social workers are the most likely professionals to carry on with the work.

INVOLVEMENT OF PARENTS

Legislation and guidelines within the UK firmly stress that parents should remain a part of the child protection process. Parents must be invited to the case conference, unless it can be shown that there is a very good reason why they should not be there. One or both parents might be excluded if there is reason to suppose that they are likely to become violent or very disruptive. At the case conference, parents can hear the views of everyone else and they can contribute their own views. However, they do not participate in the conference decision making.

Any professional involved in a case conference needs to understand what the experience can feel like from the parents' point of view. It is very stressful as is all the investigation. Parents can feel seriously outnumbered around the table and especially threatened if the police are present – as they will be if the suspected abuse could lead to criminal prosecution.

Some local authorities have developed the use of family group conferences as a way to involve the immediate and extended family in steps to protect a child or young person. This meeting does not replace the child protection conference and any decisions have to be carefully considered, so that the child's well-being is assured. The family group conference can work well when there are other family members who are willing and able to take on specific responsibilities for a child or young person at risk.

THE CHILD PROTECTION REGISTER

The conference decides on the basis of the evidence whether to place the child on the local child protection register. The register is maintained by the local social services on behalf of all the agencies involved in working with children who have been abused or who are judged as being at risk of abuse, and for whom there is a need for a child protection plan. It is also possible for the NSPCC to maintain the register on behalf of the local authority.

Children can be put on the register as early as birth, or even before birth, but there would have to be sufficient evidence for such a move. The key point is that children, whose names are placed on the register, are judged to be at risk of abuse. The children have not necessarily been abused already, but all the information gathered for the case conference leads to a decision that abuse is a real possibility. There may be very strong indications for some children that they have already been abused.

Children can only be placed on the register if the following criteria for registration are met:

▶ There must have been one or more identifiable incidents that can be described as having adversely affected the child. These incidents might be something that was done to a child, or failures to act on behalf of a child.
▶ The professional judgement is that further incidents are likely involving this child.
▶ The abuse must be categorised under one, or more, of the four types:

neglect, physical injury, sexual abuse or emotional abuse (refer to Chapter 1 for definitions of these). In Scotland, non-organic failure to thrive is a separate fifth category, distinguished from other forms of physical neglect.

If a child is not placed on the register, there may still be further work with the family, led by the relevant social worker or involving local family support services, including early years or school settings. The investigation will be written up in the family's file but no further steps will be taken within the child protection process.

If the child's name is placed on the register, other actions must now follow:

▶ A core group is formed of the professionals most involved with the family. This group will not be very large and the aim is that it should not be unwieldy. (See under Step 5 for more details).
▶ A named person has to take responsibility for this case and ensure that the necessary planning and further assessment is undertaken. The person who leads may be called by different titles, for instance, the key worker or the case co-ordinator. He or she will most likely be a local authority or NSPCC social worker.
▶ A child protection plan must now be developed specifically for this child.

Usually, there is only one child protection case conference and the work is continued by the core group. Another case conference would only be called if there was evidence that procedures have not been followed properly. Another reason would be if it becomes clear that all the relevant information for the decision had not been shared at the time of the first conference.

THE CHILD PROTECTION PLAN

In good practice, professionals do not focus most of their energy on identification and investigation of children at risk. Children will be protected and helped through actions that follow. When faced with children at risk, the involved professionals have several options:

▶ They can start a child protection inquiry under the requirements set out in the relevant Children Act or Order. A comprehensive assessment of the child or young person will often be important to identify how best to help. The earlier investigation is only to establish whether the child is being abused or at risk of abuse. The first, briefer investigation does not necessarily point to appropriate actions to take about the abuse and risk.
▶ They can look at the possibilities within family support services. Each of the Children Acts and Orders in the UK is concerned with children in need as well

as child protection. There are possibilities for support services covered in the legislation: Part III of the Children Act 1989, Part II of the Children (Scotland) Act 1995 and Part IV of the Children (Northern Ireland) Order 1996.

▶ There are also possibilities within the child welfare services, including a placement in a community or foster home.

These options are not on an either/or basis. A child protection enquiry often leads to developing use of family support services as the way to safeguard or promote the child's welfare. With younger children, the support services might include attendance with their parent(s) at a family centre, home support for parents or placement of the child in a daily early years setting.

Early years, school and out-of-school practitioners are sometimes worried that a child protection investigation is very likely to mean children are taken away from their families. Parents can be very anxious that their children will be taken into care. But this is an unusual course of action, because guidelines stress that children are to be left with their families, unless there is clear evidence that their welfare can only be safeguarded away from home.

Only in exceptional circumstances will social workers take emergency action and remove children to a foster family or residential home. Social workers can take legal action to make the children the responsibility of the local authority, if children are judged to be suffering, or likely to suffer significant harm, are not receiving reasonable care or are out of parental control. Other legal action can be used if there is reason to believe that a child has been abducted or taken away from those who have parental responsibility. Sometimes parents agree voluntarily that the child(ren) might be looked after for a period of time.

Discussion and reviews of child protection practice have expressed concern that the balance can be too much towards investigation and not enough on intervention through family support. Good practice is seen as a process that blends inquiries with the provision of family support services. Some local authorities have looked carefully at how to shift practice towards an integrated child protection and family support work system. Early action and preventative work is then stressed more than swift reactions when a crisis point is reached in a family.

Step 5: Meetings of the core group

The core group will consist of the key worker, most likely a social worker, and other professionals directly relevant to this family. The group also includes the parent(s) and the children, if they are judged to be old enough to be involved. As with the child protection conference, there would have to be a very compelling reason for not inviting the parent(s).

The core group meets on a regular basis (fortnightly) and has to develop and carry out detailed plans, including:

▶ Developing the child protection plan, which includes the need to identify objective criteria about protection for this child.
▶ Implementing the child protection plan.
▶ Ensuring that there is a comprehensive assessment of the child and family. The case conference has only decided that on the basis of the initial investigation there is cause to put the child's name on the register.
▶ Ensuring that all the elements of the plan are implemented.
▶ Setting up a matrix, which is a pattern of formal monitoring of the child's welfare and well-being. The matrix lays out who will see the child on which day of the week.

ASSESSMENT OF THE CHILD

Part of the child protection plan may be a comprehensive assessment of the child. This action includes gathering information from all the agencies who know the child and family and can include a developmental and/or medical assessment of the child. Any assessment must also include the views and wishes of the children and young people themselves.

Good practice is that any assessment directly involving the child, whether a developmental assessment, an interview or a medical examination must be undertaken with respectful concern for the child, both in their physical care and their feelings. No assessment, at this stage or at the earlier investigation stage, should further add to a child's distress or feelings of being used or abused. Any collecting of evidence should always be balanced against avoiding further trauma to the child. Some child abuse inquiries have made the specific point that children should not be subject to repetitive and long interviews, nor to repeated medical examinations.

Medical examinations would not always be part of the assessment of children at risk. A medical examination of a child would be undertaken for specific reasons, such as to:

▶ Detect traumatic or infectious conditions.
▶ Evaluate the nature of the abuse.
▶ Provide evidence including forensic proof.

▶ Provide a developmental assessment that could provide a benchmark on children's future health and development.
▶ Reassure children who fear that the abuse has seriously damaged them physically.
▶ Start the process of recovery for an abused child.

A medical examination, including the use of X-rays, does not always produce clear-cut results, for instance about how an injury was caused or whether it is accidental or non-accidental, beyond 'reasonable doubt'.

A comprehensive assessment is presented to the first child protection review meeting or less often to a reconvened case conference. The core group is responsible for taking action on the basis of the assessment, always bearing in mind the child's wishes, feelings and perceptions.

Step 6: Reviews

Children do not just remain on the child protection register forever as you can see from the statistics on page 7. Every six months there must be a review, the aim of which is to assess whether the child's name should remain on the register. This review would include all those with relevant information including the parents and the child(ren) if they are old enough. The first review for a child is usually at a shorter time gap, perhaps three months after the child protection conference.

DE-REGISTRATION

The child's name is taken off the register under the following possible circumstances:

▶ The original factors that led to registration no longer apply:
  ▶ the child is still at home but the risk is reduced through work with the family
  ▶ the child is away from home and the source of the risk
  ▶ the abusing adult or young person has gone
  ▶ assessment and analysis shows that child protection is not necessary
▶ The child and family have left the area and the area to which they have moved has assumed responsibility for the case.
▶ The child at risk is not longer deemed to be a child. In England and Wales when young people have reached the age of legal majority (18 years) or got married (between 16 and 18 years). In Scotland, children are de-registered when they reach 16 years and in Northern Ireland at 17 years.
▶ The child has died.

If the review decides that the child's name will be taken off the register, work can continue with the child and family, involving whichever professionals and services are appropriate. The child and family may still need help but the child is judged not longer to be at risk.

How well does the system work?

Lessons from public inquiries

In England and Wales a special case management review must follow the death or very serious injury of a child whenever child abuse is confirmed or suspected. This type of review does not have to be made public. The deaths of children while the local authority is involved with the family have sometimes led to more public inquiries and reports. Scotland does not have the case review system but does undertake public inquiries. The changes brought about by the death of Maria Colwell in 1974 are described on page 2. But subsequent tragedies have brought the names of other children into the public arena. The separate deaths of Jasmine Beckford, Tyra Henry, Kimberley Carlile and Kennedy McFarlane may be familiar to you. But other children have died or been very seriously injured and their cases have not been reported nationally.

It is important that everyone involved in child protection shares the same value base and sees themselves as working together, with different roles but towards the same goals. The national reviews and consultations over child protection practice have highlighted the risks of poor or unbalanced professional practice. Unfortunately, the child protection system still fails some children and some departments responsible for this work are seriously under resourced. The public inquiry, reported in 2003, into the death of Victoria Climbie in North London showed that tragically some of the potential problems described in this section still undermine effective child protection.

There have also been public inquiries following investigations into child abuse when opinions have been divided, for instance, the sexual abuse cases in Cleveland, Rochdale or the Orkneys. Inquiries also usually follow the discovery of substantial abuse at residential institutions or day care settings. For instance, the physically abusive 'Pindown' system used by Tony Latham in Staffordshire children's homes, or the Kincora children's homes scandal in Northern Ireland.

Public enquiries address the particular circumstances surrounding a child's death or the discovery of large-scale abuse. The impact of high profile cases is to unsettle everyone, not only those in that area. The experience of tragedy or the discovery of professional misconduct can shake general morale and confidence. Yet, the enquiries have lessons for good practice that need to be addressed. The Department of Health for England has commissioned reviews to identify the practice implications of the series of enquiries. The key points that have emerged are equally relevant for early years, school and out-of-school practitioners as they consider their role in the whole process of child protection

FOCUS ON THE CHILD(REN)

It is very important to be aware of the state and development of children as individuals in their own right. In some cases that ended in tragedy for the child, professional attention seemed, with hindsight, to be too much on the parents' problems and experience of stress. The needs of children should never be overlooked in order to maintain a good relationship with parents, or any other adults. A criticism made in the public inquiry on the Cleveland sex abuse cases was that the children themselves ran the risk of being lost in the flurry of diagnosis and counter-claim. A telling phrase from that report is still quoted: 'The child is a person not an object of concern.'

PROFESSIONALS MUST WORK WELL TOGETHER

Inquiries have stressed the great importance of inter-agency working: that all the professionals involved with a child or family must discuss, consult and share information in such a way to protect child. During 2002 two public inquiries made it clear that children are still lost as a result of poor inter-agency working, amongst other failings. Two children died through abuse and neglect: Victoria Climbie at the hands of her aunt and partner and Ainlee Walker by her parents. In both cases, information about the child was overlooked or not pursued and fell between different agencies. Abusive parents or carers also exploit any gaps by moving between services and refusing to co-operate with professionals.

Some inquiries have highlighted the dangers for children if their protection is weakened by unclear boundaries for inter-agency work. Relationships between the different professionals and the levels of intervention need to be guided by written procedures. Some inquiries have pointed to competition and hostility between professionals as one reason for the mis-management of a case. Arguments between professionals are unproductive, but a failure to raise issues can be just as dangerous. The phrase 'professional dangerousness' has been used to describe the situation where the actions of child protection professionals can fail to protect and even make matters worse for children.

The phrase 'system abuse' is used to describe the disruptive effect on children when the investigative process in child protection causes significant distress. Inquiries followed the removal of children from the family in Cleveland and the Orkneys. The inquiry reports in both cases were critical of how the children were taken into care and the manner in which they were repeatedly interviewed about the alleged abuse.

More than one inquiry has pointed out the necessity of using observations and assessment by people who see the child(ren) regularly. If all the different reports and knowledge of children are brought together, then the seriousness of the situation for the children can be far more obvious than depending on one perspective. This finding suggests the great importance of consulting group settings where children are seen on a regular basis, sometimes daily.

Avoid unrealistic optimism

Adults would often rather think well of other adults – that they would not deliberately harm their children or place children's needs at the bottom of their list of priorities. Yet no professional can afford to be guided by what has been called 'the rule of optimism': the wish to think the best of people, despite evidence to the contrary. It is important not to be unduly pessimistic about a family, and certainly not to work on unsupported assumptions of likely failure because of the family's social, ethnic or religious identity. However, some inquiries have pointed to the risks that followed from professionals' over-optimism that a parent, or other adult, could cope, or that the parent's view of the situation was the most reliable.

Maintain a professional objectivity

Professionals within any of the branches of social, family and child care have to manage a blend of caring and detachment. They have to avoid becoming over-involved with the family, overlooking the needs of the child(ren) in order to protect a working relationship with the parents. No practitioner should resist acting on concerns about children because 'it could damage my relationship with the parents'. There are serious risks if professionals become over-involved with a family. They may overlook the significance of family patterns of behaviour because they are focusing on single events or crises. These risks are multiplied if a social worker is operating without sufficient support.

The crucial need for support

No practitioner should operate in child protection without clear lines of support. All practitioners, but especially those who are less experienced, need easy access to regular supervision. The judgements and decisions that need to be made in child protection are rarely straightforward and consultation and weighing up different perspectives will be crucial. Good quality supervision and professional support should also offer a way of dealing properly with personal feelings and values, including cultural and religious issues.

Concerns about a family need to be acknowledged as do any worries about the professional's own personal safety with a particular family. Children are left at risk if social workers or other practitioners feel intimidated or threatened by a family. The risk is multiplied if practitioners deal with their fears by failure to persist in visits to see the child. Realistic anxiety about personal safety appears to have been yet another factor in the avoidable deaths of Victoria Climbie and Ainlee Walker. A proper support system should swiftly challenge the situation of how can any children be regarded as safe when they are living in households which the professionals are scared to visit.

APPROPRIATE ANTI–DISCRIMINATORY PRACTICE

It is appropriate that professions such as social work should actively seek to recruit members from across ethnic and social groups. The handling of any child protection case should include proper knowledge and understanding of the cultural and social background of the child and family. However, children are not protected by crude racial matching of professional and family. A black professional, loosely defined, is not going to share the same culture, faith or language as every family who is also defined loosely as black. More sensible, detailed considerations are needed.

Furthermore, anti-discriminatory practice cannot mean tolerance of treatment of children that damages their health or development. An appropriate respect for families, combined with effective protection of children, has sometimes been a hard balance to maintain. The task can be especially difficult in under-resourced social work departments and where teams have become highly anxious about being labelled as racist. Some similar issues can affect early years, school and out-of-school teams and these are discussed in the section from page 89.

A BALANCE BETWEEN INVESTIGATION AND FAMILY SUPPORT

A recurring dilemma when there is any concern of possible child abuse is deciding at what point an investigation is started into a family, institution or an individual. In the second half of the 1990s there was shift towards what was called a 'lighter touch', trying to explore possibilities of family support and not moving at too greater haste into the investigation process. This discussion has been called the 'refocusing debate' and has worked to find a new balance in the child protection system between using the investigation sections of the Children Act 1989 and family support.

How may you be involved?

Practice varies considerably between different areas. But, in general, there has been a stronger tradition of involving schools and teachers rather than early years and out-of-school settings. It is hard to explain this division unless you link it to the general care-education divide and the view that school staff are professionals and other practioners are generally not. I disagree with this view, but it exists and influences the poor practice that can leave non-educational settings out of the child protection process.

However, there have been steady changes that make it far more likely now that early years and out-of-school settings will be recognised as important sources of information and support within child protection. It has been required for some time that schools have clear written procedures for child protection and a designated member of staff responsible for co-ordinating work between the school and other agencies. The local social services has a duty to inform a school if a child on the school roll is placed on the child protection register, or if the child starts school. The school must monitor the child's attendance and development and report any concerns to the local education authority. It is also the school's responsibility to inform the keeper of the child protection register if the child changes school.

There is now a greater recognition that most children attend some kind of early years setting before school age and that many children experience out-of-school care. Two strong themes in good practice for child protection make it likely that non-school settings will be more involved in the child protection process, especially when their teams show their knowledge and professionalism (see the discussion on page 88).

1 Inquiries and guidelines stress that the focus on the child must never be lost in concerns about adults within the family. Early years settings have worked hard to develop partnership with parents alongside a clear focus on children and their development. Early years settings usually keep developmental records of children and see them on a regular basis, sometimes daily. Out-of-school settings will keep different kinds of

records but share the regular contact with children that can be so vital to their well-being.

2 Reviews of practice continue to emphasise that professionals must work together and social workers, or other key practitioners in a core group must draw on all the agencies involved with a child and family. This will often include early years and out-of-school settings.

You are more likely now to be involved with your local child protection team than in the early 1990s. You should be closely involved and consulted if you work in settings that have a selected population such as family centres and other early years settings of which family support is an integral part of your work.

There are no equivalent expectations of non-educational early years settings, nor a requirement that the setting be informed in the same way as schools. You may be involved by your local team, but there is no official line similar to the position if you work in a nursery or primary school. You are more likely to be involved if you work in settings that have a selected population that brings in more families who are deemed to be at risk and children who are 'in need': for instance, family centres or local authority children's centres.

POSSIBILITIES OF INVOLVEMENT

Practitioners in school and out-of-school services can have an important role to play in child protection. However everyone needs to be clear about what should be done internally and what should be referred on to social services. No practitioner, however experienced or senior in a setting, will undertake an investigation, as described on page 53. This part of the work is the job of the social worker. However, there are a number of equally important ways in which you might be involved in the child protection process:

▶ Concerns might be raised first within your service. You are in an important position to be aware of the development and well-being of individual children.

▶ Good practice in any early years setting is to keep records of children's attendance and of their developmental progress. So, you may be the first professional to become concerned about a child's failure to thrive physically, difficulties in development or the changing behaviour of a previously happy child.

▶ Practitioners do not have to make the judgement whether a child or young person is being abused. You would never start a child protection investigation yourself but you, and your colleagues in a team, could be crucial at the early stage of exploring the seriousness of a concern

▶ Your first awareness of a problem might be when you are contacted by a social worker or child protection co-ordinator because concerns have been raised elsewhere about a child who attends your setting or family home if you work as a childminder.

▶ If a child is on the local child protection register then the social services should inform and involve your setting to ensure the full protection of the child. You may be asked to monitor this child's attendance and development and report any concerns to the social worker in charge of the case. You might be asked to tell a social worker immediately if a child fails to arrive as agreed or if the parent intends to move the child to another setting.

▶ In early years settings, your usual written records of children and their development will be important for a child who is at risk. But you may also keep other factual records including exchanges with the child and parent(s).

▶ You might be asked to be present when a child is being interviewed regarding concerns about possible abuse. When you know a child well, your presence might be very reassuring in what could otherwise be a confusing or distressing experience.

▶ You, or a senior colleague, may present reports at a case conference or later review of the case.

▶ Work with a young child and the parent(s) in an early years setting may be a specific part of the child protection plan that is developed when the child's name is added to the child protection register. Certainly, placement of the child in an early years setting should not be the end of the work with the family. The key social worker should continue in contact with you.

▶ Schools and out-of-school services have an important part to play within the boundaries to their services. Schools have a pastoral side but may sometimes have to balance how much time can be given to parents who are very needy.

▶ You may have an important role in supporting parents and continuing to work with them. Some families may work most closely with the duty social worker but some parents may have developed a good working relationship with you. A parent may turn to you to explain what will happen or appreciate your company at the case conference.

▶ It is possible, although unlikely, that you may be called upon to give evidence in criminal proceedings (see page 167). Most abuse cases do not reach the courts, so only a few readers of this book will face the experience of being a witness.

3

Policies, procedures and good practice

Early years, school and out-of-school practitioners have a very important role to play in a comprehensive approach to child protection. Practitioners within the different services have regular contact with children and with their parents. Child protection should never be seen as an internal concern, but neither is it a matter just for outside specialists such as social workers. The part that practitioners play in child protection requires the following:

▶ Knowledge and understanding of the whole framework of which you are a part. Chapter 2 describes the child protection system as a whole.
▶ Understanding your role: how you could be involved, as well as what you will not be doing.
▶ Knowledge of the policy and procedures of your setting – what you do within your service and what is expected of you as part of your job.

Policy and procedures

Good practice in early years, school and out-of-school services involves clear, public policies. A policy on child protection should be in place, regardless of the children and families who use your service. It is not the case that only centres and services dealing with vulnerable families need to address child protection. Attention to this area is part of good practice for everyone. In the different aspects of your work **policies** lay out the key principles that should guide and inform good practice and **procedures** will describe the details of the steps that should be followed. It is likely that your child protection guidance may include principles and action within the same material. Consequently, this section refers to written guidance as child protection procedures.

Procedures on child protection should be in place as a matter of good practice. You do not, for instance, wait for children to have accidents in your setting before you decide on procedures on first aid. All your staff should know where the first aid materials are kept and safe steps to follow in a minor or apparently more serious injury. In the same way, it would be very poor practice if any setting postponed any consideration of child protection until some crisis developed.

You are not, of course, trying to assess whether the kinds of families you meet are likely to abuse their children. There are no easy predictions in child protection, because there is no social class, ethnic or religious group for whom anyone can say with confidence that these people are likely, or unlikely, to abuse or neglect their children. Additionally, families that have taken good care of their children can be shocked to find that someone else, trusted by the family, has abused the children. So detailed procedures should be in place whatever the area you work in, the families who use your service or the kind of service you offer. As with any other policy on good practice, the guidance on child protection in your setting should be drafted so that it is straightforward to use:

▶ The procedures should be written down in a format that is easy to read and understand for all the team, including any volunteers. The concerns and guidance for action apply to everyone.
▶ The procedures should be public, in that they can be consulted by parents or any professionals involved your setting or service.
▶ Key issues in child protection should be communicated to parents as part of establishing a good working relationship between families and your service. So, for instance, general material about your setting and initial conversations with parents are an opportunity to communicate that you have obligations to address and report serious concerns about children.
▶ Any policy should be open to discussion and review. Certainly if you are drafting a policy for the first time, it is a good idea to set a date, perhaps six months ahead when the policy will be discussed in detail and sensible revisions made.

Practitioners who work alone

Some readers will work on their own, within a family home. Childminders and foster carers work within their own home and nannies within the children's own home. As an individual practitioner, you would not be expected to have lengthy written procedures. It is important, however, that childminders, foster carers and nannies, are aware of their professional obligations in child protection and have information about whom they should contact locally.

Throughout this chapter, there is acknowledgement of the rather different situation of practitioners who work on their own.

Child protection procedures

Any procedures need to be worded and communicated in a positive way. You do not want to give the impression that all parents, practitioners or volunteers are seen as potential abusers. Such an approach would be very disheartening and would not reflect the genuine level of risk for children – the majority of adults will not abuse children. The procedures need to be presented positively as part of how you care for children and your awareness that child abuse is a reality within our society. The procedures make clear your responsibilities within the broader framework of child care and education and that the team is accountable for their own actions.

For a group setting your child protection procedures should lay out in a clear way the responsibilities of the team, including:

▶ The duty of staff to work towards prevention of child abuse and to react appropriately to any concerns.
▶ A summary of signs that should concern a practitioner, but which are not necessarily proof of child abuse. This part of procedures would not be lengthy and could well be a brief summary of material that is available in another guideline document.
▶ What to do when staff have concerns and what not to do. The role of practitioners is to deal with the immediate situation involving a child or adult and to pass on concerns. Procedures should make clear the difference between talking with a child or parent and undertaking an investigation (which is the role of a social worker).
▶ The steps that will be followed when there is reason for concern, the balance between confidentiality and obligation of teams and individuals such as childminders to pass on concerns.
▶ The ways in which early years, school or out-of-school practitioners might be involved as contributors to a child protection investigation.
▶ Ways of supporting a child, and parent, who is involved in the child protection process. This section would acknowledge the support role but not go into significant detail.
▶ The responsibilities of the setting on child protection, duties under a legal framework that affect everyone in child care, early education and playwork.
▶ Details of who should be consulted locally: the local social services department, a local branch of the NSPCC or the police child protection team. Procedures should make it clear who should be contacted under what circumstances, if there is a choice.
▶ The policy on keeping records, good practice in observation and written reports and the policy of sharing records with parents.

▶ Issues of security in the setting, including who has responsibility for collecting children at the end of the day or session and visitors to the centre.
▶ The procedures for making checks on new staff and volunteers. A system for dealing with criticisms of staff practice, or allegations of child abuse.

Good practice in child protection involves making supported judgements about children and your concerns about them. Clear child protection procedures are necessary so that everyone understands the framework in which you are working. But no procedure, however good, will make decisions for you. Written guidelines give you a framework in which to work and should indicate how to consult, seek support and pass on concerns appropriately. The most experienced professional in child protection is still in the position of making carefully considered judgements based on what is known and what can reasonably be predicted.

ACTIVITY

If you are in post, look at the child protection procedures of your setting. If you are on work placement as a student, then talk with the head or manager about reading their procedures.

You can consider some or all of these questions:

1 Do the child protection procedures cover all these issues raised in this section? If not, how might any gaps be covered?
2 Are the procedures effectively shared with all the adults involved in your setting? For instance, are you an early years setting with volunteers or parent helpers? If you work in a school, are the specialist teaching assistants or playground support staff fully informed and involved?
3 How often are the procedures updated for changes in names and contact details for named people who should be contacted over child protection issues?
4 If your setting has no proper procedures then, with the agreement of your manager, start the process of drafting an appropriate set.

Any written policies or procedures should be available in the main languages spoken in your neighbourhood. For some settings, this task may be very straightforward, but, if you work in a diverse area with many languages and written scripts, the translation task may be daunting. This issue will arise with all written material originating from your service, so it is wise to contact local translation and interpretation services. Bilingual practitioners or parents may be able to help in the work, but it would be wise to obtain a second opinion on translations, especially with such a sensitive topic as child protection.

Some parents, or carers, will not be literate or may be very reluctant readers. So practitioners should always be ready to explain in words – for any aspect of good practice, not only child protection.

Steps in child protection for practitioners

A possible plan of action, with options, is given on page 72. If your own group setting does not have such a flow chart, you could use this plan as a working chart from which you develop your own. Minor concerns will often be resolved within your setting and through conversation with parents.

▶ However, you should find out well before there is a crisis exactly how the child protection system works in your area.

▶ Your first step is not automatically to call social services. In a group setting, or as an individual practitioner, you would most often talk with the parent(s). The exception is if the current situation, or past events with this family, genuinely support a belief that the child is at immediate and significant risk. See also page 82 about partnership with parents.

▶ Readers will be in different situations regarding who they can consult about concerns, that are not emergencies. In a group setting, you should be able to have a swift discussion with a more senior colleague or your manager, as well as a confidential discussion with a room colleague, if you have one. In schools and some early years settings there will be a designated child protection officer on the staff team. In this case, you can discuss with this person.

▶ If there are serious concerns, then you need to know already the telephone number and, if appropriate, the name of the person to contact. This person would most likely be the duty social worker, or possibly the local NSPCC, if they are prominent in child protection in your area. Even out of normal working hours, there should be emergency social work cover at the end of the telephone.

▶ The police have an important role in child protection (see page 52), but it is very unlikely that the police would be your first contact. The exception would be if a parent, or other carer, were attacking a child or other person within your centre and the behaviour was so aggressive, that it was unsafe for staff to intervene. You would then call the police as you would for any incident where safety was a serious concern.

Possible flow chart for early years, school or playwork practitioners

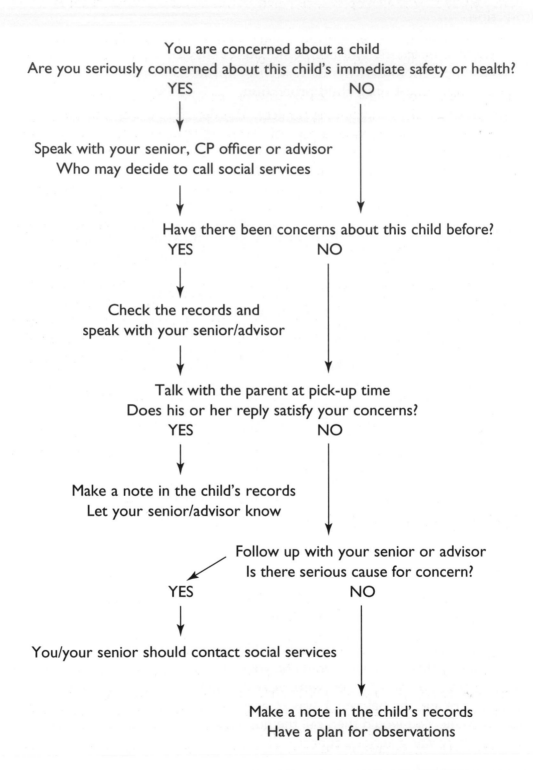

You are concerned about a child
Are you seriously concerned about this child's immediate safety or health?
YES   NO

Speak with your senior, CP officer or advisor
Who may decide to call social services

Have there been concerns about this child before?
YES   NO

Check the records and
speak with your senior/advisor

Talk with the parent at pick-up time
Does his or her reply satisfy your concerns?
YES   NO

Make a note in the child's records
Let your senior/advisor know

Follow up with your senior or advisor
Is there serious cause for concern?
YES   NO

You/your senior should contact social services

Make a note in the child's records
Have a plan for observations

▶ If a concern is sufficient that you have discussed the matter with the parent(s), then it is appropriate to make a note in your written records.

If you are a practitioner working on your own, then you will need to look at the plan in a different way, although covering the same steps.

▶ Childminders should have access to a named person who locally is responsible for the childminding services. The development of childminding networks has usually created a post of childminding development worker, or a similar title. In some areas, childminders are offered a full programme of training, which should include child protection.
▶ As a foster carer, you are working with children who are already vulnerable, although not necessarily abused. Foster carers should have had clear information about child protection through pre-care training and should have easy means to contact a social worker or a foster care link worker.
▶ Practitioners working as nannies can be the most alone if child protection concerns arise. As an unregistered early years service, nannies do not easily have access to the advice and information resources of other practitioners in early years settings. But there is no reason why you cannot find out details of early years advisors, with a view to extending your knowledge of local child protection and establishing a possible way to discuss concerns in confidence.

Practitioners working on their own can, like any other concerned adult, phone the NSPCC in confidence. The national helpline for adults or children is 0808 800 5000 Some duty social workers will listen on the telephone and give advice, without insisting on names. Local teams vary and some are not able or willing to offer time in this way.

Adult responsibilities

Staff behaviour

All group settings need clear guidelines for the behaviour of staff and volunteers. This kind of policy has links with child protection but many of the issues are about more general good practice with children. The main issues include:

▶ A positive approach to dealing with children's behaviour and any misbehaviour. Staff need to understand what are acceptable and unacceptable approaches to discipline. (More from page 192.)
▶ The standards of behaviour that are expected of staff in their work with the

children and some sense of what is non-negotiable and what is more a matter for individual style. Guidelines would also be applicable to parent helpers, volunteers and young people on work placement.

▶ All settings need to have discussed the issues of appropriate and inappropriate physical contact with children. This issue is particularly important in the physical care of young children or older disabled children. (see page 178.) This discussion also leads into respect for children and not imposing adult needs for emotional support or affection onto the children.

▶ Appropriate touch is also a feature of physical contact within discipline when children may need to be restrained for their own safety or that of others.

▶ Senior staff should monitor the programme of activities for the children – what is done and how.

It is also good to monitor any local trips that staff made with children. It should always be clear what staff have planned in a local trip, where they are going and the purpose of the trip. One reason why such outings should be monitored is because a few abusers within early years settings have used trips out as the opportunity to abuse children. However, the vast majority of unacceptable trips with young children will not be abusive in intention or result, but will be a poor use of time with the children, for instance, trailing them round shops that are only of interest to adults. Good practice for outings with older children relates also to their safety, appropriate levels of supervision and adult expertise with equipment or resources.

Organisation of the work

Attempts to organise a setting to minimise the chance of child abuse have to be considered realistically. Some settings have made firm ground rules that children should always be with more than one person or that male practitioners should not undertake any intimate care of children.

In many settings it is completely unrealistic to insist that there must always be more than one adult present with a child or group. This type of recommendation unfortunately suggests that all staff are potential abusers. Yet it does not remove all possibility of abuse. Single abusers are the more common pattern but abusers have been known to work with one or more colleagues. The limitations on male practitioners are misplaced for several reasons – see page 80.

Unfortunately, there is no definitive way of organising that will remove all possibility of abuse within a group setting. However, procedures for checking staff and an atmosphere in which children and adults feel able to raise concerns will be a more reliable way to work to prevent abuse and poor practice. You will find more on these issues on page 75.

A focus on the children

The emphasis of any early years, school or out-of-school setting must always be on the children and their well-being. A setting with a strong community focus probably has to keep an especially strong hold on this perspective. The same is true of centres that offer work experience to students or other young people. An early years, school or out-of-school setting is not a therapeutic community for staff or volunteers. Nor is it the children's primary role in life to create training opportunities for adults and young people.

▶ The supervision system in any setting should be used to support any practitioner whose health or emotional well-being is leading to stress at work. But you should never lose sight of a practitioner's daily practice with the children. If stresses from the practitioner's home life are leading to poor practice, then the children's safety and well-being has to be the prime concern. If a choice is forced, then the well-being of the children is more important than sympathy for adults and a wish not to upset them by challenging poor practice or changing their work duties.

▶ Volunteers can be welcome and may be crucial for the running of some group settings. But, no centre should tolerate bad practice from a volunteer, perhaps on the grounds of 'We can't make a fuss, she's giving her time for free.' Of course, poor practice from volunteers, much as some concerns about practitioners, will not always be at the level of child abuse. A senior practitioner might have to deal with a volunteer who is regularly impatient with the children or insists on table manners that are culturally very specific and therefore inappropriate.

▶ Early years and community centres are sometimes contacted by other local organisations who ask for an individual to be placed with them because working with children might help this individual. Heads of centres must not feel under any obligation to agree to such requests. Volunteers should only be accepted because they are suitable to be with children. You might have sympathy for this person's needs but your decision has to be whether the children will benefit.

New staff

PROTECTING CHILDREN FROM HIGH RISK ADULTS

Thorough checking is not only about the activities of paedophiles; children are also harmed by adults whose poor practice moves into physical or emotional abuse or neglectful treatment. There are two broad types of checks that should be made before anyone is accepted to work in close contact with children or young people.

▶ There should be a police check for any relevant criminal conviction that would make someone a direct risk to children.
▶ There should be a check for any background information from previous employment or voluntary work that raises serious questions about a person's suitability or practice. On this kind of check, there need not have been any criminal investigation or caution. The named person could have been dismissed or otherwise removed from a post because of serious concerns about how he or she behaved with the children or young people.

Organisations or group settings have to contact the relevant body for their part of the UK and apply for disclosure of information. Generally, the fuller disclosure of unsuitability, as well the police check, would have to be undertaken for any person who would be in regular close contact with children or young people, through work in early years settings, as a childminder, in school and out-of-school care and residential children's homes.

If you work in England and Wales, the Protection of Children Act 1999 established the Criminal Records Bureau(CRB). The CRB has the task of bringing together the data held in the Police National Computer and information on the lists of people unsuitable to work with children and young people held by the Department of Health (the Protection of Children Act List) and the Department for Education and Skills (known as List 99). Responsibility for the CRB was given to a private company, Capita, and in 2002 there were major delays in getting the checks through the system.

In Scotland, the Protection of Children Bill introduced an index to list people unsuitable to work with children in 2002. The organisation Disclosure Scotland handles the criminal records checks and the index.

In Northern Ireland the Pre-Employment Consultancy Service (PECS) register was placed on a full legal footing by the Protection of Children and Vulnerable Adults Bill 1999. This service again covers police checks and persons unsuitable to work with children. Cross border issues are a serious concern for Northern Ireland, since unsafe adults move between the Province and Eire. Child protection professionals in both countries are working hard to get their vetting systems coherent and enable communication between teams across the border.

Organisations and settings have to register with the relevant body, to validate their right to ask for the information about a named individual. You should talk to your local advisors if you are at all unclear about how to proceed. Good practice would also to be honest with prospective employees and volunteers that these checks are a non-negotiable part of the process.

Childminders and adult members of their household are all checked, as are foster carers. Nannies are not currently subject to any checks, so families have to use their own judgement, as well as follow up a nanny's references and curriculum vitae. The only exception is when nannies work with three or more families, in which case they are judged to be working effectively as childminders. Nannies are then required to go through the childminding registration and inspection process, that would then include the full checks.

GOOD PRACTICE IN RECRUITMENT

Even when it runs smoothly, no checking system can be 100 per cent effective. Police checks will only show incidents when an individual has been cautioned or convicted. Lists of people judged unsuitable can only be updated when somebody has been identified in bad practice. So, good recruitment procedures for group settings are crucial.

▶ Use written application forms for everyone, including volunteers.
▶ Take up at least two written references and ideally follow them up by telephone, but especially if there are any doubts.
▶ Explore any doubts about the people whose names are given as referees: what they say or how you are required to contact them, for instance a mobile number rather than workplace that can be independently checked.
▶ You should look carefully at the curriculum vitae of any applicant and reassure yourself about any unexplained gaps or swift changes of job. Verify qualifications whenever possible.
▶ Ask for proof of identity, preferably something that contains a photograph, or request a National Insurance number.

Unsuitable individuals may still get through careful recruitment systems or people develop bad practice while in post. No system is 100 per cent effective, but sloppy checks or recruitment procedures put children at a higher risk.

HIGH RISK INDIVIDUALS IN THE NEIGHBOURHOOD

People convicted of serious sexual offences are subject to a sex offender order that means that they have to:

▶ Notify their local police of their name and address and any changes to that information. This information is kept by the police on what has become known as the sex offenders register.

▶ Follow specific restrictions on their behaviour, for instance staying away from children's settings like a playground, or refraining from seeking employment with children.

There is as yet no central register for sex offenders but recent proposals for England may establish a national database listing violent and sex offenders.

Local panels and committees operate in the four nations of the UK to manage information about known sex offenders who pose a risk to children or young people. The panel or committee has the power to disclose information about an individual to an organisation or group, if that person were in contact with, or working to get in close contact with, children. There would not be a more public disclosure, and members of the public cannot access the police register, because of the real dangers of civic unrest. Events in some parts of England during 2000 showed that violent neighbourhood action could result from information – true or false – about paedophiles living locally.

Induction process and continued support

Checks on staff and volunteers are an important part of good practice in group settings, but this step is only one part of effective child protection. All staff and volunteers should have copies of the centre's policies. The implications for practice should be explained in more than one conversation, if necessary.

▶ Staff need to be clear about guidelines on good practice, for instance about a positive approach to children's behaviour, their physical care or trips out of the setting. Such support is sometimes overlooked for volunteers, but is equally necessary.

▶ Paid staff should have a job description – it is a legal requirement. But parent helpers and other volunteers could also be given an outline of what they are expected to do and the limits to their responsibilities.

▶ Staff and volunteers should know how they will be offered and can ask for support and that it is good practice to ask rather than assume, when you are uncertain.

▶ Any adult or young person who is working with the children in your centre needs to recognise that poor practice will be challenged, as indeed good practice should be encouraged. Everyone has to keep within the good practice boundaries. It is irrelevant for the children that someone is volunteering their time or present only for a fixed work experience slot.

▶ Teams sometimes need to think more carefully about explanation and support for volunteers or parent helpers. These adults need to work within good practice boundaries. Clear support may be necessarily to explain what is legitimate discussion and what is inappropriate gossip, or breaking of confidences overheard in the setting.

Visitors to a group setting

Early years, school or out-of-school settings will have a number of visitors, either those who are interested in your work or people who have a legitimate involvement in your practice, for instance, members of the management committee or parent governors in school.

Good practice is to keep track of the number of visitors, since too many adults can be a disruption for children's learning. Children, just like adults, may also resent unannounced arrivals of visitors. Clear communication to children on this issue is a matter of respect. Good adult practice also enables older children, in school or out-of-school settings, to realise that you want to know if they see unknown adults in the setting.

Child protection concerns arise in that visitors should be monitored and not simply left to wander about a centre. Any concerns raised by children, or their parents, about a regular visitor, should be taken with the same level of seriousness as concerns about any adult or young person. David Finkelhor's study of sexual abuse in day care settings in the United States established that, in something like half of the cases, the perpetrator was a regular visitor to the centre – neither a stranger nor a member of staff.

Communication and effective child protection

Child protection procedures will depend on good communication within any group setting.

▶ Practitioners need to feel confident that there are opportunities to talk with colleagues and senior staff and that their concerns will be taken with seriousness.

▶ Any centre needs a system of supervision and support for staff. Supervision should be in place not only because of child protection concerns but also to deal with any other practice issues that arise and need to be talked through for clarity or resolution.

▶ Working with a child and family can be stressful when there are child protection concerns. The practitioner has to maintain confidentiality and not discuss the family outside the setting. But it is the responsibility of senior staff to ensure that the person most involved with the child has opportunities to express worries or doubts within the team. The chance to talk should be seen as a usual part of such work and not available only 'if you're really upset'.

▶ Staff who are involved with children on a daily basis should be informed about what is happening in a child protection case by the senior practitioner, who in turn may need to make sure that the centre continues to be informed by outside agencies.

Teams need to consider limits to the 'need to know' when child protection is concerned and also that all practitioners understand when confidential discussions take place. Inexperienced practitioners may need to be directed that no personal details of the children, whether child protection is an issue or not, should be discussed outside the setting. However, even experienced practitioners may need to be alerted to a suitable time and place for confidential discussions within the setting.

Childminders and foster carers may have to manage carefully the limited explanations and information necessary for members of their own household.

Male practitioners

Early years teams have always been overwhelmingly female. It is unusual to encounter male staff in nurseries and playgroups, and primary schools usually have far more female teachers than male. The main reason for this imbalance seems to be that working with babies and young children has been seen as women's work. The job has been undervalued and pay and conditions, although they have improved, still reflect those attitudes. Children's and family centres that have multi-disciplinary teams often have more men, who may join the centre with a qualification other than child care or early education. The playwork tradition links with youth and leisure work and involves working with older children. Consequently, it is more usual to meet male practitioners in after-school clubs or holiday schemes.

The child protection focus

Until concern about child abuse came to the forefront, many early years teams were keen to encourage more male involvement in order to provide children with a well-rounded experience. However, awareness of sexual abuse has raised some difficult issues. As a consequence, some teams and local authorities have made ground rules that only apply to male staff or have failed to encourage men working in early years centres. This debate is a complicated one and there are no sure answers. This section covers the main issues and will help you to think about this area of practice, whether you are female or male.

The focus of concern about male staff with young children in particular has been that 'most abusers are male', so children have to be protected. However:

▶ The only area of child abuse in which men predominate is sexual abuse. The impact of sexual abuse on children can be substantial, but it is not the only child protection concern. Additionally, some women have sexually abused children and, where there is institutional abuse, women are relatively more prominent than in abuse by family or friends.

▶ Banning men from early years work would not deal with the fact that women can be physically and emotionally cruel to children. Munchausen Syndrome by proxy is rare, but women rather than men show this kind of psychological disturbance, which can be dangerous to the children involved (see page 15).

▶ Most sex abusers are male but most men do not sexually abuse children or young people. It is seriously unjust to develop a policy on early years employment that assumes all men are potential sex abusers.

Taken to extremes, this concern could mean that no men are allowed near children in any capacity. This exclusion would ban them as staff in early years centres, school and playwork facilities or as fathers with their own children. Such an extreme stance is unworkable and would seriously distort children's development. Human beings come in two sexes and boys and girls need both of them.

All settings need clear codes of conduct with children, which apply to female as well as male staff. The inaccurate view that children are only at risk from men overlooks the capacity of some women to ill-treat children physically or emotionally. Paedophiles sometimes spend a considerable amount of time becoming accepted before they start to abuse children. So it is important that any code of conduct should apply to all staff, however long they have been involved with the setting, and whether they are paid for their work or give their time as a volunteer. Centres also need an atmosphere in which children, colleagues and parents feel able to voice any concerns promptly and with confidence that someone will listen and take them seriously. (See page 118.)

(See page 118.)

EQUAL OPPORTUNITIES ISSUES

Discussion and argument in the UK has focused on 'most abusers are men so . . .', but this perspective on the discussion has not followed in all countries. Publications from the European Commission Network on Childcare point out that countries in mainland Europe, especially in Scandinavia, have held on to the equal opportunities focus in employing male practitioners. Child protection is a concern but is not assumed to be resolved by keeping men out of work with young children. Strong reasons for employing both men and women in the team include:

▶ Children need to relate to men as well as women who provide a positive role model of being an adult.
▶ Putting equal opportunities on gender into practice ideally needs a mixed-sex team. It is far more effective for children to learn and play alongside male staff who show a gentle side, or are good cooks, than to tell children this is a possibility, or only depend on books and posters.
▶ Male and female practitioners may well have different styles because of their sex as well as their individual differences. So long as the roles of practitioners do not become stereotyped, or one sex corners all the interesting work, then children can experience different styles.
▶ Children in single parent homes may not have much contact with a positive male figure – although of course some do. Children from homes disrupted by male domestic violence may desperately need some experience of a man who can be gentle, patient and deal with conflict without violence.

Partnership with parents

Establishing a friendly working relationship with parents is part of good practice in all the early years, school and out-of-school services. You should be aiming for an effective partnership and exploring what this means for your setting, even if you never have any child protection concerns. An open and friendly relationship with parents can, however, make a substantial difference when concerns arise about possible abuse do arise.

TALKING WITH PARENTS

Regular conversations with parents should be normal experience for them and will make them more conformable about discussing a range of issues with you. Make sure that you exchange interesting and positive experiences of their child and let them know about any minor mishaps in the centre that have involved or hurt their child. You would also exchange information about a child's health, that a child has developed a slight temperature at the end of the day or that there are two cases of chicken pox in the nursery. These kind of conversations build a relationship which communicates your interest in their child, your wish to keep parents informed and to listen to their views and information.

It is bad practice for practitioners to develop the habit of only talking with a parent if there is a problem. The result of this imbalance is that parents will, not surprisingly, be wary as soon as you bear down on them. They will be ready to defend themselves or their child against criticism. If you then have a serious worry, parents are far less likely to listen and talk with you than if you have an existing friendly relationship. It will never be easy or fully comfortable to have a conversation with a parent that arises because of an unexplained injury to the child or because the child has made a worrying remark. But it is far more possible if you have established yourself with parents as somebody who cares about the children and is not always ready to criticise and blame parents.

The first step in child protection worries would be, in the vast majority of cases, to talk with the parent. This will not be an easy conversation but it will be far more possible if you have developed a relationship with this parent which has established you as a person who will listen, as well as talk, and who cares about the child. Such a conversation could be very hard if this is the first time you have had a proper conversation with this parent, or if you have allowed a situation to develop in which you only talk with parents, or some parents, when there is a problem.

Sometimes, it will be a parent, or other carer of the child, who raises a worry with you. Again, parents are far more likely to approach you if they have developed confidence in you as someone who will listen and not overreact. Most practitioners are most concerned about the prospect of tackling parents about a worry. Staff overlook the possibility that parents may sometimes have worries: about a member of their family, a neighbour, a practitioner or volunteer. Parents may be very uneasy about approaching a member of staff, however much they feel that they must say something.

ACTIVITY

Over a period of two weeks, keep track of all your conversations with parents, however short. Note down:

▶ The name of the parent with whom you spoke.
▶ The day and approximate time.
▶ The topic of conversation and in brief what was said.

If it is possible, also keep a note of conversations when parents approach you.

Look back over your record afterwards and consider honestly:

1 Are there any parents with whom you rarely, if ever, speak? Are there some with whom it is usually only a very short exchange? What might be the possible reasons?
2 Can you see any imbalance in the reasons for which you start a conversation with parents, or with some parents in particular? Is it usually to raise problems with some, or many of the parents?
3 What can you do to redress any imbalances? Talk over your findings with a colleague. Perhaps you all find it hard to approach some of the parents, but you need to plan what to do about it.

ACCESS TO RECORDS

Parents should know that you keep an accident book of incidents in the setting and that they have access to any records about their own child. Some teams have space on records or a diary of a child so that parents can contribute their views, in agreement or disagreement. Parents will be less disturbed about any recording for child protection concerns if they can see this activity as part of the centre's good practice in keeping accurate and objective records. Centres that do not give parents easy access to their children's records are creating potential trouble. Parents may well assume that the records are biased or full of critical remarks about the children and parents.

In your setting it should be clear to parents and to any professionals with whom you work:

▶ What records you keep on a regular basis.
▶ The reasons you keep records and details of children's development. Your aims are not all negative about identifying and tracking problems.
▶ Your obligations about discussing concerns and to whom you would show records under these circumstances. Written records are not shared with everyone.
▶ How you work to ensure that your records are factual and objective.

▶ The steps you take to ensure that written and computer-based records are kept secure to ensure confidentiality and avoid any unauthorised access.

You will find more about record keeping from page 164.

CHILD PROTECTION POLICY AND PARENTS

It would be overwhelming for parents who were new to your setting if they were given copies of every policy or set of procedures and left to read them. Parents need to be given the key points about how your setting operates and told that they are welcome to look in greater detail at any policies if they wish. The key points about child protection for parents are that:

▶ Staff have a commitment to children's health and development. There is a team commitment in settings and childminders share that commitment in their practice within their own home.
▶ Part of the work is an obligation to follow up concerns about any child's physical well-being, emotional state or behaviour.
▶ Usual practice is to discuss any worries first with the child's parent or carer.
▶ If staff, or the parent(s), feel concerned that child protection is an issue, then the matter has to be referred to social services.
▶ The written records on children are open to those children's parent(s) or other permanent carer.
▶ If parents have any concerns about their child(ren) or about any member of staff, then they can raise them with a practitioner or the head of the centre, as they feel best.

These points might be drafted into a written leaflet but good communication includes spoken exchanges as well. It is important for practitioners to find a form of words to explain the ideas in conversation. Not all parents will be confident readers and some may welcome a brief discussion as well as having a written leaflet.

ACTIVITY

Using the key points suggested for communication with parents about child protection and write them into a short leaflet for parents.

1 Discuss your wording with a colleague and consider any suitable revisions. You could also discuss the leaflet with a friend who is not involved in your profession. Such a person can often be a good judge of whether a

leaflet is clear or has some professional phrases that are not in everyday usage.

2 Take the opportunity also to practise fielding likely questions about how the procedures work.

In many child protection cases children will stay in the setting that they have been attending or with the individual childminder. The exceptions are likely to be if children are taken into care because of the nature of the concerns, or if protection issues have arisen about the setting or childminder. Relationships with the parent may not be easy (see also page 152) but the day care or education arrangement for the child is more likely to continue if:

▶ There has been an open relationship established between practitioners and the parent(s).
▶ The parent does not feel judged or accused by the practitioner and feels confident that written records are accurate and not full of speculations.

Practitioners are usually more worried that a parent may be angry with the setting or individual practitioners. However, it is also possible that a parent is looking for support and trusts the practitioner to provide it. Some parents will seek help when they recognise that they are close to ill-treating their child. In some cases, the parent with whom you are working will not be the abuser (see also Chapter 5).

Working with other professionals and agencies

WORKING WELL TOGETHER

All the child protection legislation in the UK highlights the requirement that professionals should work co-operatively with each other and involve all the relevant parties in a child protection case. Social workers are key professionals in the process, but effective protection of children and young people includes more professions than social work.

All group settings, daily or residential, and individual practitioners such as childminders and foster carers, need to establish regular channels of communication that are in place before you have a crisis. Within any cross-professional contact, not only child protection, you can show other professionals that:

▶ You understand the process of child protection and your possible role in the system. You understand, and are ready to learn more, about what you can do from your professional experience, and what is the role of the social worker.
▶ Your position with the children and families gives you an insight into individual children and an opportunity to monitor worrying changes or problems.
▶ You work for good practice in keeping records and respect the appropriate boundaries to confidentiality and access.
▶ You respect the other person's professional status and anticipate respect in turn for your professionalism.

YOUR LOCAL CHILD PROTECTION SYSTEM

You need to know your local network and have relevant names and numbers easily to hand. No group setting or individual practitioner should wait for a crisis before finding out who they should contact about a child protection concern. The chart on page 72 offers one way of clarifying what should happen and in what order. This section explores in more detail how you might extend your knowledge, and that of your colleagues in a team.

▶ You will have local authority departments that offer information, advice, training and contact links for local professional networks. For early years and out-of-school settings in England, Wales or Scotland, you can contact your local Early Years Development and Childcare Partnership (EYDCP) about local organisations and networks. In Northern Ireland, you would contact the local Pre-School Advisory Group. School settings would probably contact the local educational authority, but there is no reason for you not to contact the EYDCP or PSAG.
▶ Your area may have a specialist Child Protection Team or a Co-ordinator. This person would also be a good place to start in understanding how child protection works in your area. The co-ordinator should be able to advise you about training courses or workshops that would help you or your team to understand child protection.
▶ The NSPCC may be active in your local area. This organisation is the only national children's charity that has a legal right to start or to investigate child protection issues. The NSPCC publishes useful information but may also deal with information and advice on a local basis.
▶ Your local police should have an individual or a team responsible for child protection concerns. They may go under the name of Child Protection or Family Protection Unit or Team. You should know that they exist and their number.
▶ Childminders will sometimes have the option of a local childminding network, with an advisor.

▶ Consider making direct contact with any other equivalent group setting close to you. Admittedly, private nurseries can feel that they are in competition with each other and any settings can experience rivalry when there are more places locally than children to fill them. Yet a sharing of ideas and policies on child protection would benefit everyone.

RAISING THE PROFILE OF YOUR SETTING

Generally speaking, local child protection guidelines have been more likely to involve schools in the process and to overlook the importance of early years or out-of-school settings. However, more recent guidelines have given greater acknowledge to non-school settings. Areas vary and your local child protection team may always have appreciated the important role of nurseries, pre-schools, playgroups and out-of-school care. If there is work to do to raise your professional profile, then senior team members need to take steps to show what you and your colleagues can do as part of inter-agency work.

▶ Be ready to make the move towards the local child protection team rather than sitting back and thinking 'They ought to contact us!'.
▶ Set up regular channels of communication so that you have established professional links before there is a child protection concern or crisis.
▶ Show that you understand how the child protection process works and the ways in which your setting could contribute. And that you are equally clear about what you should leave to other professionals within the process.
▶ Develop and maintain appropriate policies and procedures and let the child protection team know what you do and how.
▶ Show that you understand good practice in record keeping, appropriate confidentiality and passing on information and a professional working relationship with parents.
▶ Prepare thoroughly for any meetings, either informal ones with a social worker, or if you are invited to a case conference. Organise in advance the information you have to contribute and the facts underpinning any opinions that are expressed. You may have to be confident in presenting the perspective and observations of your centre. It will be pointless to complain afterwards that nobody asked you; you have to be ready to speak up, if necessary.
▶ The head of centre and any senior practitioners are responsible for ensuring that good practice is maintained in the centre and for coaching, supporting and organising training for staff who would benefit in any of the aspects to this part of the job. Good practice in the centre requires an atmosphere in which staff feel able to ask for help or a second opinion and are encouraged to learn from new experiences.

You will find more about working with other professionals from page 135.

Anti-discriminatory practice

What is normal in families?

All practitioners need a broad base of knowledge to make sensible and properly supported judgements. 'Normal' is certainly not just what you know from your own childhood or memories of families whom you knew then, or for families you know personally now. All practitioners, whatever their personal cultural and ethnic background, have to make the effort to extend their knowledge of family traditions and ways of raising children that are not familiar to them.

An awareness of different cultures and approaches to children has to be part of a more general awareness that adults vary in how they deal with children and what they feel is appropriate from adults to children. Some parents may be less demonstrative than you in your dealings with children. Less overt affection does not necessarily mean that an adult cares less about a child; people have different ways of showing that they care. Alternatively, you may feel that some parents may be too emotional with their children, for your taste. None of these differences may relate to cultural traditions but are more linked with particular families and their personal style. However, if you do not share a culture with a parent or know that you differ in religious beliefs, it is easy to assume that the different patterns arise from broader cultural differences. This explanation may or may not be valid.

DIFFERENCES WITHIN A CULTURE

Opinions of the right way to raise children change over time and can be very different between different social classes within the same culture. For instance, there has been considerable criticism of women who are working mothers and who use child care facilities. But there has never been a similar criticism of wealthy families who delegate the majority of child care to the family nanny. It has also been regarded as normal practice in such families to give children as young as seven years into the care of strangers for considerable parts of the year – sending children off to boarding school. Some children seem to have enjoyed, or at least tolerated, boarding school life. But this practice has continued in some families despite children's protestations that they are desperately unhappy.

In the UK there are striking differences of opinion, between people of a very similar cultural background, about the acceptability of physical forms of discipline with children. Some adults, parents and different kinds of professionals, are strongly opposed to hitting children or any other kind of physical punishment. An equally strong lobby is in favour of hitting young children on the grounds that it is all they understand in some circumstances and that denying the option for adults to hit will lead to badly behaved children (more on page 194).

DIFFERENCES BETWEEN CULTURES

Cultural tradition can be a strong influence on how parents raise their children, react towards sons and daughters and resolve matters of authority in the family.

It is regarded as normal in the UK that mothers take the primary responsibility for children, although there is more variation in this pattern than a couple of generations ago. But in some cultures, for instance some African and Caribbean cultures, it is much more usual that the care of children is shared between relatives, probably female. There is also a tradition that parents leave some or all of their children with the extended family, while the parents go elsewhere in search of work, sometimes at a considerable distance. This pattern was continued with some West African families in England who sought long-term private fostering for their children while they worked or completed studies.

So, it would be an unacceptable assumption for a practitioner to criticise a shared care family system on the grounds that 'it should be the mother'. On the other hand, the system must work for the safety and well-being of the child. A shared care system can fail children just as some mothers in sole charge have abused or neglected their children. Any professional involved with the families should still be concerned about the quality of care for children in the extended family or any private fostering arrangements.

FAITH AND ANTI-DISCRIMINATORY PRACTICE

In Northern Ireland, anti-discriminatory practice has the additional significant feature of anti-sectarianism, working against the deeply held negative views between the Catholic and Protestant communities. In child protection, as in any other service for children and families, professionals need to show respect for a faith other than their own and address any unwarranted assumptions that may arise from the long history of ill feeling between the communities in the Province.

Issues in child protection

Anti-discriminatory practice is part of general good practice in early years work. But particular issues and dilemmas can arise in child protection.

ASSUMPTIONS AND BELIEFS

Your approach to child protection concerns should include an awareness of your feelings and assumptions, just like any other aspect of your practice.

▶ In child protection it is important that you do not assume that particular kinds of families are more, or less, likely to abuse or neglect their children. You should take each child and their family as individuals and, if you have concerns, make sure that you have a sound basis for deciding there is a possible child protection worry.

▶ Consult with colleagues and with your manager. They should support you in standing back from a family and talking through what has happened and why you are worried.

▶ You might want to check that you are not more ready to suspect abuse or neglect because your relationship with the parent has never been easy or because you disapprove of their approach to discipline and their child.

▶ On the other hand, you might need just as much support and a chance to talk when you are tempted to think, 'This is such a nice family, surely they couldn't harm their child?'

▶ It would be a racist outlook if any member of staff had a working assumption that families of a particular cultural or religious background were more likely to abuse or neglect their children. Any sense of 'these people don't care about their children' should be dealt with firmly by a senior practitioner. The practitioner would be expressing prejudiced attitudes, regardless of whatever group he or she belonged to or the identity of 'these people'.

▶ On the other hand, practitioners need support in exploring their concerns when they do not share a cultural or religious identity with the family. Staff may be so concerned that they might be thought racist or in some other way prejudiced, that they may back off concerns that should be explored. Senior practitioners will be very important in guiding the team through what can be some delicate issues.

▶ Any kind of assumptions about a family need to be checked and possibly challenged, in a positive way, through discussion in your centre and through the supervision process. A practitioner might assume that a lone parent will be without any family back-up but some lone parents have a very effective network of family and friends. In contrast, perhaps another practitioner assumes, without asking, that the struggling Indian mother will be fine 'because all Asians live in an extended family, don't they?' But this mother may be on her own without any possible family support or feel for some reason that she cannot access help from family and friends.

▶ Language and understanding can be an issue in sensitive conversations, even when practitioner and parent share the same language. People use their words, the expressiveness in the tone of voice and all the accompanying body language in varied ways. Differences of culture and social class are often reflected in what is said and how, especially if emotions become involved.

▶ If you do not share a language with a parent then you need to know who is this parent's preferred interpreter. This choice is another issue that needs to have been resolved early in the relationships, before you face a difficult conversation.

The key point is that assumptions can be misleading and may put children at risk. Unchecked assumptions might be racist, but are not inevitably so. You need to be ready to ask yourself, or accept the question from colleagues, of 'What is my basis for assuming this?' 'What makes me so sure?'

Undoubtedly, if you work alone, it can be less straightforward to find someone with whom you can discuss in confidence. Childminders may be part of a childminding network, but even if you are not, the childminding development worker or advisor might still be pleased to help you weigh up this issues. Foster carers should have access to a social worker or link worker, who is specifically responsible for professional support of any kind.

KNOWLEDGE

You need to take account of different ways of raising children and dealing with day-by-day difficulties. It would not be justified to assume that the way you were brought up, or the way that you and your colleagues deal with the children, is the only right way. You need to be open to other possibilities and this should be your approach, whatever your own cultural or religious background.

It is good practice to be ready to learn more about different cultures and beliefs but you need to extend your knowledge with a broad base. You can use several different approaches:

▶ Learn from other people: talking, asking questions and listening to colleagues, parents and friends who have a different experience and knowledge.
▶ However, do not expect everyone to be an expert and handle your questioning with sensitivity. Imagine how you might feel if you were asked searching questions about 'Is this really normal in your culture?' or 'Does everybody do this with their children?'
▶ Learn from reading and by watching relevant television programmes.
▶ Take advantage as well of training courses and workshops.

ACTIVITY

The main aim in learning more about cultures other than your own is to develop general knowledge, so that you have a reasonable basis for understanding to what extent a family is following a cultural or religious tradition and how much is a purely family style. Obviously, the two intermingle in many families.

Think carefully about three or four families whom you know well and who share your own cultural background. These may be families you know through work but think also about one or two families whom you know through personal contact.

1 If someone from a very different cultural background met each of these families, how far do you judge it is possible for the family to take them as representative of your culture?
2 Would you tend to say, 'In some ways, yes but in some ways, no?' If so, in what ways?
3 Do you feel it would be misleading to generalise from these families without further experience? What could this tell you about the risks when practitioners feel they know a particular culture or a religion from contact with a small number of families?

BE CAREFUL OF GENERALISATIONS

Knowing one or two examples of families from a particular cultural, national or religious background are not a safe basis for feeling that you now know all about this group. If you met a few families from Devon, you could not assume that you were well-informed about all family life in the West Country, let alone the rest of England or the UK. Yet people do sometimes think that contact with a couple of Indian families somehow informs them about Indian traditions as a whole, with no grasp of the tremendous diversity in culture, religion and social status that exists within the large group of families within the UK of Indian origin.

You should also be careful about developing beliefs about any culture from working with families who are under stress. Families experiencing some form of crisis are not usually behaving the way that is normal for them in calmer times, let alone typical of the culture or religion to which they belong.

EVERYONE NEEDS TO LEARN

Some thought needs to be given to genuine anti-discriminatory practice – in general and not only in connection with child protection. There is considerable diversity within groups defined by ethnic group, cultural background or religious faith. It is not good practice to assume that any black practitioner loosely defined will somehow understand and be the best person to work with any black family. There is far too much variety within such a broad definition. A black practitioner may well have empathy with others who have experienced ill-treatment as a result of racism. But this possibly shared experience does not provide detailed knowledge about another person's culture, nor even guarantee a shared fluent language.

Group settings need to avoid any assumptions that rough matching of ethnic group of practitioner to parents may ease the situation with a parent when there is a delicate issue to broach. Good practice in the setting and an effective key worker system will be the most important issues. Black practitioners will not necessarily be in tune with every black family, any more than white practitioners will feel in agreement with any given white family. You have to ask why should anyone expect this level of empathy? The terms 'black' and 'white' cover a tremendous variety of individual people and cultural backgrounds

So, unless they have specific experience and knowledge, practitioners of African-Caribbean origin, for example, will not be any better equipped than a 'white' colleague to relate to a Somali refugee family, a Mandarin-speaking Chinese family or a family from Bengal. Senior practitioners and other team members need to be clear about appropriate experience or individual characteristics. For instance, it would be appropriate use of a team member's skills, if that person shared a fluent language with a parent, who was otherwise ill at ease or limited in what could be expressed in English. You need to speak up if you find yourself expected to have unrealistic levels of knowledge on the basis of your own culture, religion or simply your skin colour.

Challenging cultural traditions

Checking your assumptions about a particular family is harder when you do not know the culture very well. Among many other tough questions, you are also asking yourself whether you are observing a cultural tradition that you have misunderstood. However, ill-treatment of children cannot be excused by assuming or even concluding on the basis of good information, that the parents' actions are led by cultural tradition or by deeply held religious beliefs.

Anti-discriminatory practice in child protection has to hold a delicate balance. You should not reject other ways of child rearing because it is not your culture's way, but equally so a practice is not made acceptable because it is associated with a long cultural tradition. No individual practitioner should try to weigh up such complex issues on their own. It is sensible and professional to consult your head of centre, advisor or the other people involved in the child protection system (listed on page 54). Social workers face similar issues and need to be supported through an effective supervision system. Such dilemmas are not only faced by early years, school or out-of-school practitioners.

Children from a wide variety of different cultural backgrounds can and have been damaged by their family's actions or inaction. Whatever the strength of a cultural tradition or a religious belief, the same kind of questions hold as you weigh up what any individual parent is doing or not doing with regard to a child. Bear in mind that in a child protection case it will not be your personal responsibility to come to conclusions about abuse. But you will be able to pass on to the child protection team your concerns and care can be taken to understand the possible impact of the family's culture or religious beliefs on what is happening.

▶ Questions have to be asked like, 'what is the impact of this practice on the child?' or 'what is the experience of the children in this family?'
▶ No cultural tradition or religious belief should result in harm to a child or endanger their health. For example, parents' strongly held views about physical punishment do not excuse injuries to their child. See also the discussion about female genital mutilation on page 16.
▶ Even when you are uncertain about a family's cultural traditions you should never overlook visible physical injury to the child. Be wary when a child's explanation of the injury does not match what his parent(s) are saying or when other records that you keep of the children raise concerns independently about this child's health or development.
▶ It can be hard to put your own strongly held beliefs to one side when a family's approach is very different to your own. But you can work to be objective, and not swayed by assumptions, when you follow good practice in record keeping in your centre (see page 104). Make sure that you are up-to-date with children's development and their patterns of behaviour. Good observation skills and assessment will help you to focus on the child: regardless of what seem to be the parents' child rearing practices, how is this child progressing?
▶ A balanced overview of a child's well-being and any child protection issues has to include a cultural perspective. But all practitioners need to be on their

guard against an uncritical acceptance of a family's way because it is assumed to be, or definitely is based in cultural or religious traditions.

Scenarios

You can use the following examples to explore some of the issues raised in this chapter and to stimulate discussion about your own practice and settings of which you have most experience. You can think over the examples and make notes for yourself but, ideally, use some in discussion with colleagues or fellow-students. For each scenario you should consider:

▶ What are the main issues in this situation?
▶ What is unclear from the information so far? What more might you need to know in order to understand better what seems to be happening?
▶ What would be a sensible first step if you were facing this situation?
▶ You might want to return to some of the examples when you have read Chapters 4 and 5. You will find a short commentary on these scenarios from page 225.

Natasha

Natasha is four years old and her family came to England from Jamaica when her mother was still a child. Natasha lives with her mother and two aunts. Other relatives live within two streets of her home. You have become increasingly concerned because neither you, nor Natasha, ever knows who will pick her up from nursery school and some days it is up to half-an-hour after the end of the session before anyone arrives. Natasha always recognises the person and seems content to go but has said to you, 'I wish Mummy or Auntie Tess would pick me up.'

This week the arrangements for Natasha have become even less predictable. On two mornings you found her in the nursery front yard when you came to work, an hour before any child should arrive. You spoke with the aunt who arrived in the afternoon and were told, 'I can't help it. I have to get to work and you're here anyway aren't you?'

In the middle of the week, the nursery's handyman strikes up a conversation with you about Natasha. 'They live two doors down from us. Poor little sod, nobody watches out for her. One evening she was wandering on the pavement in her nightie until one of them shouts out the window at her. She wants to come in and play with our two and that's fine by the wife. So, she phones up and half the time Natasha's Mum doesn't even know she's gone and the aunties think my wife's odd for calling anyway. These people don't know how to look after kids properly. Now my wife is home with ours . . .'

Aaron

Aaron is three years old and has been in the playgroup for two months. On his left hand, he has an extra finger, which is floppy and does not work like a finger. Aaron does not seem to be too worried and his mother has explained that they are waiting for surgery to deal with the problem. You have noticed that a new practitioner seems to avoid being close to Aaron and has visibly shuddered when she looked at the boy's left hand. In the garden you notice her ignore Aaron's outstretched hand as he asks to be jumped down from the climbing frame. Today, you overheard this practioner say to a parent, 'It's horrible. That floppy thing gives me the creeps.'

Ann-Marie

Ann-Marie has attended your nursery for nearly three months. Her parents are fundamentalist Christians, who were initially doubtful about the nursery's behaviour policy. Her father especially made a strong case that children needed firmer discipline than the nursery appeared to provide. Ann-Marie came in last week with severe bruising to her bottom, which became obvious because she winced when she sat at the table to play. When you asked her father about the bruises, he was evasive, saying, 'You wouldn't understand. Children need guidance and Ann-Marie is very wilful.'

Ann-Marie did not return to the nursery for three days by which time she no longer seemed to be in pain. Today you notice red welts on Ann-Marie's palms and she is unwilling to explain what has happened beyond that she was 'very naughty'. At pick-up time Ann-Marie's mother is initially apologetic about an unspecified 'accident' to her daughter. Then she blurts out, 'Anyway my husband says you should respect our beliefs and what we do in our own home. We've got a copy of your equal opportunities statement. Respect us then!' And she rushes off with Ann-Marie.

Greg

You have been hearing an increased amount of noise from the room next to the one where you work with your group of children. A student on work placement appears to have taken a dislike to one of the children. She always calls him 'Gregory O'Connor', although he is known as Greg to everyone else and children in the centre are not usually addressed by their first and family name. Over the last week most of her shouting appears to have been aimed at Greg and you thought you heard something like, 'Dumb Irish tinkers'.

Your colleague next door has been showing the student how to complete the centre's developmental records on children. As you passed the door of that room you saw the student propel Greg into a chair and say, 'Right, Gregory O'Connor. Let's see all the things you can't do.' Matters come to a head when you are in the room briefly as lunch is being served and are chatting with Greg. The student ignores you, leans over to Greg and shouts very close to his ear, 'You shut up, Gregory O'Connor! No talking at mealtimes!' You say to the student, 'I was talking with Greg' and she just stares at you.

Monica

You are an experienced childminder and have cared for Monica since she was a young toddler. Monica is now nearly six years old and you are about to take responsibility for her younger brother, a baby of nearly five months of age. Monica's family have been strict vegetarians and you have been happy to ensure that her food in your home meets the family's requests. Monica has been healthy and full of energy until the last couple of months. Her family now explain that they have shifted to a new kind of vegan diet and want you to do the same for Monica, as well as following their food guidelines sheet as you help to wean the baby.

You are concerned when you see the family's food list, because the diet is very restricted even for vegan and seems to depend on excessive levels of vitamin pills. You are very uneasy that Monica, let alone the baby, will have nutritional deficiencies in some ways, yet could overdose on some vitamins and minerals. You had planned to talk with the parents about Monica's health, because she has become very listless, normal scrapes take a long time to heal and she has had a sequence of colds. A conversation this evening has not gone well. Monica's mother became very irritated and demanded that you respect the family diet or else she would find another childminder. You do not feel that partnership with parents can mean that you follow requests that could endanger Monica or her baby brother.

Kayleigh

You are a nanny to a family in which there are two younger children, for whom you are responsible and an older half-sister, Kayleigh, who is often in your household at weekends, but lives with her mother a few streets away. You have got on well with Kayleigh and she has chatted to you in a confidential way, but not over any subject that caused concern. Recently, you have seen Kayleigh out on the street at times when she should be in her secondary school. You have asked friendly questions about, 'No school today then, Kayleigh?' and received non-committal answers or unlikely explanations about being 'out doing a project'. You have now seen her twice with the daughter of a family in your street. This young teenager is known to truant and in your view runs with a 'bad crowd'. You do not want to appear to tell tales on Kayleigh, and she has never been your responsibility. But you are now concerned that she may slip into serious trouble and that at least one of her parents should be told.

Ciaran

You are a specialist teaching assistant and also undertake break time duties in the primary school playground. Ciaran is now eight years old and, in the time you have know him, has been mainly a quiet child who has occasional outbursts of distress and sometimes anger towards other children. Ciaran has gravitated towards you in the playground, although he says very little.

Recently, your school has spent funds on restructuring the school grounds to create comfortable seating and Ciaran has taken advantage of the new areas to sit and chat with you. One lunchtime he started by talking about a television drama last night that featured family rows, but soon you got the impression that Ciaran was talking about his own family. You have been very careful not to lead the conversation in any way. Over the last week you have become sure that Ciaran's mother and father have serious rows, that Ciaran and his younger sister have been hurt at least once, that they are distressed and frightened, yet under pressure to say nothing to outsiders.

Yesterday you made notes of what had emerged so far and discussed the matter with the teacher responsible for child protection in your school. This teacher trusts your skills and suggested that you continue to listen to Ciaran and that she would discuss with the head what should be the best next step. Today, the teacher has had an uncomfortable conversation with you in which she has passed on the head's instruction that you are to stop talking with Ciaran and any further conversations about his home situation must be undertaken with her, as the designated child protection teacher. Neither you nor your colleague judge that the head's instruction is appropriate for Ciaran. You want to support and protect Ciaran, but would rather not go directly against the head.

4

Child protection in action

Part of your role in the whole process of child protection will be the work that goes on within your own setting or practice as a childminder. This chapter focuses on what you can do, and some reminders of what you should not attempt to do on your own. Undoubtedly, the pattern of work will be different, depending on your position and work. The role of a head of centre or senior practitioner is different from those who work face to face every day with the children. Both roles are equally important.

There is a considerable amount that you can do, usefully and properly as an early years, school or out-of-school practitioner when possible child protection concerns arise. You can listen, talk and make sense of what has emerged through the broad base of your knowledge and observation. What you definitely do **not** do, however senior or experienced you are, is to start a formal investigation relating to child protection. That job rests with the social worker who will lead a child protection case.

When you have concerns

Keeping a perspective on child abuse

Child abuse is a serious issue and has strong emotional overtones for anyone who cares about the well-being of children. Practitioners who are coming to terms with the possibility of abuse need support, most likely from senior colleagues or an advisor, to hold a realistic perspective.

'IT COULDN'T HAPPEN HERE'

It is sometimes easier to be convinced that child abuse is a problem that happens elsewhere. Yet it is important that practitioners allow for the possibility that child protection issues could arise in their setting – wherever they work and whatever the range of families whose children attend.

You may be reluctant to consider child abuse because you cannot believe that this parent, or a colleague, could possibly ill-treat a child. Of course, you should neither suspect nor condemn out of hand, but neither should you push aside concerns because of an inaccurate image of the kind of person who would abuse children.

You may also be worried about being wrong in your concerns. It is responsible of you to allow for doubts, but it would be against the children's interests if those doubts led you to do nothing. Your setting's written procedures (see page 69) should be clear on what steps you take and whom you consult.

Doubts and worries are natural, as are concerns about making unsupported accusations of anyone, but children will be placed at risk if you allow such doubts to stop you voicing a worry about a child. Nor can you assume that 'surely someone else will notice and speak up'. Perhaps nobody else will notice, or perhaps you are the only person whom this child has told about their experience. Expressing concerns is not the same as making allegations of abuse. Group settings need a team atmosphere in which practitioners can raise low-level concerns without the anxiety that matters will swiftly get out of hand. Careful observation and communication with parents will resolve many concerns.

You are not having such doubts just because you are an early years or out-of-school practitioner. Other professionals also have to deal with these feelings and weigh up possibilities. Clear procedures are in place for how social workers should proceed, because even specialist training in child protection does not enable anyone to make very personal decisions about how they will act.

'Child abuse is everywhere'

Chapter 1 included a detailed discussion of warning signs of different kinds of child abuse that should alert you to the need to explore further. It is important to take your own concerns, or those expressed by children and parents, with seriousness. But it is also important to exercise some caution and not leap to swift conclusions.

It is good practice to recognise that you need to take some further steps, but poor practice to decide swiftly that you are definitely dealing with a case of child abuse.

▶ There can often be more than one possible explanation for an incident that concerns you or for something worrying about a child's behaviour or development. A troublesome, anxious or developmentally delayed child may be experiencing a number of stresses, which may or may not include abuse. Some action may need to be taken, including a careful discussion with the parents, but there are not inevitably issues of child protection.

▶ There are no quick and easy checklists for child abuse. Some practical leaflets describe worrying signs in brief but you need to remember that careful observation and discussion will raise a number of 'if's and 'but's. You are most usually looking for patterns rather than single incidents. Be very wary of any booklets that claim to be providing certain signs that are evidence of abuse.

▶ Especially remember that worrying signs are not a simple two-way street. Some children who wet the bed are reacting to the distress of being abused, but **not** all bedwetters have experienced abuse. Children, who have been reliably dry at night, sometimes start to have wet sheets because they are very worried and the stress leads them to regress in this skill. The bed-wetting is a sign of children's distress and the need for emotional support. However, the cause may be upset at hearing their parents argue or serious difficulties with their schoolwork.

▶ It is important that teams do not dismiss the possibility of child abuse, with the claim that 'we don't have those kind of families here' or that 'no practitioner would ever behave like that, so the child must be mistaken'. Yet a team must not become so concerned about the likelihood of abuse, of any kind, that all problems or accidents are believed to be caused by child abuse.

If you are a senior practitioner, your role will be to help your team to keep alert to child abuse and also to keep the issues in perspective: most children are not abused. You will be in a different position if your centre specialises in working with families under stress or if your referral system is designed to respond to concerns about families. Teams in specialist settings, such as family centres or residential children's homes, can reasonably assume that the children and families are more vulnerable than the general population. However, such teams still need to weigh up what they hear, see or are told, because, even in an at-risk group, every problem is not always about child protection.

The source of your concerns

There are several different ways in which you may be alerted to the possible abuse of a child in your care:

▶ You notice something that makes you worry – either a particular incident or the pattern emerging from your observations and records of a child.

▶ The child says something, does something, or the child's behaviour has changed in a way that catches your attention.

▶ A child's parents may confide in you – something about themselves or their concerns about another person involved in family life, or a member of your own team.

▶ Someone else approaches you with their concerns – another professional or a non-family member, such as a friend or neighbour.

Through your own thinking, discussion with a colleague or your senior and then through appropriate recording, you need to become steadily more clear about:

▶ What exactly is concerning you and your reasons for concern. You need to reach a specific description.
▶ Why your observations or what you have been told is a source of concern, why does it matter.
▶ Or that an incident has occurred, but you are not seriously concerned and these are the reasons why.

Your observations

Observing children

Good practice in early years settings is to keep accurate and descriptive records of children's development, interests and behaviour. These records are invaluable in keeping track of children's progress, identifying areas in which you can offer a child positive help and in sharing information with parents. The main reason for setting up records and for observing children is to monitor their learning and general well-being. Your main aim is not to have a child protection check. However, good quality records of individual children and your own alert observations can highlight patterns that you should be ready to explore further. For example, a child who used to play with interest and enthusiasm is now quiet and withdrawn. Or another child seems generally unwell, with cuts and bruises that take a long time to heal.

Your developmental records could be very important in assessing concerns about a child. Certainly, some reviews of practice in child protection have stressed the importance of keeping a detailed view of how a child is progressing and behaving on a daily basis.

Practitioners, who work alone, such as childminders, foster carers and nannies, may keep equally useful, although less formal, records. A daily diary can work well to note down short observations of a child or keeping track of their health and well being. It is advisable for foster carers in particular to keep a separate record for each child, even for siblings in your care. Some childminders are now also recruited specifically to work with the more vulnerable families and their children. Your notes will be important should there be a child protection case and it is essential that you can easily access how you have tracked this individual child, without having to remove references to other named children.

School and out-of-school settings are unlikely to keep the same kind of developmental records on all children that are good practice for early years settings. It will be good practice when you work with older children to be ready to start such a record as soon as there are any concerns about a child or young person.

OBSERVING PARENTS OR OTHER CARERS

Most practitioners will not be making formal observations of parents or other carers of the children. The exception will be if you work in a specialist family or children's centre, where your contract with the parents is that they attend as well as their children.

In a family centre or other specialist setting, you will keep written records of conversations and some interactions with parents or other key carers of the children. Such records should be part of your partnership with parents, in the same way as work with families who are not at risk. There are two main exceptions to parents' access to written records about their children and themselves.

▶ It is regarded as usual practice that practitioners in a family centre or a residential children's home, and also foster carers, will sometimes make more informal personal notes. Such notes might be tentative ideas for how to support parents or help the child, or could be information that is of uncertain relevance for the moment. Good practice is that any such notes should be kept separate, but not be a method to maintain a secondary file on a family. After a short period, probably no more than a couple of months, such notes should either be made part of the main file or shredded, since they are not relevant.
▶ The basic principles of data protection and access are that individuals should have straightforward right of access to their own files, or those on their children. This civil right is limited if the judgement is that reading the files could result in serious harm to this person or to other people. This exception is activated if the child and family are involved in a child protection case.

Informal observations of parents and conversations will often build a fuller picture of the child in a very positive way. Children are often not the same with their families as they are in an early years centre, because the two settings are different. Partnership with parents is part of good practice and within this framework it is important to have conversations with parents about their children or what is happening in the centre. These discussions should be taking place as normal daily events when there are no problems or worries whatsoever (see also page 121.)

Schools and out–of–school settings may have regular, daily contact with children, but there is usually less informal conversation with parents than can be the situation in early years settings. Staff in the early years of primary school have sometimes found that they need to be more out and about in the playground at the beginning and end of the school day. Their presence can mean that parents become accustomed to informal exchanges and do not assume that an approaching teacher means trouble. Out-of-school care teams need to do their best with the end of session, when admittedly many parents are tired and in a rush to get themselves and their child home.

Your informal communication with parents and your observations of them with their children may give rise to concerns that should be explored. Some possibilities are that:

▶ You are concerned that these parents rarely speak positively of their child. Their approach does not seem to be one of modesty but more rejection by word and action. You have never heard them praise their child and they criticise him as a matter of course.
▶ These parents, or grandparents in charge, have very high expectations for this child, which seem to you to be inappropriate given the child's age. The demanding expectations are linked with criticism of the child for failing to meet the family's standards.
▶ In a family where there are several carers of the child you become concerned that nobody seems to be keeping an eye on what is happening to the child. Each carer is saying 'I don't know' or that they think someone else is dealing with an issue. You are now worried that the child's health or development problem is falling through the net.
▶ Parents handle their child roughly in your sight – perhaps pushing and shoving their child(ren) into their coats. Perhaps a mother has been seen to drag her son along with such speed on the nursery path that the child falls over.

You need to be aware, especially if you are not yourself a parent, that all parents have bad times when they are not as thoughtful as they should be towards their children. You are looking at a pattern here and finding out if the harsh words are only in your presence, or if this week has been particularly stressful in the family. Some parents are considerably harder on their children if there is an audience, especially of people whom the parent thinks might judge them negatively.

When children say something

Sometimes, your first source of concern will be what a child says to you. The child may confide a worry to you about what is happening at home or the actions of someone in particular. Alternatively, an important confidence may follow from your question, such as, 'That's a big bump on your forehead, David. How did that happen?' The following guidelines will help you when a child confides in you. This pattern is appropriate whatever the confidence the child is sharing, but the approach can be especially important if the child's words raise the worry of abuse. When children say or show something that alerts you to likely or possible abuse, their communication is called a disclosure.

Listen

The most important skill you can offer is to **listen** to what the child is telling you. Good listening should be a skill that you continue to develop in all your other work with children and it is the most valuable when a child starts to confide in you.

▶ Give the child your full attention and listen to the words. This moment may not be the most convenient for you, but recognise that today this child or young person has become able to tell you something that really matters.

▶ Hear the words children are using and the way they share this confidence. Watch children so that you can also 'hear' what they tell you through their facial expressions and whole body language.

▶ Communications that emerge as disclosures are certainly not always 'big' events. A child or young person may initially say very little, or make a short comment or question, to judge your reaction, before continuing.

▶ Be guided by the children or young people, and do not press them to talk for longer than they want. The conversation finishes when they wish. Resist any temptation to feel you must get more information. If you are responsive now, they may well return to talk in confidence another day.

▶ Avoid imbalancing the conversation towards many questions from you; it will put undue pressure on the child. (See also page 109 about open-ended questions.)

▶ Children may choose a time when they can speak with you without being overheard, but sometimes you may need to create a confidential space. If other children come to get your attention you can courteously ask them to wait with, 'I'll be with you shortly, Andrea wants to have a word with me' or 'Can you just let Delroy and me talk in private for a while'.

▶ Children and young people sometimes deliberately pick a time when your attention as an adult is partly elsewhere. Foster carers and practitioners in residential children's homes often find that a child will start to talk over a shared domestic activity like washing up or when adult and child are driving somewhere. Some children do not want full eye contact and the fact that you have to keep your eyes on the road is an advantage.

Communication will undoubtedly be less straightforward when children have disabilities that affect their ability to express themselves in words. If you work with children who have communication difficulties, then you should be learning alternative forms of communication such as signing. A joint project by Triangle and the NSPCC recognises that many signing and image systems have serious gaps for children to communicate about personal safety or experiences of abuse. They developed a booklet to help in this area – available from NSPCC Publications Unit, Weston House, 42 Curtain Road, London EC2A 3NH (Tel: 020 7825 2500 – check for current price), or download from www.howitis.org.uk

This child or young person has chosen to confide in you. Practitioners who work in a daily or residential group setting sometimes wonder if they should stop a child who appears to be sharing a disclosure, in order to bring in a more senior colleague or the designated child protection officer. If the conversation does become a disclosure, then you will need to speak later with someone else. However, respect for the child means that you allow them to talk as they wish and do not bring in a colleague to take over or because you feel you need a witness to the conversation. If children have found it difficult to speak up, then passing them on may stop them talking altogether.

Everyone in a team must have had the training to feel able to cope with this situation and offer support to the child or young person. Continued in-house support from senior practitioners can help staff to understand how good quality communication skills are needed, and not highly specialist skills at this stage. In a school setting this support and training must be extended to specialist teaching assistants and the playground support staff, who are not always treated as full team members in every primary school. Children will sometimes approach a trusted class teacher, but they are just as likely to talk with someone else who is non-teaching staff. Children do not choose on the basis of a professional hierarchy. They talk with adults on the basis of relevant individual qualities such as friendliness, ability to listen and show empathy and a track record of respect for children's concerns.

Avoid cross questioning

An appropriate and supportive conversation for children is one in which the adult follows their lead and stops when the child wishes. It is important to avoid cross-questioning children since a series of questions can direct a delicate conversation in an unhelpful way. Concerned practitioners may feel 'But I must find out everything', yet this very pressure is likely to reduce a child or young person's willingness to speak.

▶ Keep any questions you ask as open-ended ones, not questions that push a child in specific directions. You do not know exactly what has happened or how the child feels about the experience or worry. Leading questions tend to be guided by your guesses or unsupported suspicions ('Did Daddy do this to you?') and risk distorting the communication.

▶ Children are suggestible and they may start to say what you appear to want to hear. It is your responsibility to hear what they want to tell you, in the way that the children want to tell it. You need not feel responsible for gathering loads of information. If something worrying has really occurred, then there will be a time later for exploration of more detail, led by a social worker in a child protection investigation.

▶ Asking lots of questions may also pressure children to give you more details than they wish at the moment. Children, especially those in distress, also may agree to specific questions just to stop a persistent adult questioner and end the conversation.

▶ Some child protection inquiries have criticised social workers for persistent and directive questioning of children. So, this aspect of good communication is something that everyone has to keep at the top of their mind.

Use open-ended questions

You can avoid cross-questioning by appropriate and kindly use of your language.

▶ Depending on what the child tells you, you might ask the kind of encouraging question that is part repetition of what a child has just said or a comment left unfinished. For instance, perhaps a child says, 'My big cousin is nasty to me' and you could follow up with 'Nasty in what way, Sandy?' or a similar phrase.

▶ A child might whisper, 'Somebody hurt me' and, if you ask quietly, 'You say somebody hurt you?' (with that question mark in your tone of voice), you may not even have to ask the more specific question, 'Who hurt you, Daria?' This kind of gentle questioning is sometimes called **reflective listening**.

▶ Depending on the flow of the conversation, other open-ended questions might be 'You say you were frightened?' or 'What has happened to make you cry?' You can also simply encourage a child by your open and attentive expression and simple questions like 'Yes?' or 'Anything else you want to tell me?'

Dealing with feelings

Avoid telling children or young people how they are feeling. Listen and look, rather than try to guess their emotional state.

▶ Listen to what children say about how they are feeling: 'I'm cross with him', 'She makes me cry and she doesn't care' or 'He says I'm a bad girl, that nobody will like me anymore'. Show empathy and support for the child, with comments such as, 'You're feeling cross now?' or 'I will always like you, Mario. Please tell me what has happened'.

▶ Children can have many competing feelings, especially when they are being abused or neglected within their own family. Their feelings of family loyalty may struggle with their distress. Some children are afraid of being held responsible for any negative consequences following their disclosure, such as the exposure of a loved parent's abusive partner or even the break up of their whole family.

▶ Children who have been sexually abused by a known and liked person can have very muddled emotions. What would otherwise be proper expressions of affection have become distorted by with inappropriate sexual contact. A child's sense of pleasure at the affection may be struggling with half-understood feelings that the physical form of expression was not right.

As you listen, you may be feeling anger, shock or distress. But you cannot assume that the child necessarily shares your emotions. Children may feel all of these and more, but you can only find out by listening, by gently watching their expression and body language.

It is also important that a child or young person does not feel overwhelmed by your reaction. It will have been hard for them to tell, children do need the additional burden of feeling that now they have shocked or distressed you. You do not have to pretend to have no emotional reaction at all; that would be unrealistic and confusing to the child.

Support and reassure

Children who disclose troublesome secrets need reassurance from the adult, but you should not give any promises that you cannot keep.

▶ You should show your support and affirmation of the child by the fact that you listen and follow the child's lead in the conversation.

▶ Sometimes, you should give specific reassurance, such as, 'This isn't your fault', 'No, I'm not cross with you at all. I'm so glad you told me what's happening' or 'Of course I still like you and I want to help you with this'.

▶ It is not for you to criticise the person who has hurt the child. In some cases of child abuse, the abuser is a loved relative and the turmoil of mixed emotions is part of the whole problem for children. You can still reassure the child with more general support such as, 'Kitty, nobody should make you this upset' rather than laying blame with, 'Your Grandad is a bad person'.

▶ Avoid questions like 'Why didn't you tell me before?', because they are much more about adult upset on hearing about a long-running problem than concern for children. The reasons why children have not disclosed until now may emerge later. For the moment, their reticence is less important than the fact that they have now told you. 'Why?' questions will almost certainly put the child on the spot and are unhelpful – avoid them.

▶ You cannot promise a child that you will keep disclosures about abuse as a secret. You have a responsibility to take such concerns further. Your next step might be to talk with a more senior practitioner, with the child's parent or to consult with someone else. Explain to children, in words appropriate to their age and understanding, what you are now going to do.

▶ You cannot promise children that someone who has hurt or abused them will necessarily be punished – whether within the family or by law. You can promise that you will take the matter further and see what can be done and that you will listen to children when they want your time again.

DIFFERENT KINDS OF CONFIDENCES

This section assumes that what children say to you does emerge as a possible disclosure of abuse or neglect. Sometimes of course children or young people want to talk about issues of great importance to them, but you realise that child protection is not an issue. The same good quality communication skills will be appropriate and help you to enable a child to talk and explore what can happen next.

For example, eight-year-old Charlotte may wish to confide that she was not entirely truthful about how the pots got smashed in the garden of her after school club. Charlotte knows that lying has complicated the situation, perhaps led to the wrong person being blamed, but how can she resolve it now? Children and young people sometimes want to confide troubles within the peer group, with a confidence that adults will not just charge in and make matters worse. Older children and young teenagers listen to the news and are sometimes very anxious about national or world events. They want to express worries with an attentive adult who will not dismiss or try to avoid their questions.

ACTIVITY

You may find it useful to recall a time when you wanted to tell somebody about an experience of emotional importance to you. This memory need not necessarily be something from your childhood, but could be from your adult life.

1 How did the conversation go with the person in whom you confided? Did they listen to you? What made you feel that they were really listening?
2 What kind of comments did the other person make? What was helpful to you? What made you feel unsupported?
3 Did they ask you any questions? What kinds of questions were helpful and which were not?
4 Did they ask, what seemed to you, too many questions? How did you feel on the receiving end of lots of questions?
5 Looking back over the conversation that you experienced, what lessons have you learned that can be applied to delicate conversations with children?

If possible, share some of your general thoughts with colleagues or fellow-students. Be considerate of each other as you discuss these issues. If your colleagues are sharing a difficult experience with the group, they will not want to be criticised or cross-questioned now about their memories and feelings.

CONSULT AND MAKE NOTES

Children should not have to repeat a conversation to a whole series of adults in your setting after a first disclosure. When a child has confided in you, you need to consult a more senior practitioner or advisor who will help you to identify the best next step. As the person in whom the child confided, you are responsible for making notes on the conversation as soon as possible, and certainly with no more delay than later in the same day. Your notes should include specific details of the conversation:

▶ When and where did the child talk with you? Were you alone with the child? Were any other staff or children within hearing? Did anyone else contribute to the conversation?
▶ What did the child say to you – as accurately as you can recall. Do not note down actual words in inverted commas ('…') unless you are certain that those are definitely the child's own phrases.
▶ Your impressions and opinions can be valuable because you know this child. But support them with your reasons, for instance, 'I believe Sandy is very upset. When he said to me "My big cousin is nasty to me", Sandy was twisting his hair around one finger – the way he does when he is really distressed.'
▶ Do not add guesses or speculations to the written report – about the child's feelings, likely abusers or judgements about the possible truth of what the child has said. Keep your report factual and opinions supported with 'because …'

Notes of this kind are following more general good practice in accurate written reports. An accurate and descriptive record will be just as important if the concern turns out to have an explanation that is not worrying. A careful approach, taking into account what you know and what you do not, can support you in a delicate conversation with a parent that perhaps starts with, 'I was worried/confused/taken aback by something that Tanya said to me today …' If there becomes reason for serious concern and steps start to be taken in a child protection investigation by social workers, then a responsible and specific first record will be important for any future work.

But is it true?

One of the major steps forward for children in child protection has been that what children say is now given much more weight. The prevailing assumption of previous generations was that children were unreliable, especially if set against adult(s). Children, especially young children, were assumed to muddle fact and fantasy and be prone to lying. Unfortunately, some adults, even professionals, still persist in this belief.

In child protection there has been a significant shift to a working assumption that what a child says is true. However, there are several, subtle issues intertwined in this aspect of good practice. I have laid out these issues one by one below. It is worth reading this section more than once and discussing the points with colleagues, because it is not good practice to move to a naïve view that everything children say is literally true. You would not behave in this way in other aspects of your practice and nor is it appropriate for child protection.

▶ Your responsibility is to take seriously what the child is saying to you. You show this seriousness and your respect for the child by all the guidelines for active listening given earlier (page 107).

▶ Adults should not doubt or dismiss what a child says just because it seems unlikely, the adult mentioned seems so nice or even because the child has been known to embroider the truth on other occasions.

▶ It is equally important not to turn the previously disrespectful attitudes towards children on their head and take the child's perspective as the absolute truth without any more exploration. People sometimes promote an over-simple line of 'Believe the children; children never lie about abuse'. There needed to be a reaction to tendencies to disbelieve children, but the situation is more complex than such simple statements.

▶ Children, just like adults, have their own perspective. They are giving you their view of events, which you should respect and take seriously, but there is a big difference between taking further the concern of 'Delia told me that her evening sitter shows her "naughty pictures"' and that of 'Delia's sitter is definitely abusing her'.

▶ It is very unlikely that children will lie about abuse. They are far more likely to have difficulty in telling you, especially if the person harming them is part of their family or someone the child knows is liked and respected. But it is possible that a child may say only part of what is happening or can only try to express some of their distress from a complex and troubling situation. So, the assumption that the child has told you the whole truth in one conversation could be a harmful conclusion to draw. Perhaps the child has told you only what she has managed to get out this time and there is more to tell.

▶ Although it is unlikely that children will lie about abuse, there have been cases when children have become entangled in adults' bitter relationships and what the children say has reflected what an adult wants to have believed. There have been legal cases where children, usually older ones, have been badgered by one parent into false accusations against another, as part of vicious custody disputes.

▶ It also has to be accepted that older children and teenagers have sometimes made false allegations against teachers, foster and residential carers. Some children have not really understood the consequences of such claims. Others appear to have been so distressed and angry, as a result of their own disrupted experiences, that they are keen to spread that emotional damage.

In summary, children's disclosures to you should be given the same respect as the worrying confidences of a fellow adult. What they say should be taken seriously, but not fixed as the whole truth that is to override anything that anyone else says, or as the final facts of the case.

What stops children telling?

Children do not always speak up about abuse or distressing experiences, such as being bullied. There are a number of reasons why children may not tell, or may not persist in telling.

▶ Young children may not have the language to express their upset or confusion. They may lack the actual words and so what they say does not carry the meaning they want to communicate. Adults may also not understand what a child is trying to tell them, or the possible meaning seems so unlikely that the adult does not take real notice.

▶ Making sense of communication can be especially difficult when children and young people have severe learning or physical disabilities that affect communication. You need to use signing and image systems, although with great care, to ensure that you are not over-interpreting what the child communicates.

▶ Adults or young people who abuse sometimes make direct physical threats that ensure children's silence. The abuser may threaten to hurt the child if they tell or make realistic threats towards someone else for whom the child cares.

▶ Abusers also make emotional threats, which can be just as effective as physical ones. They may say that, if the child tells, then the family will be broken up or the abuser will lose his job. Sexual abusers may claim that nobody will believe the child or that others will think the child is 'bad' or 'dirty'. The aim of these emotional threats is usually to make the child feel inappropriately responsible for any unhappy consequences of telling – 'It will all be your fault!'

▶ Children who have long experiences of abuse or neglect may simply assume that this is normal. They believe that it happens in all families or that that it happens to 'bad' children like themselves who deserve ill-treatment.

▶ Children who are having difficulty telling, for whatever reason, may try to tell in ways that are hard for adults to 'hear'. Perhaps children say very little or make a throwaway comment that could be taken several different ways. They will not say anymore if the adult's reaction seems uninterested or dismissive.

When parents or other adults say something

Worries that may have child protection implications can arise because of what an adult tells you. There are several possibilities:

▶ Parents may speak with you about their own child. The concerns may relate to this parent as an individual, to a partner or other family member or to other people involved with the family.
▶ Alternatively parents may express concerns about another child in your setting, or this parent's deep worries about the other child's family.
▶ Parents may be expressing direct concerns that something is amiss. Alternatively, what they say in passing could ring warning bells for you because it links with other incidents or information, unknown to this parent.
▶ Parents, or other adults who visit your setting, may communicate concerns or wish to clear up issues about the actions of a practitioner or volunteer.
▶ Concerns might be raised by one of your colleagues, a volunteer or another professional who regularly visits your setting (a doctor, speech therapist or child psychologist).

A positive approach when an adult tells you something of concern has many features in common with good communication with children.

▶ Listen with care to what you are being told. Give this adult your full attention and ensure that you understand what is being said to you.
▶ Ask open-ended questions in the same way as described on page 109 for listening to children. You might repeat part of what the adult has said, but with a question implied by your tone or a few words of encouragement. For example, you might answer with 'So, you've seen Marsha's mum hit the child a lot recently?' or 'You say you're really worried about the baby. Tell me what's worrying you so much.'
▶ You do not have to work out now the truth of what you are hearing. You should take seriously what you are told. Take it with seriousness even if what the parent says seems unlikely to you or you do not want to believe it.
▶ Listen carefully and do not dismiss what you are told, even if the general view is that this parent is a gossip, dislikes the accused person or in your opinion tends to make a fuss.
▶ A parent, or a member of staff, who raises many child protection worries that prove to be unfounded needs to be challenged in private conversation with a senior member of staff. There may be a number of possible underlying explanations. For instance, this adult may believe an unrealistically high

estimate about the prevalence of child abuse. Alternatively, a parent or colleague may be seeking attention through raising concerns. Frustrations with such a person should not be handled by automatically disbelieving them.

▶ An adult may ask you to keep what they say a secret or ask that you promise to keep their name out of any further enquiries. You cannot make either of these promises. Remind a parent of your setting's policy and obligation to pass on any concerns about children. But you may also be able to reassure the parent that your next step will be to talk with your senior. You will **not** move immediately to phoning social services without any further consideration.

The same skills of communication are applicable if you work on your own, but your next steps will be different from working in a group setting with colleagues – see the discussion on page 119.

THE LIMITS TO CONFIDENTIALITY

Adults who are the first to raise child protection concerns are often understandably worried about the personal consequences that may follow. You and your colleagues may feel just as uneasy as any parent who approaches you with such a worry.

However, social services cannot go ahead with a case if the only concerns are being expressed by anonymous sources. The process is very different from investigative journalism, when a newspaper article may well present some evidence without naming the source. Furthermore, local authority guidelines stress an open and accountable process. Concerns cannot be entered or used as supporting material in an investigation if the informants are anonymous. Another point is that, in many cases, parents will have a good idea of who is likely to have expressed worries about them or their children – whether this is a member of staff or a neighbour. No possible useful work is going to be done with the family in your setting unless you own the concerns you voice.

The NSPCC are willing to accept anonymous referrals, although they prefer to have as much detail as possible. If you are talking with parents who insist on keeping their name out of any report, you could advise them to contact the local NSPCC. However, it would be sensible for you to inform your senior practitioner of the conversation.

Consulting colleagues

Concerns that are relevant to children's well-being should be shared appropriately in your setting. Your first step may vary slightly, depending on the nature of your concern, exactly what you have noticed or what someone else has expressed to you.

Some possibilities are:

▶ You may discuss what you have heard or noticed with your room colleague, so that you can both gain some perspective and draw on your more general knowledge of the child and family.
▶ Such a conversation must, of course, be confidential and out of the hearing of either the children or parents. This kind of discussion is not appropriate for general staff room conversation, nor for snatched exchanges in corridors or the toilets.
▶ Pressing concerns should lead you to make sure that you talk the same day with a senior practitioner, your head of centre or an advisor. If you are yourself a senior team leader, you might still want to talk in confidence with someone. A head of centre might welcome a conversation with the deputy in order to weigh up what has been brought to their attention.
▶ Sometimes it is wise to raise a worrying pattern of concerns in a room meeting or some other staff session in which you discuss the progress and behaviour of individual children. However, you should not postpone pressing concerns for days until you have a scheduled meeting.
▶ Persistent but vague worries about a child, parent or a colleague might be best raised during supervision, when a senior practitioner should help you to explore what exactly is troubling you and what might be done. Not all settings have a thorough supervision system. You would then need to approach a colleague or senior practitioner, explaining that you need to speak in confidence with some urgency.
▶ Large early years settings may have a designated officer who specialises in child protection. Schools should have such a person, but in many early years or playwork settings you would talk with the head of centre.

The possibilities outlined above highlight how important it is that general good practice is in place in your setting before there is any crisis, or potential crisis, in child protection. All group settings need a positive atmosphere in which practitioners feel able to talk about concerns for the children, even if those worries are vague and hard to identify. Practitioners should support one another and senior practitioners specifically support the staff through informal conversations as well as regular supervision.

Support and supervision

You may be the colleague or senior staff member to whom another practitioner turns for a helpful conversation. You can offer support by using effective communication:

▶ Listen to what the other person is telling you, without prejudging the issue one way or another. (You will notice that the advice to listen continues to come up throughout this section.) Child protection is a topic on which everyone's feelings can become involved and listening with care is a good way to avoid premature conclusions: rejecting or accepting the reality of a worry on a mainly emotional basis.

▶ Ask questions that encourage the practitioner to say anything else that is relevant, but do not direct too much. You might ask, 'What else did he say to you?', 'Did she give you any more details about the baby's screaming?' or 'What sense do you make of this – given what you know of the child?'

▶ A practitioner who comes with a vague, although persistent concern, may need some help in exploring the worry. You might comment, 'I understand you feel that Joan [a colleague] humiliates the children. Can you give me an example of what you mean – something that's happened recently?' Or 'You say that this morning brought your worries about Karen to a head. Can you talk me through what happened – step by step?'

▶ You are not trying to make a firm assessment of the truth or any assertions or the seriousness of concerns. As a more senior practitioner you are gathering information on what has happened, has been said and what sense you make of it given your general knowledge of this child, family or practitioner.

▶ Encourage the other practitioner to make their notes on the conversation now, if this work has not yet been completed.

▶ Support this practitioner in preparing how she, or he, will speak with the parent. The issue needs to be raised with the parent(s), if it was not them who approached the practitioner in the first place. If matters have arisen because of something the parent said, then the practitioner needs to be ready for a follow-up conversation about what will, or will not, be happening as a result in the centre.

If you work on your own

Your options will be different if you work in a very small group setting or are working on your own as a childminder, foster carer or nanny.

▶ In a very small early years or out-of-school setting, you may not have a senior practitioner with whom you can talk. Perhaps you and one other person run the group. You need to talk together, of course, but then you will want to consult someone in an advisory position. Every local area must have somebody who is responsible for early years and for out-of-school settings. The job titles may vary but you should be able to get the information from your local Early Years Development and Childcare Partnership (EYDCP) or the Pre-School Advisory Group in Northern Ireland.

▶ If you are a childminder you could use a similar route, although there should be someone with local responsibility specifically for the childminding service. You will certainly have a support worker if you are part of a childminding network. Foster carers should have their own named support or link worker, who can be consulted.

▶ Nannies are the most isolated individual practitioners. You would still follow the general good practice about talking with parents. If you needed objective, outside advice, you could contact the local advisory sources in the same way as any practitioner. Many of the national children's charities, including the NSPCC, have helplines that could support you in making sense of your concerns if there is nobody with whom you can talk in confidence.

Continued relationships with parents or co-workers can be delicate or difficult in a group setting where practitioners should find support from colleagues. But relationships can be especially hard when you are working alone as a childminder or foster carer in your own home or as a nanny in the family's home. Depending on what has happened, you may find that the working relationship, or your job if you are a nanny, is no longer viable. However, if you are relating to the non-abusing parent in a family abuse case, or if the abuser came from outside the family, your continuing relationship with the parent(s) may be a very welcome support to them. As a foster carer, you should have support easily available, because you work with children whose families are already identified as vulnerable in some way.

Talking with parents

Assuming that it has not been the parent(s) who raised a concern with you, good practice is to speak with the parent(s) as soon as possible after a problem or concern has arisen. The only valid reasons not to talk with parents before taking any other steps would be that you and your senior genuinely believe that the child is at risk of serious harm from the parent, or that there are good reasons for thinking that the parent will have an extreme and violent reaction to what you say. In such a case the safety of you, your colleagues and the children is paramount. Your judgement, on the basis of sound information, which you can explain clearly to other professionals, is that the child's immediate safety requires that you contact social services to set other procedures in motion.

If there is any doubt about talking with parents as the most usual first step, then remember that communication with parents, or children's other primary carers, represents good practice, in line with all the child protection legislation across the UK. Each Children Act and Order has as key principles that professionals should support parental responsibility and work in an active partnership with parents (see Chapter 2).

Whatever the exact nature of your concern, the conversation with a parent is unlikely to be easy or comfortable. On the other hand, you may get a straightforward and credible explanation to your question. Parents may be pleased that you have spoken up because they share your concerns and want to do something about them. The appropriate action may not need to go further than your setting because no child protection concern arises. Perhaps the key issues are about the child's development or an understandable behavioural reaction to family stress or bereavement.

The value of partnership with parents

Without doubt this kind of conversation will be far more possible and easier if you have taken the trouble to build a friendly working relationship with parents. Such a relationship gives parents a different context in which to make sense of your question about Sandra's bruises on her thigh or Mike's puzzling remark about 'seeing a strange man's willy'.

Perhaps you have taken time over the previous weeks or months to ask the parent's opinion on matters relating to the child. You may have asked about non-confrontational personal matters such as food preferences or ways that you and the parent together might boost the child's physical confidence. Conversations of this kind will have established you as someone who relates to the child as an individual and to parents as people who matter.

There may have been incidents in the setting when you have had to explain to a parent how the child sustained a minor injury and what was done at the time. Alternatively the incident might have been one in which the child became emotionally upset about a story or an altercation between other children. This openness creates a two-way relationship where you have shown you believe that parents have a right to be informed and offered explanations.

Your previous approach will make it more likely that a parent will react positively to your query. A good working relationship with parents may also mean that Mike's mother tells you, without your having to ask, that yesterday she and her son had an unpleasant encounter with a flasher in the park or Sandra's father describes how his daughter fell out of the tree-house at the weekend.

You should never avoid talking with parents because:

▶ You are too busy. It is crucial that you make the time and, if necessary, colleagues or a senior practitioner must rearrange their time to enable you to have an uninterrupted conversation with the parent.
▶ You are concerned, perhaps for good reason, that the parent will get angry or abusive. Being shouted at is not a pleasant experience but you need to face this possibility for the sake of the child. Look also at page 123 on an assertive approach.
▶ You cannot believe that anything like this could possibly happen in this family, so you are going to ignore the whole incident. There are no certainties as regards abusers in child protection work, so you must take further appropriate action.
▶ You are worried about the consequences if your concerns are groundless, that you will spoil a friendly relationship with the parent that has been hard to establish. One of the criticisms of poor social work practice has been when a social worker puts undue priority to maintaining a good relationship with the parent, as a higher priority than the welfare of the child. All the UK child protection legislation stresses that the welfare of the child must be the most important consideration and should therefore take priority over adult feelings.
▶ You want somebody else to deal with the difficulty and so you refer on immediately to the social worker on the grounds that they will sort out the matter if there is anything serious. This step is not appropriate and would be bad practice. A simple conversation with a parent might clear up the questions, whereas going straight to social services, without good reason, will immediately place matters on a more serious footing, and undermine trust between the setting and the parents.

Undoubtedly some teams have gained the impression that even minor concerns should be passed immediately to the social services. Sometimes this message has been given through child protection courses, with the rationale that talking with parents raises the possibility that abusers will cover up the evidence. It is worth repeating here, as has been emphasised in other sections of the book, that good practice is to talk with parents, unless there are sound reasons not to do this. Teams would be hurt and probably angry if parents' first reaction, about concerns related to the setting, were to contact social services rather than have a conversation with staff.

Assertive communication

Anything that you say to parents needs to be in your own words and so come across as a genuine communication. There is no format that is always right or that will avoid any awkwardness or unpleasantness. However, there are better, as well as unwise, ways of expressing your concern or question. Your aim is for clear, honest and **assertive** communication. You need to avoid both a passive, unduly apologetic approach or an aggressive and confrontational line.

BE CLEAR IN YOUR OWN MIND

Decide what you want to tell or ask a parent (or other relevant carer).

▶ What exactly is puzzling you about what the child said or did?
▶ What and where are the bruises, cuts or other marks?
▶ What patterns of behaviour from the child have concerned you, what is happening or not happening?

Which of your feelings are relevant and could appropriately be voiced? Some examples are:

▶ 'I'm uneasy about the games Jamie tries to play with two other children.'
▶ 'I'm confused about what Tara said. What kind of sense does it make to you as her mother?'
▶ 'I'm concerned that Alan is so often upset when your au pair picks him up. It's like he's a different child from the days that you or your husband come.'

It is unlikely to be appropriate to add apologies like 'I'm sorry but ...' or riders like 'I'm sure there's a perfectly simple explanation' or 'Please don't think I'm interfering but ...' The communication will be more straightforward if you express the facts and any relevant feelings simply. It is appropriate to apologise if there has been an accident involving the child or something has happened that should not have occurred. For instance, perhaps one parent's child was inadvertently left in a locked classroom when the rest of the nursery group were taken off to see a video.

PRACTISE IF IT HELPS

If you feel it would help, then take the time in the day to consider with a colleague or senior practitioner what you will say to this parent at the end of session or the day. A second perspective can be helpful if you feel uneasy about the impending conversation or if you are not coming to terms with your difficulties in working out what you will say.

You could practise what you will say, either in your head or out loud with a colleague. Keep your message simple, for instance, 'Wai has several big bruises on her upper arms. Do you know how they came about?' Or 'Davie said an odd thing to me today. He said, "The ghosties will get me if I tell about Uncle Ned". He seemed very upset. What sense do you make of it?'.

When the parent arrives to pick up the child:

▶ Ask to have a word in private if it is not easy to talk away from other parents and children.
▶ If the parent wants to rush off, you may need to press with, 'I appreciate you're in a hurry, but I think this is too important to wait until tomorrow/next week.'
▶ Say what you have to say and listen to the parent's reply.
▶ Be ready to repeat your question or statement if the parent seems not to have listened or understood.
▶ Have a conversation that opens up the topic and be ready to make an arrangement to talk further with the parent in the very near future, if this seems appropriate.

Accidental or non-accidental injury?

There are no certainties in any guidelines over non–accidental injury. But there are a number of features in a conversation with a parent that could put your mind at ease, or alternatively add to your existing concern. The same considerations hold if you are a senior practitioner in conversation with a member of staff, who was responsible for the group when an accident happened. Such conversations will not occur only with parents.

Children can inflict a range of injuries on themselves without adult intervention. Every setting will have had accidents, sometimes serious, in an environment that is supposedly child-centred and child-friendly. So, it is important to remain open-minded and not to leap to conclusions because you do not like or trust the parent – or the practitioner. But also do not convince yourself it must be alright in order to avoid a difficult conversation.

Injury of a child as the result of a genuine accident is likely to have some or most of the following features:

▶ The parent (or other carer) acted swiftly to help the child, with appropriate first aid or seeking further medical help. Some people are prone to panic, but what happened after the panic subsided? (If a team member seems less than competent in a crisis, then this practice will have to be addressed through in-house support or training.)

▶ After a full conversation, the explanation of the child's injury makes sense: given the nature of the injury, the child's age, what you know of the child (some children are reckless) and their overall development. But again do not just be persuaded by your knowledge that these individual children are lively and fearless – were they being properly supervised?

▶ The description of the incident given by all the individuals involved, including the children if they are old enough to talk about what happened, is very similar, i.e. there is a consistent story about what happened.

▶ The children's appearance or demeanour do not suggest that they are fearful of their parents or carer, or neglected by them.

You would suspect non-accidental injury if the pattern varied significantly from the above. But be aware that genuine anxiety of parents can show itself in many ways. People are generally now very aware of child abuse and so parents, in a family where nothing wrong has happened, may seem uneasy. Perhaps they are genuinely worried that matters may get out of hand and that they will be accused of maltreatment.

The results of talking with parents

You may talk with parents and they give a reasonable and plausible explanation of what had concerned you. Good practice would still be to make a note in the child's record of the conversation. This is easier if you and the parents have a continuing relationship of openness and shared written records.

Alternatively you may talk with parents and your concerns are not put to rest. Perhaps what they say only adds to your concerns or the parents are relieved you have opened the subject and make a disclosure about themselves or someone else involved with the family. The same guidelines for good communication apply as were outlined on page 117, including the reminder that you cannot keep a disclosure about possible abuse as a secret. Tell parents what you will be doing next and when you will speak with them again.

Observations, records and reports

The material in this, and the following section, 'Working with other professionals', overlap slightly with other parts of this book. It is necessary, however, to place these important issues within the context of exactly how they are dealt with in group settings or by individual practitioners.

Good practice for child protection

Observation and record keeping is an integral part of quality standards for all settings and your contribution to child protection will draw on this area of good practice.

As an involved practitioner, you should be observant of the children – what they do, what they enjoy and how individual children usually react. You will not notice everything in a busy group, but you should be alert to what is happening and be ready to focus your attention on individual children or activities.

Informal, daily observations of young children within a setting should be complemented by more structured observations that build up a descriptive record of children's development and behaviour. Any setting should be able to make a substantial contribution to questions about a child's physical well-being, development and patterns of behaviour. You are absolutely **not** tracking children in your setting just in case child protection becomes an issue. What is needed is a positive focus on what children are able to do and how their development progresses over time. This focus will be the most helpful to any children who are at risk.

Child protection inquiries following the serious injury or death of a child have sometimes emphasised the danger, and perhaps a tragic outcome, when nobody appears to have kept track of the children. Perhaps the various professionals involved have been weighing up the parents' abilities to cope, the likely truth of competing explanations of what has happened or subtle issues of cultural patterns. In all these important facets of child protection monitoring, somebody must focus on the child. When children are attending an early years setting or regularly going to a childminder, your records and observations may contribute that crucial focus.

If you become concerned about a child, then do not wait for other professionals to ask for your contribution. Be ready to offer the perspective that your knowledge can bring to the child's well-being and perhaps their safety. If you are a senior practitioner or head of centre, then make sure that you develop contacts within the local child protection system (see page 136). As a senior, it is also your responsibility to develop your team so that practitioners feel confident to present their observations and summarise their records of a child.

The contribution of any practitioner is not going to be the final word on whether a child is being abused. Your input will be part of informal early enquiries or a more detailed investigation. Practitioners should be able to contribute to a discussion, with the support of a child's records. Your contribution may support the need to worry about a child or may place isolated concerns in a more positive context. The following examples show how early years practitioners might contribute verbally to a group discussion in a meeting about a young child.

Example One

'Yes, we have become concerned about Emma's behaviour. When we look back through our records for her, she seems to have become more and more unhappy over the last two months. She is tearful and gets upset about minor difficulties when nobody is cross with her at all. During the last fortnight, her key worker has noticed that Emma has been picking at her skin so much that she has raw patches around her fingernails and on her scalp. This week we approached Emma's mother with our concerns, but we haven't got much further than her Mum saying that there are what she calls "family troubles" at the moment.'

Example Two

'No, we're not worried about Hamid's weight. Our records for the last six months show that he makes steady gains and he eats a balanced diet. His general health is good and minor scratches heal quickly. When we observe his play, Hamid has plenty of energy and he keeps up with children of his own age. The health visitor is right to say that Hamid is on the lowest percentile for the standard weight charts, but the entire family is shorter and smaller than average. Hamid had some frustrations when a couple of children tried to baby him in their games but he's been able to deal with that, with some discreet help from his key worker. We are happy to keep monitoring Hamid, but we want to avoid the weight business becoming a big issue. Hamid's mother asked to speak with the key worker this week and she seems to feel harassed by all the visits and questions about her son.'

Practitioners who work with young children may be the most likely to keep track of health and development. However, school and out-of-school settings remain in a strong position to keep a close eye on the well being of older children, who still cannot be expected to manage all aspects of their health and care.

The examples above are given in the kind of language you would use in spoken communication. Written communication is phrased differently and practitioners are often asked to write in a way that avoids the 'I' and 'we' that is natural in conversation. There is further discussion about written records below.

Records and child protection

When child protection becomes a possible issue, then good standards in written reports still apply in the same way as any recording. You should consider:

▶ **What** you need to record
▶ The reasons **why** you are recording this information
▶ Good practice in **how** you record
▶ Issues of confidentiality of reports and of appropriate access to them.

FACTUAL INFORMATION

Good written records should be honestly factual. Opinions are important, as long as they are supported (see later in this section), but a good and useful report does not muddle up facts, opinions and interpretations.

Your written record has to report the facts as they are known. This emphasis is crucial whether you are writing a few sentences of notes in an on-going record or several pages in a summary report on a child. You may be describing any of the following:

▶ What happened, where and when? Give dates and times if appropriate.

For example: perhaps a teenage older brother has been observed to hit and drag the younger sibling he picks up from nursery. Who saw this incident? When did it occur? What happened before the blow was struck? Where were the siblings when the elder struck the younger one? Has there been more than one similar incident? What, if anything, did anyone from the nursery do or say?

▶ If a child's behaviour has concerned you, then describe what you observed. Support your observation with an explanation, not necessarily very long, of your reasons for concern. If your concern focuses on a pattern of behaviour or observable changes in a child's more usual reactions, then exactly what have you seen or heard, and when?

▶ If you write up what someone else has told you, perhaps a parent or concerned neighbour, then make it clear in your report when you are documenting what somebody else says they have observed.

For example: you may not have direct experience that 'Emma's parents are having awful rows'. More accurately, what you are reporting is that 'Emma's next-door neighbour [name] spoke with me on [date] to say that he is "very worried" because he hears "all these screaming matches" through the wall between his home and the Davisons'.'

▶ Avoid quoting words or phrases unless you are sure that this is exactly what was said, whether it is a child or adult. If you are uncertain of the exact words then be honest and write that the child, or adult said 'something like ...' The more prompt you are in writing up your notes, the more accurate your memory will be. Certainly, do not tidy up a child's words, or those of an adult. If what was said is open to more than one interpretation, then this ambiguity must be maintained.

▶ If a child's physical well-being is in question then be specific about your observations. Perhaps a child regularly arrives in wintertime wearing lightweight summer clothes. Note down the days and what the child is wearing, do not leave a vague note of 'Gabrielle's clothes are inadequate for the weather'.

▶ If a child has injuries, then make an accurate record of the nature and extent of the bruises, cuts or other marks. You could use a simple outline figure of a child, front and back versions, to sketch the location of any injuries. Do not draw any conclusions that you are unable to support, especially do not make guesses about the possible cause of any injury.

For example: you might write that 'there were four bruises on Ansel's upper arm and one under the arm'. You should not claim that the marks are from a fierce grip on the child's arm unless you have a sound reason. A series of small, round, inflamed marks on Ansel's back might be cigarette burns. But what independent evidence do you have? If you have no basis for a considered guess, then do not go any further than a description in your report.

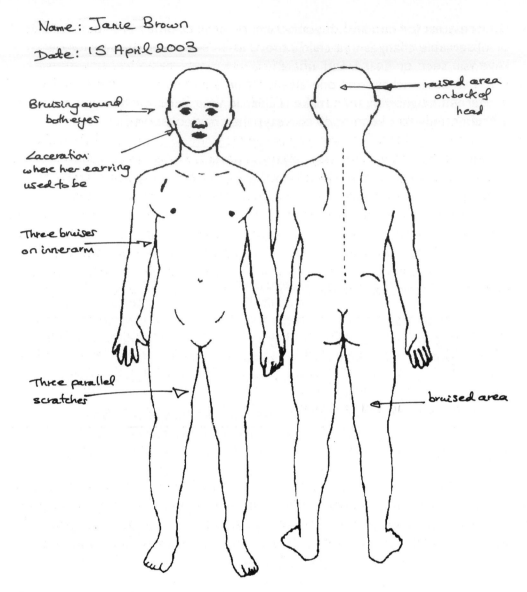

Name: Janie Brown

Date: 15 April 2003

Bruising around both eyes →

Laceration where her earring used to be

Three bruises on inner arm →

Three parallel scratches →

raised area on back of head ←

bruised area ←

▶ Use only sketches and a written description. You should not be asked to take photographs, especially of the parts of a child's body that would usually be covered by clothes. Assessment in a child protection inquiry sometimes involves photographic evidence. But everyone who is part of such an inquiry must be aware of children's dignity and their right not to be subjected to more intrusive investigation or recording than is absolutely necessary.

▶ Of course, you will not always be in a position to see a child unclothed. Babies and very young children need a level of personal care that involves changing their clothes. Some disabled children continue to need a high level of adult support with personal care. School-age children may have reason to change for games.

▶ But some early years and out-of-school settings do not have routines that would make it likely for you to see a child in less cover than lightweight summer clothing. You would not, of course, pressure a child to remove clothing. But you might as a kindly question if a child is rubbing their leg, as if in pain or says, 'my tummy hurts'. Children who have had genuine accidents are often only too keen to show you their scrapes or bruises.

▶ Write down as literally as you can any explanation that the child gives about the injury, and in the same way, what the parents say when you approach them.

▶ In a group setting, and in specialist work like foster care, you should have some guidelines to help you with written reports. Some prefer that practitioners avoid personal words such as 'I' or 'we'. You can word phrases in a different way, for instance, 'I am still concerned about ...' can become, 'there is still concern about ...' or 'This explanation does not address the concerns because ...' In any report, it must be clear who is writing or has made the observations by the name at the end of the report.

> *For example*: your observation of a lacerated area on a child's leg might then be supported with the notes that: 'Sian and her father both said that the family dog bit Sian on Saturday night. Mr Evans told May (key practitioner) that he took Sian to Casualty immediately. The doctor cleaned the wound but said that no stitches were necessary.'

TIMELY RECORDING

You should make your notes about a concern for a child as soon as possible after your observation and certainly within the same day. The longer you leave it to make your written record, the greater the chance that you will forget details. Another possibility is that you may start to lay your own interpretation over events.

Timely recording is an important issue for all professionals. For instance, if child protection, or any other cases, reach court, then professionals giving evidence are often asked to be specific about exactly when they made their notes. Records written up many days after important events are far less credible than prompt recording.

SUPPORT YOUR OPINIONS

You, and your colleagues, have personal experience of individual children and a broad base of general knowledge about child development. You will draw on one or both of these sources when you weigh up, with colleagues or your senior, to what extent there is cause for concern. The important point is that you share through your written record how you reached a judgement and do not simply give the judgement itself – 'we should be worried' or 'there's no cause for concern'.

Factual description will be very important in reports relevant to child protection but your opinions are also of value, so long as you give your reasons. There always needs to be some sense of 'because ...', whether you write that actual word or not. Some of the examples already given in this section include supported opinions. There is a great deal of difference, in terms of the quality of the report, between 'Fazila's parents neglect her' and 'We have been concerned about the standard of Fazila's care from her family because she wears the same clothes, including underwear, for over two weeks at a time. Fazila has become distressed because other children do not want to sit next to her and say that she smells. Fazila is in regular pain with her teeth, which we have mentioned on three occasions [dates] to her mother but there is no sign that the child has been taken to the dentist. Fazila is usually very hungry on Monday mornings and eats several helpings at breakfast. Her hunger seems to lessen as the week goes by ...' And so on.

Sometimes it is not easy to put your finger directly on what concerns you. It is important to pursue strong feelings of unease or work to become more specific about gut reactions. A colleague may be able to help you or your senior within a supervision session. It can help to be asked questions like, 'Can you describe for me the most recent time that you felt very uneasy about this child?' Open-ended questions can help you to become more specific about who was present, what happened or who said what.

Sometimes your uneasiness may be fuelled by what does not happen. For instance, perhaps a child's mother rarely seems to react one way or another – happiness when the child is excited or sympathy if the child is distressed. You would not conclude from this pattern that the child was necessarily subject to deliberate emotional abuse. An equally possible explanation, to allow for until there is more information, is that the mother is severely depressed. The parent and family might need and welcome support. Such input might be the best way of ensuring the well being of the child.

It is often possible, with the help of a colleague to identify the firmer observational basis of a gut feeling. This observation can then be written into the report. If you cannot identify firmer ground then you should not write vague and unsupported feelings in a report such as 'Nobody in Liam's family seems to care about him' or 'I'm certain there is something very wrong in the Brownlow family.' If you cannot support a comment, then do not write it in the report. You are leaving yourself, and the setting that you represent, open to accusations of unfairness to a family or being prejudiced against the parents on some grounds. If you are expressing criticisms with no obvious evidence, then perhaps you are working from unreasonable or ill-informed assumptions about this family. However, some gut feelings will have a strong basis in your observations and knowledge of individual children. You need to identify the basis and make it explicit through description and examples.

CLEAR WRITTEN STYLE

Any records need to be written in a clear and concise style. Child protection reports are no different in that way from good practice for any written records.

▶ If your records are hand-written, then make sure that your writing is legible and check the spelling of words if you have any doubt. If you work on a word processor, then make sure that you use the spell-check function.

▶ Make it easy for anyone to follow the flow of your report. Ensure that any narrative about a child or family goes in the right order, with dates or times next to the incident in question.

▶ Use headings if that is appropriate and consider making a list of bullet points for clarity if you are describing a series of incidents or concerns. It can be easier to follow this kind of list than a description all within one long paragraph.

Senior, or more experienced, practitioners need to be ready to help colleagues improve their style in any written reports. Feedback needs to be constructive:

▶ Offer specific suggestions on how practitioners could improve a particular report and avoid non-specific criticisms. For instance, it is very discouraging to be told bluntly, 'Your report is far too muddled. You'll have to re-organise it before we let the social worker see it'.

▶ You need to be specific about why the report is 'muddled' and in what ways it can be improved. Practitioners also deserve positive feedback about improvements made in their writing skills so far. Support often involves talking about the situation prior to suggesting that a colleague reworks the report.

▶ In the given example, the practitioner needs to be told, 'You have identified well that you have three main concerns about Tom, but the report is hard to follow because your concerns appear in bits throughout the report. And your descriptions are often separate from the dates you give. Let's start with your worry about Tom and the games he tries to play with Natalie'.

▶ Use of headings can help to give consistency in written reports. Practitioners who work with vulnerable children and families may well have proformas on the computer, into which information is typed.

Confidentiality and access

When you write records it is important to remind yourself that parents will be able to read what you are writing. Do not be less honest because of this realisation but be ready to support everything you write.

Parents should know the setting's policy on records because you should have told them early on in the relationship. A clear statement about records should be part of written material on any setting. Parents should have straightforward access to the records of their own children. Older children and young teenagers should also have access, although the guidelines can be less clear for this age group. Access is a civil right supported by legislation and is only over-ridden when there is good cause and one such reason is when a child protection case is ongoing.

Anyone else should only have access to records about children on a clear need to know basis. If child protection issues are raised then the children's records, or more usefully, summaries of them could well become an important part of material on the child and family. The setting's accident and incident book, or developmental records of children might be a crucial support in assessments of whether a child's development and behaviour is a source of concern or not.

Talking about reports

Other professionals may read your full reports on a child and a clear, well-written report will make their task easier. Good quality reports will also support a confident stance with your local child protection team that your setting has a vital contribution to make to the process. You may find that your own local team is only too ready to involve your setting and listen to your perspective. However, some readers who work in early years settings and not in school may still have to establish themselves with other professionals who are less than positive or knowledgeable about the input of early years or out-of-school settings. Make sure that everything you contribute to the process is professional.

At some point you might have to present a summary of your report on a child to a group of other professionals, perhaps at a case conference. It may not be appropriate to work your way through the entire record. The meeting needs highlights and a summary. Prepare yourself before the meeting and make summary notes that will guide you. You will probably need to cover the following:

▶ The nature of your concern about the child
▶ Information supporting your concern
▶ What you have done in your setting with the child and parents
▶ Any changes, for better or not, that you have observed in the child

It is worth communicating clearly to the meeting that the centre would welcome suggestions in further work with child or parents and that you would like, and expect, to be kept informed so that you can contribute to the protection of this child.

Working with other professionals

Child protection legislation within the UK makes it a legal requirement that different agencies should work together for the well-being of children. Reviews of good, and poor, practice in child protection have stressed the great importance of people from different professional backgrounds and agencies working in co-operation and mutual respect. Children can fail to be protected when adults do not communicate with each other and make the effort to work together.

If the concern about a child arises within your setting, then the head of centre will make the decision about contacting someone outside the setting (see the discussion on page 71). Sharing your concerns with other professionals should be done with the parents' knowledge, since you should have spoken with the parent(s) as soon as you became concerned. The parent(s) may not always be happy about your passing on your concerns – they might prefer that you kept silent – but they should be informed about the steps that you are taking.

There are few circumstances in which you would be justified in immediately contacting another professional without the discussion with a child's parent. You might call the police if a parent were attacking the child or members of staff in your setting. You might call a doctor if a child was seriously injured or showed signs of needing urgent medical attention. Talk with members of your local child protection team for some clear guidance on any circumstances that they feel would justify an immediate call to the team.

From your own perspective, the features of good inter-professional co-operation are that you:

▶ Learn about and know your role and that of other professionals in the bigger picture of child protection. Work to understand the boundaries of your role: what you do and when you should hand over to another professional.

▶ Set up regular channels of communication so that you have established some professional links before a crisis (see also page 69).

▶ Work to be assertive and confident in your professional approach and, if you are a senior practitioner, support your team in becoming more confident about their contribution to child protection.

▶ Know what the child protection team's expectations of your setting are as regards your work with this individual child and family. What, exactly would they like you to do and with what goals in mind? When should you be reporting back?

▶ Know exactly what other members of the team should be doing. Who is taking the lead responsibility on this case within your own setting?

Some teams or individual practitioners may need to address doubts about how their own skills are regarded by other professionals in the local area. There is greater respect now for early years, out-of-school, foster and residential practitioners, but still some distance to go. You cannot force other professionals to change their minds, if they undervalue the contribution of your experience and knowledge of individual children or young people. But you can, by persistently behaving in a very professional way yourself, make it ever harder for other people to hold this view.

▶ Be ready, do not wait to be asked and offer your opinion through carefully considered words and good written reports.

▶ Speak up in meetings about children rather than complaining afterwards that 'nobody asked me'. Make sure that you, or the setting's representative, is prepared to speak about a child or family. Show your knowledge and considered opinion about this child.

▶ Act in advance by ensuring that the representative of your setting has a slot on the agenda of the meeting. Talk with the chair of the meeting or find out whom you should contact from your appropriate local advisor or development worker.

▶ Make sure that all these moves are undertaken in the professional spirit of 'we have something to contribute'. Avoid any sense of criticism like 'Why do you deliberately leave us out?' If your contribution has been overlooked, it may not have been a deliberate slight by the child protection team. Early years and out-of-school settings still have to establish themselves against a broad tradition that has undervalued care, and still does in many ways.

▶ Within meetings or discussions that happen at your setting, make it clear that you will keep communications open with the other professionals and that you are confidently expecting the same courtesy. You would not expect to be contacted on a daily basis about a child, but you should be given updates so that you know what is happening with the child and family and you can review your work in the setting.

▶ In any work that is part of the child protection process, you will need to establish common goals and discuss any apparent differences in approach or terminology. But respect any remaining differences between your work and that of the other professionals, including social workers. Your roles are not the same and the jobs are different.

Scenarios

These are short examples of the kinds of situations you might face. For each example, consider one or more of the following questions. (Do not feel you have to work through them all in one sitting.)

1 What might you say to the child in this situation? Practise actual phrases rather than general ideas. You could make notes or try out a sentence with a colleague or fellow-student.
2 What will you say to the parent at the end of the day or session? Again, try some actual sentences. In a student group, you could work some examples into a short role play, with the support of your tutor.
3 What should you say to a more senior colleague? Or what should you raise, if you are the more senior practitioner and your team does not seem to take the situation seriously?
4 Should you make a note of what has happened? If so, what key points should you write?

You will find a short commentary on the scenarios from page 227.

Sergio

Four-year-old Sergio has been persistent in trying to grope the female practitioners in your centre. When you started at the centre two weeks ago, you were warned never to turn your back on the boy, but this was explained as 'macho Italian stuff – it's the family'. Within a week you have noticed how practitioners stand with their back to the fence out in the garden and a couple have held Sergio away. Today, Sergio tried to push his hand up your T-shirt.

Sally

A parent asks to speak with you. Sally, her child, is not in your group, but in one run by Richard and Jessica. She says, 'I know it's awkward to ask you, but I'm worried that Richard is leaving. We've always been a bit concerned about Jessica. She's very fierce with the children. Our daughter says some amazing things when she's playing with dolls, and it's not the kind of stuff that we say to her. Richard seemed to keep a balance, but now he's going. Could you get our daughter moved into your group?'

Rory

Rory is two years old and seems to have a lot of accidents at home. His mother, who runs her business from home, has offered a reasonable explanation for each incident so far. You know Rory as a bold child whose curiosity and self-confidence can lead him into risky situations even in the day nursery. This morning Rory has a very large bruise on his forehead and you ask his mother what happened. She replies, 'I think he pulled out the kitchen steps to get to the biscuits. He must have fallen off. It was a while before I realised.' You ask, 'Oh, weren't you in the kitchen with him then?' She looks a bit embarrassed and then says firmly, 'I had an assignment to finish. I can't turn down work and you won't have them later than 6.30. And his father won't watch him.'

Owen

In a conversation over lunch at your centre, three-year-old Owen is talking about the new baby that will come soon. Owen is talking with affection, 'I pat the baby in Mummy's tummy. Her tummy's very big and knobbly. I see it in the bath'. Your colleague asks Owen with some surprise, 'Do you and Mummy have a bath together?' He replies, 'Oh, yes. We have wet cuddles in the bath.' You have never been concerned about Owen or his family but your colleague talks with you later over coffee. She says, 'Don't you think we should report this. People shouldn't have baths with their children. It isn't right.' She shudders and looks very uncomfortable.

Yvette

Yvette is seven years old and attends your after-school club. Her mother dresses Yvette is what you feel are inappropriate clothes for a girl her age. She wears mainly crop tops, tight short skirts and her shoes often have little heels. Yvette wears nail polish and has three ear rings in each ear. You have become increasingly uneasy hearing Yvette's comments about someone called Martin. Yvette has said things like, 'I'm his little princess' and 'Martin is going to get me a CD player if I'm good.' Yvette seems to become even more flirty with your male colleague than previously. He has just said to you that Yvette wanted to sit on his lap this afternoon. He made an excuse to get her off, because she seemed to be wriggling back very firmly against his crutch.

Winston

Fifteen-month-old Winston often seems to be grumpy in the morning but today he was very out of sorts and wandered around in a daze until lunchtime. When his mother picks him up you ask whether Winston has been unwell. She replies, 'I think we overdid the sleeping medicine.' You look puzzled and she continues, 'Winston is an awful sleeper. My mum said to give him a tot of sherry. She said that was what she used to do and it didn't do us any harm. I was having a terrible time and one night I started to shake him. So I thought the sherry would be safer.'

Olwyn

You are the specialist support assistant for Olwyn who has learning and communication disabilities. Olwyn is ten years old and her developmental level is estimated to be more like a six- or seven-year-old. Olwyn has managed with support in mainstream school, but her pattern of behaviour has now raised concerns. Olwyn appeared to have learned some of the boundaries between private and public behaviour, but has recently started to masturbate when she is in the classroom. You also recently found her without her underwear in the boys' toilets and a couple of sheepish looking boys just leaving.

You speak in confidence with a colleague as you consider your next step, and your colleague takes the view that Olwyn is showing immature behaviour as part of her disability. You feel, however, that this is a new and different pattern and that it should be taken seriously. You are also uneasy about how Olwyn behaves towards the new driver on her transport to school. You find it hard to identify quite what is awry, but are concerned to hear that he also runs a specialist sports club that Olwyn attends. You do not want to make a fuss about nothing, but equally you do not feel that her behaviour should be explained away as part of the disability.

Jerome

You are the class teacher for Jerome, who is thirteen years old and the eldest of a family of four. His mother has a history of alcoholism and has been violent in the past. The family has had a great deal of social work input and the view of the current social worker is that Jerome's mother has turned the corner on her alcohol problem and is better at dealing with her anger and her own memories of childhood abuse. There is a new partner in the household and he is regarded as a stabilising influence.

You have a private conversation with Jerome because his standard of work has fallen in the subject for which you take him. But you are also aware that your colleagues, like you, have found that Jerome is missing most deadlines now on homework. Initially, Jerome appears surly and full of unlikely excuses. You have had a good relationship with him, so you look doubtful and ask, 'How are things at home, then?'

Bit by bit, it emerges that family life is far from stabilised. Jerome appears to take most of the responsibility for his siblings and his mother wants to talk at length to him about her own abuse as a child – conversations that he finds distressing and embarrassing. Jerome resents the new partner for trying to take over, as if he is their father and says that this man and his mother have started heavy drinking sessions. The family social worker rarely, if ever, talks with Jerome. You are concerned about the weight on Jerome, but are very aware that his abiding fear is that he will be split from his siblings, if it becomes clear that his mother cannot cope.

5

Working with individual children and families

Children's experiences of abuse and neglect are very varied and so there is no single pattern of how best to help them. There are, however, some practical guidelines that enable early years, school and out-of-school practitioners to take a positive approach. Many of the suggestions in this section are grounded in good practice with all children, whether or not they have had distressing experiences.

Working with the children

Consult other professionals

Good contacts between your service and the local child protection team should include practical discussions about the contribution of your setting and your own skills as an individual practitioner. If you are still building an effective working relationship, perhaps the setting will have to make some active moves. If you are the manager, or senior, then do not just wait for the social worker to call you.

You might want to discuss any of the following:

▶ Is there anything specific you would like us to do within the setting? Are there any particular checks that could be carried on with the child, or anything within our records that could be helpful?

▶ What suggestions would you make about how best to help within your setting, or home, from your knowledge of the child and the family?

▶ It will be helpful to know whether other specialist input is being offered to the child or family, in order to support your relationship with the child. You are not, of course, asking for confidential details of counselling or therapy. With some shared information, you will perhaps know the identity of 'Lisa' who apparently talks with this child every week or the 'clinic' that 'Mummy has gone to this weekend'.

▶ Therapy for children, including play therapy is a specialised task and no practitioners should attempt to undertake any form of therapy unless they have been trained. But not all children or young people, who have been abused, want or need special therapy. They can be well supported by what you offer within the ordinary day or session with a child.

Practical monitoring and physical care

Usual good practice for observation and physical care may be sufficient for some children who have experienced abuse. However, when children have been injured or seriously neglected, you may be asked to monitor or support children in a more specific way. You may be asked:

▶ To ensure that the child has been brought into your setting for the agreed days or sessions. Unless there is a specific agreement, school age children will be expected to attend every day. You need to know whom you should contact, if the child is absent beyond a particular time.

▶ To check a child for bruises or new injuries. Make sure that any checking is done with respect for the child and an awareness of the sense of bodily dignity of even young children. Have an honest and simple answer ready for when a child asks you why you are doing regular checks.

▶ To weigh children or keep a record of what they eat in your setting or family home.

▶ To keep a record of children's clothing, whether this is appropriate for the weather or check that a young child is in a clean nappy or underwear that is not soiled.

Usual patterns of care for younger children can be extended within the age range, if children have physical or learning disabilities that limit their ability or understanding to take on much of their own personal care.

Supporting the children

The key guideline is to treat children as normally as possible, without pretending that nothing has happened.

You will not be able to treat children who have been abused in exactly the same way as children whose life experience has been less disruptive and distressing. However, it would not be good practice, in any case, to attempt to treat all children in exactly the same way. Sensitive practitioners should respond to children as individuals, tuning in to what they say and being sensitive to how their abusive experience may be reflected in their play, conversation and behaviour. You should be able to draw on your general skills with children in how you work with and support a child who has been abused.

AFFIRM THE CHILD AS A WORTHWHILE INDIVIDUAL

An experience of abuse or neglect can make children seriously doubt themselves and the trustworthiness of adults. Children need to feel, or learn to feel through positive experiences with adults, that someone cares about what happened and will support them from now on. You can help in the following ways:

▶ If children say critical things of themselves, you need to offer positive emotional support. Avoid saying simply to the child that 'It's not true'. Neither will it be supportive to deny the child's feelings with, 'You don't think that, really'. Clearly the child does think such negative thoughts, or has reason to believe that you might.

▶ You can acknowledge that the child has expressed a strong feeling with a phrase like, 'It must be difficult for you to feel that way'. You do not have to agree with the child's negative remark but can say warmly 'I like you' or 'I don't think you're a bad boy.'

▶ In your continuing relationship with the child, you can show your positive feelings not only through what you say, but also in how you behave to the child. Smiles, encouraging nods and attention given to children's comments and activities all communicate to them that you value them, enjoy having them in your group or class, or like chatting with them in the school playground.

▶ You can express emotional warmth and affection to children who doubt themselves and also to children whose behaviour, shaped by their experience, is hard to handle.

▶ As with all children, you should be guided by the individual in how close they want an adult to be or how much they want to be touched. No adult should push a child further than the child wishes for hugs, hand holding, sitting on your lap or any other simple physical expression of closeness appropriate with young children. (See also the discussion on page 184)

▶ Take the time to bring in a very distrustful child and do not feel that your skills are in question. Some children may take a long time to open up and you have to be pleased with small successes.

▶ Children need your support and sympathy, but pity is rarely a helpful emotion to express, to a child or adult in distress. Avoid talking about children in hushed tones or expressing the message of 'Poor little Emma', whether you communicate through spoken words or your body language.

▶ Make sure that you involve children in decisions and ask their opinion as you should with any child. Even if it takes time before a child believes you really mean what you say, keep trying.

Listen and be ready to talk

Children do not forget about distressing events just because adults avoid talking about the topic. What is more likely is that children will conclude, perhaps correctly, that the adults are reluctant to talk. In the absence of any clear message, children may also conclude that adults are cross with them or believe the children did something wrong or are dirty children. Emotionally damaging thoughts can grow in a child's mind if nothing positive is being communicated by adults who should care.

The ways in which you may be able to offer time and attention will vary according to your work. Ideally, you would respond when a child starts to talk. However, there may also be times when you have to say carefully to a child or young person, 'I really want to hear what you want to tell me, but there is no way for us to have privacy until (give a time). Can we please talk together then?'

Listen and be ready to talk in the following ways:

▶ It is important for you to provide children with a chance to express their feelings. But do not press them to talk at times or communicate in ways that are not the child's choice.
▶ Some children who have experienced abuse may want to talk with you. Others may never say much at all about their experiences. Their feelings and confusions may emerge through their play and you can help them in that situation (see page 189).
▶ The guidelines on page 109 about listening, open-ended questions and being guided by the child will all be useful.
▶ Some children may tell you about events that not only distressed them, but also shake you when you hear the details. You may be most stunned by a child's apparent indifference to a catalogue of ill-treatment – she thinks this kind of misery is normal.
▶ You can show your sympathy and acknowledge children's feelings. It can be appropriate to show a child that what happened was not acceptable. But your own feelings must not overwhelm the time you spend with children or young people. Your feelings, perhaps anger or distress on their behalf, should not become a burden for children. If you have strong feelings that are hard to resolve, then find an opportunity to talk about your reactions in confidence with a colleague, senior or advisor.

EXAMPLE

Angie, who has seen angry rows between her parents, is talking with Jane, her key worker at the after-school club.

Angie: Do you shout at Mark [Jane's partner]?
Jane: No, I don't. We try to talk about things when we disagree.
A: Do you yell at Bella [Jane's child]?
J: No. I try hard not to.
A: My Mummy shouts at Daddy all the time.
J: Yes, I realise that. But not all Mummies and Daddies shout at each other.
A: Mummy yells at me and I haven't done anything.
J: Yes, I know. You hear a lot of shouting, don't you, Angie?
A: Mummy says I'm a 'useless little cow'.
J: I'm sorry your Mummy says that to you, Angie. I don't agree with her at all. You're a real help here and I like you very much.
And so on . . .

COMMENT:

Jane accepts Angie's questions about her own family life and answers honestly. Angie is asking and not prying. But on other occasions with inappropriately curious questions, Jane could decline to answer with a comment like, 'That's private to me'.

Conversations with older children and teenagers will range over broad topics and they are often genuinely interested in your personal and family life. In daily and residential settings, as well as an individual practitioner, it is appropriate that you share some personal information. You are working with children and young people in a professional capacity. But, when children have a friendly relationship with you, they regard you as a person, who should relate to them as individuals.

Support children through play

It is usual for children to weave personal experiences into their play so events in the lives of children who are abused may also emerge through different play activities in your early years setting, or out in the playground at school.

Unless you have specific skills in play therapy, you should not set out to use play with children to help them through their experiences. However, a sensitive practitioner can be supportive by responding to opportunities that arise naturally. It is also important that you relate to abused children in play as you would to any child: enjoying their successes and satisfaction and looking for opportunities for them to learn. It will not be helpful to seek deep meanings in every drawing they do or find greater significance in rough physical play then you would for another child.

Deal positively with behaviour

You need to continue to act as a responsible adult with obligations to the whole group as well as to any children who have experienced abuse or continuing distress.

Children will need your understanding of the likely impact on their distressing experiences. You may well have to adjust your expectations for development, behaviour and outlook that you would usually bring to a child of this age. But children will not benefit from a tolerance that is without limits. In the long run, it is unhelpful for children if they are permitted to behave in highly disruptive or unacceptable ways and no practitioner steps in. Perhaps the child's abusive experience is seen as an excuse. Alternatively, practitioners may be genuinely concerned that setting some limits to behaviour and holding expectations of children may add to their burdens. In fact, it can reassure a child to see that adults take responsibility and act in a predictable manner. You need to set and keep to boundaries for the children's behaviour and to show that your own actions are within limits.

Children whose lives have been very disrupted have even more need of a predictable early years, school and out-of-school environment. Predictability will mean reassurance. Children may have experienced unpredictable or highly punitive control from parents or other carers. Perhaps the unpredictability has been fuelled by the parents' use of alcohol or drugs. A child whose life has been very disrupted may need a clear structure in her day. It may be even more important to her than to the other children that she knows what will be happening and that there are no surprises.

You need to be prepared for individual reactions from children. Some children who have witnessed bouts of domestic violence may be distressed by even mild altercations or expect fierce words from you for minor mistakes. The children will need a great deal of reassurance as they learn that you do not react like their aggressive parent(s). They may need to hear this message directly from you, 'I'm not cross. Everyone makes mistakes sometimes' or 'It's not a big thing, Barry. We can put it right together'. However, children who have experienced domestic violence may show the opposite behaviour, a readiness to use fierce words and aggressive actions. You will need to step in with a firm, 'It's alright to be cross. It's not alright to hit people'.

Children who have been abused should not be allowed to dump their misery, anger or inappropriate behaviour on other children. It is unfair to the other children and will not help the abused child in the long run. You should follow the same kind of guidelines as you would with children who import aggressive ways of behaving into the centre or whose family experience has taught them that they can have whatever they want, without regard for others.

▶ Take a positive line in guiding this child's behaviour with the underlying message of 'I like you, Ansel. I don't like what you did to Marianne'.
▶ You might offer alternatives for action, explain simply why one course of action is not allowed.
▶ You may need to show and encourage other ways that a child can handle frustration, distress, showing affection or trying to make friends.
▶ You can be practical on behalf of the child, always balancing any 'please don't do that' with guidance in words and actions towards 'I'd rather you behaved this way'. (More on page 192.)

When children have been sexually abused, they may bring inappropriate behaviour into the setting. The child may seek over-intimate contact with adults or with other children. You need to hold what can be a delicate balance between the twin messages of 'I like you and I am happy to have you close to me' with 'The way you want to touch me is not the right way between a child and an adult'.

Other children and parents in the group

When one child brings her problems into a group, the other children may need to be reassured that you are aware of what is happening. They will feel that your behaviour is fair to everyone if they can see you deal with disruptive or inappropriate behaviour. And they will feel confident you are taking responsibility for the group, if you move swiftly to deal with a child's distress. Other children can be protective and caring towards each other and may well react well to simple explanations that do not break confidences. Perhaps you might explain, 'It's okay Melissa, I know you didn't say anything mean to Cameron. But he gets upset if people shout at him. Just try saying things in a normal voice.'

If a child's abusive experience is emerging through behaviour in the group, you may also have to give some explanation to other parents. You would never break confidences about the child or family, so it can be useful to consider what you say. Explanations should never become excuses and parents should not be expected to tolerate their own children's bruises or distress because another child is experiencing problems. Explain simply to concerned parents that you are aware of what is happening, that you are taking steps to deal with the situation and you appreciate their having spoken with you.

In a small community, some parents may be well aware of the stresses in a particular family. You would take a professional stance by listening with care to any concerns expressed by other parents or information about a household. However, it would be important not to allow such exchanges to slip into ordinary or regular conversation.

You should also be prepared to talk with children and their parents if there has been alleged or proven abuse by a practitioner, volunteer or visitor to the centre. (See page 162.)

Working with parents

Your work with parents may take several forms:

▶ Trying to continue a working relationship with parents who are alleged to have abused or who have admitted ill-treating their child.
▶ Supporting non-abusing parents who are distressed and confused that their partner has abused the child(ren).
▶ Working with parents whose child has been abused by somebody else, either within the family, a trusted person allowed contact with the child, or less usually a stranger.

For many readers you will be working with parents through general supportive conversation and keeping in close touch about their child. Only practitioners in more specialist settings, and those with additional training, would undertake either counselling or more therapeutic work with other adults. But a very great deal of support can be offered through usual good practice with parents and other carers.

Offer a welcome

A friendly face and a continued welcome to your setting may be exactly what some parents want and need. For parents whose life has been turned upside down, their child's nursery, school or out-of-school club may be the one setting that remains constant. Non-abusing parents may really appreciate a place where they and their child are treated as normally as possible. You will be available to talk about the difficulties if they wish, but otherwise you are still there to show parents the collage their daughter completed or tell how their son was such a help in reorganising the store cupboard.

Some parents may be angry with you, because it was the setting that first raised concerns about possible abuse. But it is possible that you will get through the anger and be able to offer support (see 'parents' feelings' later in this section). The anger of some parents does not, of course, subside and you have to continue your contact with them in as civil a way as possible.

Parents do not necessarily turn against their child's setting or individual practitioners like childminders, even if it was you that first raised the concerns. Parents may feel that, despite mixed emotions, their key worker, the child's class teacher or the head of centre is basically on the side of their child and family and will be supportive.

A formal or informal parents' group may offer a great deal to depressed or isolated parents whose stress and loneliness has contributed to neglect of their children. Company or support from other parents and practitioners will not solve all their problems, but it can help.

Talking and listening

Some parents may wish to talk with you about what has happened and is yet to come. Use your skills of listening, of open-ended questions and of offering ideas without telling parents what to do (see page 154). You can be helpful and still be honest about what you do not know and cannot make happen. You should not attempt detailed individual work, for instance trying to counsel parents, unless you genuinely have the time and have been trained in the proper skills.

A PRIVATE CONVERSATION

Generally speaking, these supportive conversations should be private. So you need to find a time to talk without the children in earshot. It is almost inevitable in a busy setting that you may try to have snatched conversations, but it is unwise. Parents may have deep and confused feelings, they may become distressed or angry (not necessarily with you) and they may talk about their child(ren) in the hearing of other children or parents. If what seemed to be a quick question about information is turning into what ought to be a longer and private conversation, then you should halt the parent and explain – something like, 'I want to give you some proper time, but it's impossible now. Can you can come back at . . . ?'

PARENTS' FEELINGS

The strong feelings that parents express will vary between individuals, depending on the circumstances of the abuse: the type of abuse, the alleged abuser, the emotional state of the child. There is no single blueprint for how parents may feel. They may express any of the following emotions and their feelings may change over time.

▶ Shocked and unable to take in what has happened. A non-abusing parent may still find it hard to believe what has occurred. An abusing parent may feel stunned that matters got this much out of hand.

▶ Angry that someone else has abused their child. Or an abusing parent may feel angry that justifiable discipline has been called abuse or that a child's word is believed over an adult's counter-claim. Parents may feel angry with the person(s) who first raised the concerns, even if they also feel a sense of relief. Anger has to be directed somewhere and a non-abusing parent may initially find it hard to be angry with a previously trusted partner or friend. Sometimes anger is directed, at least initially, towards the child. It is neither rational nor fair, but in a seriously disrupted household the child is sometimes blamed.

▶ Guilty about not realising earlier or not facing nagging worries about a child's physical or emotional state. A non-abusing parent may fret over why the child did not tell and you may need to explain the many reasons why children often do not speak up about physical or sexual abuse (see page 115). An abusing parent may feel very guilty about what has been done and may be willing to accept help – of course, not all abusers feel this way.

▶ Relieved that the abuse has been discovered and is being challenged. A neglectful parent may feel many other emotions but still feel that it is better to get help than to struggle.

▶ Doubt in a parent's ability to protect their children. Non-abusing parents whose child has been ill-treated by a trusted relative or friend can feel a serious loss of confidence about their own judgement. In cases of sexual abuse, for instance, children can have been abused for some time and have said nothing – or what they have said was not recognised as a serious cry for help. When the facts emerge, the non-abusing parent(s) are faced with a time of weeks, months, or even years, when their perception of events was completely wrong. This kind of discovery of abuse has been likened to bereavement or loss.

▶ A conflict of loyalties between the child and the alleged abuser, when this person is part of the family. Allegations of physical or sexual abuse can drive a wedge between members of a family. And you need to remember that sometimes possible abuse turns out to have a non-abusive explanation (see page 11).

▶ Shame and embarrassment about what has happened and that family life has become public. Once a child-abuse investigation starts, professionals have the right and obligation to ask many questions that intrude into what otherwise are private family matters.

▶ Distress and pressure from other family members, or local people who are not being supportive. Non-abusing parents may have to deal with relatives and neighbours who want to disbelieve the child, who blame the parent or who feel that the whole matter should have been dealt with by the family or immediate community.

You will support parents if you acknowledge their feelings and recognise the mixed and changing emotions. You are not saying that they are right to feel that way (for instance, in appearing to blame a child for keeping the abuse a secret) but you show that you have heard what they said. You may be able to put an alternative perspective, for example, explaining why children can have such difficulty in telling. Recognise also that once an abuser has been removed from a family or denied any more access to a child, the situation does not suddenly snap back to what was normal before the crisis. The child may have distress and mixed feelings to work through and so will the non-abusing adults of the family. Everything is not suddenly back to normal once more.

If parents are angry with you or with your team as a whole, you again need to acknowledge that anger, rather than try to argue or get angry in return. There is no sure way to deal with anger and defuse the power of that emotion, but the following guidelines will help:

▶ Stay calm and do not answer the parent's anger with your own angry replies, or counter-claims that the parent is being unfair.

▶ Show that you recognise their feelings. You are not saying they are right to be angry. Nor are you agreeing that their view is correct, perhaps that the centre is to blame or that all social workers are idiots.

▶ Listen to what parents are saying – what has made them so angry? They may be expressing themselves in a very emotional way, but can you hear what has fed the strong feelings?

▶ You can test the waters to see if the parent is ready to listen but it is unwise to push explanations or logic unless the parent seems receptive. You might be saying, 'I can see that you're angry. You feel the social worker won't answer your questions. Do you want me to explain what happens next?'

▶ You still have a responsibility for children in the setting, who can become distressed and frightened by adults who appear out of control. A furious adult or one who is using violent or offensive language may need to be told firmly, 'I can see how angry you are. But I can't have you upsetting the children. I will talk with you outside the room.'

▶ All practitioners have a right to their own safety and any setting should have clear procedures on how staff come to a colleague's aid when an altercation gets out of hand.

Advice and information

Your aim is to share information appropriately with parents, so that they feel more in control about their side of what is happening. Support them but do not take over, or carry out tasks that the parents could do. It will be unhelpful if you make them feel even more out of control of their family life than they already do.

THE STEPS IN THE CHILD PROTECTION PROCESS

If there is an investigation ongoing, then parents should be kept informed of what is happening in the process. The assigned social worker should also be ready to explain to parents, but they may prefer to talk with you, as somebody they already knew before this crisis emerged. Make sure that you understand the child protection process, so that you can explain to parents what will happen next and that some events (for instance, taking children into care) are definitely not inevitable. You can ensure that parents know about case conferences and their right to attend. Explain your role in such events and that although the parent may appreciate a friendly face, you have to give the centre's impartial report as a contribution to the meeting.

PARENTS AT CASE CONFERENCES

Normal practice is that parents are invited to case conferences on their children as part of the child protection process. Parents are not obliged to attend but there would have to be very good reasons for them to be excluded.

Professionals of different backgrounds have been wary about the impact of parents attending case conferences. And certainly there was a time, before partnership with parents became an accepted aspect of good professional practice, when parents were not involved as a matter of course. Reviews of parental involvement in case conferences have raised a number of positive consequences as well as acknowledging that professionals may not always feel at ease.

The presence of parents, listening to what is said, can push professionals at a case conference to support their opinions in a proper way. With parents watching and listening, there is less likelihood of unsubstantiated opinions or offhand remarks about the family. Discussion can be more focused and objective. Parents can see the process for themselves and, at least sometimes, will feel reassured that it is fair and people are not condemning them out of hand. Parents should also see the different professionals working together. When parents are present, the conference members can listen to the parents and gain some understanding of how far they are likely to be motivated to take part in the treatment plan for this child or to co-operate in any monitoring of the child's health or development.

Despite possible positives of having parents within the conference, the focus must still be on the child's welfare. The professionals present, including any early years, school and out-of-school practitioners, have to be ready to express the more difficult issues about the child and family. As the practitioner who will give a report, you should not be making comments that will surprise and shock a parent. You should have had the difficult discussions with the parent prior to the case conference. Nevertheless it can be hard for any professionals to listen and appreciate parents' distress or fear about what is happening. You may be discomforted by an articulate defence by parents of their actions or a verbal attack about professional assumptions or attitudes.

SUPPORT IN CHILD CARE SKILLS

Parents whose abuse has largely arisen through ignorance of their child's basic needs may accept help within your setting. Children's and family centres are organised so that contracts can be made with parents for their attendance as well as that of their child. Other settings may not have the time and space to offer comprehensive work with parents. A setting has to look carefully as what can realistically be done, without reducing the quality of work with the children. One setting may be able to offer regular time and long conversations to a parent, perhaps a suitable group. Other settings cannot hope to organise this kind of work but can provide a friendly face, a listening ear and short conversations about children and ways of dealing with their needs.

Home visiting schemes can be a great support to families under stress and those who would welcome some guidance on child care and play with their children. Home visitors, from schemes such as Home Start, are part of a broad based family support service; they do not, of course, only visit families about whom there are child protection concerns. Some early years and school settings are able to offer supportive parents' groups, that can cover a range of issues and again are not only for families about whom there are serious worries. In some areas, specialist family support workers will be assigned as a response to child protection concerns. In that case, the family can be well aware that noticeable improvement in the well being of their children is essential, if more serious intervention is not to follow.

Some parents may genuinely have very little idea about children's physical and emotional needs. The problem may have arisen because the parents are very young themselves. Some adults had a disrupted childhood from which they have no useful memories of how to treat children well. In other families, serious stress may have overwhelmed the parents and blotted out concerns for their children. Depending on the other calls on your time and energy, you may be able to offer advice on some of the following:

▶ Basic child care such as food, clothing and hygiene. Any suggestions have to be realistic, given the parent's family circumstances and finances. In this area, as in any other aspect to child care, it will not help simply to suggest that parents follow the model established in your setting. Your centre is not a family home, let alone one under stress. If you have no experience of caring for children at home (whether your own or in work as a nanny), then talk with colleagues who can extend your understanding.

▶ Information on the usual range of development and behaviour for young children. For instance, that most two-year-olds do not follow what they are told every time. It is normal for children to want adult's attention and if they cannot get it in pleasant ways, they will become disruptive one way or another.

▶ You may be able to share some ideas on a positive approach to handling children's behaviour, for instance, about being consistent, using encouragement and the willingness to compromise. In this area, and any other aspect to children's lives, avoid any sense that you always get things right or that there are certain answers. You are offering good ideas that work enough of the time to make the effort worthwhile.

▶ Parents may need to find some enjoyment in being with their child. You may have ideas on how they could play together, but again make sure that any suggestions are sensible for this parent's family life. She or he may need ideas about how to involve a child safely in domestic routine, a suggestion about watching a suitable television programme together with the child or simple and free activities like going to the park.

A consistent theme in this kind of help is encouraging parents to put their child's needs much more to the forefront of their lives. Keep realistic goals for your input and what parents can manage, learn and do, given their state of understanding and pressures. In the end they will chose whether they follow your ideas or specific advice and they need to feel that they are becoming more competent, rather than finding you as a person who knows everything.

It is worth recalling that a wide range of families abuse or neglect their children. It is not only families in poor or deprived neighbourhoods who put their children or young people at risk. Some two-parent families with substantial incomes place such a high priority on the adults' careers that the children are left with inappropriate or insufficient care and supervision.

Different issues can arise when older children and young teenagers are at potential risk. In this case, family support may be more about setting boundaries for an older child who is allowed dangerous levels of freedom or who is expected to manage unrealistic levels of domestic responsibility and childcare.

However hard the parents are trying, you still have to see what is the impact on the child and your records of a child's development and behaviour will reflect any changes. You can offer warmth and support to parents but with the clear cut goal that changes are necessary for the child's sake. You are not just offering a woolly sympathy for parents. You need, with support in your setting, to be impartial and objective about parents' behaviour with their children. You cannot remain neutral about children's welfare.

It is not your responsibility to try to make parents take advice or change negative patterns of behaviour with their children. The most important lesson for some parents is to learn that they are responsible for the consequences of their own actions and that they have to stop trying to shift the responsibility or blame onto other people.

SHARING IDEAS FOR CARE OF AN ABUSED CHILD

The confidence of non-abusing parents in their own skills can be severely shaken. They may be trying to make everything up to the child with treats or abandoning normal family ground rules. Or perhaps a parent feels that the child needs the security of positive family boundaries but is being overruled by someone else in the family. You may be able to help a parent in the importance of support for a child's distress that may flex a little, but does not overturn previous ground rules. You may be facing similar problems in your setting, although this will not necessarily be the case as children react differently in the various settings of their young life.

▶ Listen to this parent's dilemma and, if it might help, then explain how you are handling the child's behaviour in the setting.

▶ Describe how you affirm your care and liking of the child whilst being prepared to step in over disruptive or cruel behaviour to other children.

▶ On the other hand, abused children may become very quiet and inward-looking. Explain to the parent how you are giving time to the child, not trying to jolly her out of her feelings, but still encouraging any movement towards the way this child or young person used to be.

▶ Parents may need to be encouraged to respond to their child's overtures in conversation. Non-abusing parents and other carers are still sometimes told that it is better not to talk about a distressing experience with their child or teenager, on the 'least said soonest mended' principle. You may be able to reassure them that, although children should not be pressed to talk, parents should show that they are responsive and will listen.

▶ A child who has been sexually abused may make inappropriate physical approaches to other children, or to practitioners. Parents may not realise that such consequences could follow from their child's experience.

▶ You can offer support by acknowledging the seriousness of this kind of behaviour, but explain that it is not unusual for sexually abused children. Explain to the parents how you are dealing with the behaviour, whilst showing respect and care for the child.

DOMESTIC VIOLENCE

In order to help parents, you have to have some understanding of the situation that they are facing. The experience of domestic violence is often very complex. People who have very little experience of the problem often say, 'But surely, she could just leave'. Women, or the smaller number of men, who are on the receiving end of domestic violence often have few if any options of where to go. Despite the violence, he or she may still be attached to their partner and hold onto the hope that he, or she, will change. They may excuse violent actions as explained by drink or stress, or feel that they in some way provoke the outbursts. Parents in violent homes are also often afraid that their children will be taken into care, if the full extent of the violence emerges. The violence then remains as a family secret into which the children are drawn.

You may not be the person to help directly but you could be invaluable in alerting a parent to other sources of help and support. You may be able to boost parents' confidence by reassuring them that they do have resources for the children, when the failure to protect them from a violent partner may have seriously undermined this confidence. Parents sometimes also have mixed feelings, seeing the violent partner in the actions of one or more of the children.

Sometimes parents need to be alerted to the fact that the children are affected by violence in the home. Children can suffer serious emotional distress, even when they are not physically harmed. Parents may feel that they are protecting children, perhaps by tolerating the violence and that the children are not really aware of what is happening. You may also support a parent who needs to be honest with children about what is happening or if they all leave a violent parent. Another issue, relevant to the whole staff of any setting, is that children whose fathers are violent may desperately need models of caring and non-violent men. Such a positive image may be offered if you have male practitioners or volunteers.

LOCAL AND NATIONAL RESOURCES

No setting will ever provide all services for parents. Good practice in a centre has to be understanding what you can and should offer on site and keeping your knowledge up-to-date on what is available elsewhere. Unless you work in a specialist centre, it will not be appropriate to attempt to undertake direct work with parents on complex problems, such as severe depression or alcoholism.

You need to know, for instance, the kind of facilities available locally for women with post-natal depression. If you are working with a woman frightened by domestic violence, are there any local refuges to which she and her children could go? Where can someone go locally if they have addiction problems of alcohol, illegal or prescription drugs? Do local social services, or a voluntary organisation, offer respite care for a family overwhelmed by the needs of a severely disabled child or the care of an elderly relative?

The area in which you work may be well served, at least for some of these needs, or there may be very little to suggest. You need to remain realistic – offer the advice and information that you can. Accept that you are not personally responsible for the shortcomings of any local services. Nor is it your job to push parents in using available units or advice groups; that has to remain their choice and their commitment.

SUGGESTED ACTIVITY

All settings should keep a file, updated at regular intervals, with addresses, names and details on local services and special units. You can add national organisations who offer advice over telephone helplines or practical publications. There are examples in this book from page 242. This resource is not limited to issues arising from child protection. It is a more general resource.

If your setting does not have such a folder or file, then start one now. If something already exists, then check that it is helpful for child protection issues as well as other aspects to early child care and education.

Support for practitioners

Supervision

Any staff working with a family, where there are allegations of child abuse, will be under some degree of stress. All settings should provide support through discussions about the family and careful planning to guide the approach of an individual practitioner and maintain consistency within a team.

▶ Supervision time should allow individual practitioners to express concerns, doubts or have a chance to explore aspects of the agreed approach that are uncertain or that involve new skills. Even experienced practitioners need a chance to talk through how to handle a more difficult relationship with one or both parents or the best way forward with a child's disruptive pattern of behaviour.

▶ Practitioners have feelings and you may want to air your concern for the child and distress at what has happened. A professional approach to child protection includes an awareness of your feelings and taking opportunities to talk through them. Good practice would never be to pretend that no emotions have been aroused by events.

▶ A senior colleague should also help you to define your priorities. For instance, however sympathetic you may be to the dilemmas or stresses experienced by a parent, you need to hold a strong focus on children and their emotional and physical well-being.

▶ You may also welcome some guidance in managing your time. Depending on the kind of work you are expected to cover within the normal day, you may have to limit the amount of time you can offer to parents, and be clear about when you are available for conversation and when you really are not.

▶ If you work on your own then you will need to access support that is available through the advisors or link workers.

Personal experience of abuse

A practitioner's own experience of childhood abuse or neglect can be revived by working with an abused child and family. As a senior practitioner you need to be aware that opening up the subject through in-house discussion or sending practitioners on relevant courses may bring out staff's personal experiences, one way or another. All professionals have to weigh up:

▶ In what way their own difficult experiences (not just abuse) are relevant to their work
▶ To what extent details are shared, with whom and when
▶ How they seek support for unresolved problems or distress.

The personal experience of staff is as much an individual matter as children's current experiences. What may help or be most appropriate for the practitioner as a person and professionally speaking will depend on the details of the situation.

▶ The current work may bring back memories and feelings that you believed you had resolved – what happened to you or perhaps bad experiences of having tried to tell someone when you were a child. This child's experience, or something that an adult says, has provoked your own memories, as fresh as ever.

▶ If you never told anyone about the abuse you experienced, then working with this child or family may arouse strong, perhaps conflicting feelings about events which have so far stayed with you alone.

▶ It is also possible that your memories are not of your own experience but that of someone close to you in childhood, a sibling or good friend, whose abusive experience touched you deeply as a child.

Good professional practice is to raise personal issues within supervision so that you can gain the support you need and seek a perspective that helps you to separate personal experience from how you work now with a child or family. Senior practitioners in any setting are responsible for giving time to staff and helping everyone involved to reach appropriate and supported decisions. The following points will help you whether you are offering supervision or are yourself working through memories of childhood abuse.

▶ Practitioners who themselves experienced childhood abuse or neglect should neither be regarded as too close to the topic to help a child, nor as the ideal key worker because of their own experience. There should not be an automatic decision in either direction.

▶ If your feelings about your own experience are still raw, especially if you have not disclosed your experience until this time, you may not be the best person to work with this child and family. For instance, it is not good practice in counselling on major crises such as bereavement or relationship breakdown, to help others when your own feelings are currently in turmoil. It is too difficult to unravel what is happening to you from objective and considered help to someone else.

▶ If you have strong and unresolved feelings about your own abuse, then the professional step is to seek help. Your supervisor may be able to support you in your work, but will probably not be in a position to offer the time and expertise of concentrated counselling.

▶ If you were given support as a child and your abusive experience is part of you (an unhappy memory but resolved in some way), then there is no reason why you should not be the key worker with this child and parent. It would be inappropriate to say, for instance, that a practitioner who lost a parent when young should not work with a bereaved child now. A similar line of argument has to be followed for staff who experienced childhood abuse, but whose feelings will not distort their current judgement.

▶ Use the opportunity of supervision to ensure that personal experiences are not over-influencing your judgement. For instance, perhaps you have unhappy memories of inappropriate touch when you were taken into bed with a parent or other relative. However, parents of children you know now may be letting wakeful children sleep with them or having a story in bed on weekend mornings and nothing wrong is happening at all.

Supervision can be the best context for weighing up the personal and professional issues, including whether a practitioner should share a personal experience of abuse with colleagues or parents.

▶ A practitioner should not be pushed into making a personal disclosure unless he or she is comfortable and wishes to do so. This guideline applies to any kind of personal experience in which strong feelings are also involved.
▶ The issues surrounding any disclosure of abuse should be discussed within supervision, especially if a less experienced practitioner is involved. They may not anticipate the possible consequences of sharing a highly personal experience.
▶ Practitioners also need to understand the place of any personal disclosure (not only abuse) in a helping relationship with a parent. It is very unlikely that it would be appropriate for a practitioner to share personal experiences of abuse or neglect with a parent. The personal and professional aspects are almost certain to become entangled.

A practitioner with relevant personal experience may choose to mention this issue in discussion with colleagues. Perhaps there is a staff meeting in which some practitioners express persistent doubts that 'a respected person like the Reverend Mayfield could possibly hurt his own son' or practitioners cannot understand why a child has not previously told about persistent abuse. A practitioner with direct experience might decide to put the weight of that experience against colleagues' doubts or apparent inability to understand how young children can be intimidated, even if there is no threat of physical violence.

You need to be prepared to give some details of your experience but do not feel obligated to give a long and highly detailed account. You are saying to your colleagues in effect, 'Respect my views on this. I know more than you do.' So, it is neither fair nor useful to limit yourself to 'I was abused as a child but I don't want to talk about it. Just believe what I'm telling you.' On the other hand after a few sentences of relevant explanation you could say, 'The rest is very personal and I don't want to say any more.'

Your colleagues will have mixed reactions, depending on exactly what you have shared. They may express sympathy, uneasiness or shock. Some colleagues may be curious and press for more details; some may react with 'that didn't sound too bad, what's the fuss about?' It is possible that your disclosure may lead another colleague to share unhappy childhood experiences. You have chosen to bring something personal into a more public arena. But it is still fair of you to ask colleagues not to repeat what you said outside the staff group.

You need to consider carefully, and discuss with your supervisor, the rare circumstances under which a personal experience of abuse should be shared with parents. Generally speaking, you should have a sound reason for sharing any personal experience with parents. It should be an active decision to speak, rather than sharing without thinking through the issues. In a helping relationship with parents (for any problem they are experiencing), personal disclosures need to be used positively and with care.

Your experience may provide a valuable perspective but it does not make you an expert on this child's experience. You may understand how this child might be feeling, but you do not automatically know. Any discussions about possible action must focus on the individual child and family. Do not be tempted towards a particular course of action because it helped you as a child, nor because you wish somebody had taken this approach for you.

Discussion of your experience should be brief. But the aim is to help the parent, not to gain time for you to talk or to work through unresolved issues. The relationship with a parent must not be shifted in such a way that she or he is listening to you or becoming preoccupied with your problems.

Allegations against staff

Much of this chapter has approached child protection from the perspective that risk to the child comes from outside the early years, school or out-of-school setting. However, there have been reminders that allegations may be made against staff and this section directly addresses this topic. Any group setting, daily or residential, should have clear procedures for dealing with allegations.

All settings, led by the head of centre, have to be seen to take a serious view of any allegations, by parents, children or colleagues, about the behaviour of paid staff, volunteers or visitors to the centre. Much of what you have read in other sections of the book is equally relevant when people internal to your setting are involved. Remember to:

▶ Listen carefully to what you are told, whether you are a practitioner listening to a child or parent, or you are a senior member of staff listening to the concerns of another practitioner.
▶ Gather your information, but do not leap to conclusions one way or another. You should discuss the matter with the practitioner or the volunteer in

question. At this stage, you may not have to name the source of your concern, although the practitioner may be sure who is likely to have raised the issue of his or her practice.

▶ Make accurate notes following all the guidelines for good practice from page 129.

▶ Discuss the matter with appropriate people more senior to yourself or in a position to help you find a sound perspective on the matter. A practitioner should speak with a senior or head of the setting. If you are the head, then it should be clear who needs to know about the allegation within your line management and other relevant bodies, such as a management committee or school governors. The organisation that inspects child care in your part of the UK will want to be informed if there are any allegations against staff or if a child protection investigation raises doubts about the behaviour of any member of your team.

▶ Follow the procedures set out by your setting and ensure that anyone involved – parent, practitioners and other professionals – realise that you are acting in accord with previously agreed guidelines.

There may be an acceptable and credible explanation for the questions that have been raised about a practitioner's behaviour. This explanation should be entered into the written record in the same way that you would write up a parent's account of a child's injury, when the judgement was that the matter was satisfactorily explained.

You might be reassured that neither child abuse or neglect has occurred, but more general issues of good practice have been highlighted by the incident. Senior practitioners should address relevant issues sooner rather than later, either through supervision or broader staff discussion if appropriate. Examples of poor practice that need to be challenged could be:

▶ A practitioner has been lax in informing parents about troublesome incidents between children in the setting that led to injury or failed to mention a child's accident.

▶ Perhaps nobody checked that this mother had definitely not given permission for her child's photo to leave the setting and the child's image is now to appear in a magazine article. Apart from the fact that it is for parents to give, or withhold, such permission, some parents are in hiding from violent partners and do not want to risk being traced.

▶ A parent's complaint brings to light that a practitioner does personal shopping on trips out with children and then drops into her home on the way back to the centre. This practitioner is using work time for non-professional purposes.

▶ A parent's concern might make a setting re-assess an inappropriately open-door policy about visitors to the setting or a large rota of volunteers who are barely checked.

If there is clear evidence or serious reason to suspect abuse of any kind or neglect, then procedures for dealing with an accused practitioner would have to follow the same pattern as that of suspected abuse by any adult. Depending on the severity of the accusations, a practitioner would almost certainly be suspended whilst further enquiries were undertaken.

When there are allegations of child abuse within any setting or service, feelings can run high. Practitioners may find the allegations hard to believe – and everyone has to remember that suspicions may be unfounded. The case of Christopher Lillie and Dawn Reid, nursery nurses from Newcastle, was a sobering reminder of the devastation for individuals' lives when unproven allegations are promoted as fact. Alternatively, some staff may be distressed or self-critical because they did not take their uneasiness about someone more seriously. Support will be needed from within the setting and from appropriate sources within the wider professional network.

Allegations of neglect or abuse may be hard to prove, or disprove. However, observations of a practitioner or volunteer may be sufficient to question the quality of their practice and start disciplinary procedures. Any setting should have clear written procedures for challenging poor practice. Perhaps a practitioner has developed bad habits of shouting at children, nagging or ridiculing them for mistakes. Such bad practice should be handled through supervision and practitioners be given very clear directions about appropriate behaviour with children. Practitioners also need to be firmly warned if their behaviour suggests that they have favourites among the children, or their reactions to children are influenced by a poor working relationship with the parents. Your setting should have clear policies about issues such as a positive approach to children's behaviour. Unacceptable practice can be related to the expectations made clear in everyone's job description.

This kind of discussion with a practitioner within supervision should be written up in specific terms in the practitioner's file. When a practitioner's behaviour has been called into question, the actions taken should not remain an internal matter between the practitioner and the head of centre. Other appropriate people should be informed and consulted. Depending on where you work, a manager might contact the next line manager in the service, the chair of the management committee or governing body of a school. In the case of serious concerns about the behaviour of a practitioner or a volunteer, the information should be passed on to the relevant body in your part of the UK for possible addition to the list of persons unsuitable to work with children and young people (see page 76).

If practitioners do not heed warnings and persist in bad practice then they might eventually be dismissed. However, proper procedures will have to be followed to avoid accusations of wrongful dismissal. A senior practitioner may, for instance, have to ensure that a certain number of clear verbal and written warnings have been given to a practitioner. Check out your own procedures; they will be relevant whatever the bad practice, not only alleged child abuse.

Communication with children and parents

In addition to supportive work with the children directly involved, there should also be communication with parents and probably with the other children. The head of a setting, in collaboration with the line manager, management committee, school governing body or other appropriate group should make specific plans that can be shared with the whole staff group. The best approach will depend on what has happened, how far parents were involved in bringing abuse or ill-treatment to light and the age of the children.

When children have been ill-treated by practitioners or volunteers it is important that their experience is recognised. They need to know that responsible adults took notice and have taken action on the children's behalf. Depending on what has happened, the children might be reassured that the behaviour of a volunteer was wrong and this person will not be allowed to come to the centre anymore. If there has been long-term or organised abuse in a setting, children may need specialist input supported by the care of practitioners whom they know and who were not involved. Children need to be reassured that they, or their peers, have been tricked by adults whose behaviour was wrong.

It is certainly better for a setting to be ready to talk with parents or to deal properly with questions that parents ask. The local parent grapevine will operate with speed and the only way to increase the chances that accurate information is being passed around is to make that information available. In the early stage of an investigation staff might be told to say that complaints about a named practitioner or volunteer are being taken seriously and thoroughly checked. At this time it would be important that no staff allow themselves to be drawn into gossip. An agreement reached in a staff meeting might be that further questions by concerned parents are deflected courteously with a reply like, 'I honestly don't know any more details. It's very important that we all keep an open mind for the moment. Miriam (centre manager) will send a letter to everyone when we know what's happening.' If a practitioner is dismissed then it will be wiser to give some explanation to the parents, who will otherwise speculate about the reasons. The head or manager should consult the management committee, school governing body, or other line management, about how best to phrase any communication, spoken or written by letter.

Sometimes the allegations of abuse or neglect will be unfounded, even perhaps malicious. It is important that investigations are made swiftly. Information seeking should be thorough but it is unjust when accused practitioners are left for weeks, sometimes even months, with no resolution over an accusation. All professionals must take child protection seriously, but no investigation can overturn proper procedures, nor make assumptions about evidence because of a strong belief that abuse or neglect has occurred.

Scenario

A class of seven-year-olds was taken by a supply teacher for two days when their own teacher was ill. The supply teacher was unable to keep control and, although the children were initially amused by the chaos, they became increasingly distressed by the teacher's screaming and odd behaviour. Two children who played up were chased out of the classroom and around the playground, leaving the main group alone. The teacher got into a wrestling match with one child over a book when the child would not let go. Then on the second day, the same child was slapped twice on the hands for cheeking the teacher.

On the third day the class's own teacher returned and put together what some of the children told her with reports from colleagues who had heard the screaming. With the support of the head, the teacher first spoke to the whole class explaining that she was concerned about how the supply teacher seemed to have behaved with the class and needed to find out exactly what had happened. She reassured the class that she was not trying to blame them. It was clear from some children's comments that they were expecting to be criticised for messing about with the supply teacher. The class teacher and the head spoke individually with each child in the class to build an accurate picture of what had happened. They were then able to say to the whole class the next day that the supply teacher had behaved very badly. No teacher was allowed to hit children, this person would never be allowed back into the school again and they would be sending a report on what she had done.

QUESTIONS

1 In this case, the head decided not to write to parents over the incident.
2 What do you think of this decision? If you think she should have sent a letter, what are your reasons?
3 What does the example illustrate about children's expectations of adults?

Child abuse and the courts

Generally speaking, all the professionals involved in a child protection case will work to achieve an agreement on what should happen for the welfare of the child(ren) without going to court. If a parent, or other relevant carer, is clearly taking effective steps to protect the child and accepting the help that is on offer, then the courts will not be involved. Each of the relevant child protection laws in England, Wales, Scotland and Northern Ireland has established that orders, or other kinds of legal intervention, should not be pursued in child protection cases, unless there is evidence that such steps are in the best interests of the child(ren).

So, child protection specialists should not rush to involve the legal system, but it is possible that a child abuse case in which you are the involved practitioner could go to court. The social worker in charge of the case might seek a specific order in relation to the case. Your input in discussions with the social worker might have been important in supporting their decision that an order was necessary for the well-being of the child or young person.

Civil proceedings

Civil courts are less formal than the criminal courts and the standard of proof is different. In civil proceedings for child protection, there has to be evidence that suggests **on the balance of probabilities** that a child has been abused and that a named person (or persons) is the likely abuser. In criminal proceedings the evidence has to be on the basis of **beyond reasonable doubt** – a tougher test of any evidence.

Civil proceedings in court can lead to rulings that the named alleged abuser stays away from the child or can only have supervised contact. A social worker might be involved in such contact or some arrangement might be made with your own early years setting. Alternatively, a ruling might be made that children should be removed from the family home as the only way to ensure their safety. Foster parents or the staff of a residential children's home might then be supervising the agreed contact. Civil proceedings allow for a range of steps to protect the child(ren) but do not involve any prosecution against the alleged abuser(s).

Civil proceedings are not only less formal but tend to be less confrontational than the legal process in a criminal court. But, there can still be disagreements and arguments. If an acceptable solution had been found between social workers and the family, the case would have been resolved outside the courtroom. Civil proceedings are more likely to occur when:

▶ The local authority social workers cannot reach an agreement with the family about what has or is continuing to happen to the child and the family's response to the situation.
▶ The child protection team judges that children need to be removed from the family and no voluntary arrangement has successfully been made with the parents or other relatives.
▶ Custody and access issues in a matrimonial dispute hinge on an allegation of abuse.

Children do not have to appear in civil proceedings, whereas they may be a witness for the prosecution in a criminal case (see page 172). Children in civil proceedings have an independent legal representative, different from the solicitor for the local authority and another solicitor representing the parent(s). The court also appoints a Guardian Ad Litem, who is a person who will continue to represent the child's best interests and wishes. GALs are advocates on behalf of the child. In Scotland, the independent representative for the child is known as a safeguarder. Scottish law and practice is especially strong on providing ways for children's views to be heard.

It is possible that early years, school and out-of-school practitioners might be called to civil proceedings to give evidence about a child. You might have knowledge and records of a child's physical health, development or behaviour that had a bearing on the child's need for protection. You may have observed important incidents between a parent and child, or the child may have chosen to disclose an experience of abuse to you. The procedure in civil courts is not as adversarial as criminal proceedings, but many of the key issues about being a reliable and credible witness are equally important.

UK child protection legislation allows for some strong legal steps to be taken to protect children and young people, that do not require a criminal court case and prosecution of the alleged abuser. For instance, it can be very difficult to prove beyond reasonable doubt that sexual abuse, in particular with young children, has taken place and the identity of the abuser. But civil proceedings allow steps to prevent contact between an alleged abuser and child or young person.

Criminal proceedings

Only a minority of child abuse cases reach the courts as part of criminal proceedings. A prosecution will only be undertaken when the abuse, if proven, falls into the category of a crime and there is sufficient evidence to support the case (see also page 52 about the role of the police).

If you are called as a witness

Most readers of this book will not experience being a witness in civil or criminal proceedings for alleged child abuse. It is not a frequent event, but it could happen, especially if you work in a children's or family centre that offers a service to families under stress or within the foster and residential services.

Being a witness can be an uncomfortable experience, even daunting. An understanding of the process and your role can help to prepare you for going to court.

▶ The local authority lawyer should give time to meet you before your appearance. He or she can explain what will happen and go through any practical issues about your evidence. The lawyer can alert you to the kind of questions that she or he will ask you as the case is developed.
▶ If you have any uncertainty or new information, speak up now. Lawyers' nightmares are court scenes in which their witness suddenly reveals new facts or voices doubts. The lawyer may also have some good guesses about the questions likely to be put to you by the defence lawyer.
▶ If there seems to be a delay in your being contacted, then phone the local authority lawyer yourself, especially if you are facing your first time as a witness.
▶ If you are in a service where child protection cases are more likely, then you should have access to a training workshop or course about court procedures and being a witness. You should be given general preparation before you are faced with the experience.

▶ You might also welcome a prior visit to the courtroom, so that you know in advance the general layout of the room or a similar one. Unless you have experience of a courtroom, for instance through jury service, you may have very little idea of what to expect.

▶ On the day, smart clothes are appropriate dress for attendance at court as a witness. Avoid very casual styles, even if jeans and sweatshirts are usual for your place of work.

▶ Arrive at the court with time to spare so that you do not feel rushed.

Once you are in the witness box there are some practical guidelines to bear in mind.

▶ Speak steadily and clearly. Look up and not down at the floor. Although the lawyer asks you the questions, you should direct your reply to the magistrate or judge sitting at the bench. This style can feel strange at the start but you will become accustomed.

▶ You probably need to talk at slightly slower than normal conversational pace. The clerk of the court will be taking notes and magistrates or judges usually take their own notes as well.

▶ If you could not hear all or part of a question, ask for it to be repeated. If you do not understand the question, then say so.

▶ Witnesses are not expected to remember everything by heart when they are going to be asked for many details, as you could be. It is acceptable for you to take notes into the witness box and to consult them to ensure the accuracy of your answers, for instance about dates or what a child said.

▶ However, as soon as you use notes as a witness you can legitimately be asked when you wrote up your notes – see the point about the timeliness of recording also made on page 131. Your notes can also be taken in as evidence and made available to the defence lawyer in criminal proceedings.

▶ Your evidence should be limited to what you personally observed, what you can honestly say 'I saw' or 'I heard'. Quote a parent's or child's actual words only if you are certain that those were the exact words used. Otherwise you can give the gist of what was said.

▶ Answer the question and do not move onto other topics unless what you have to say is a relevant explanation. You would normally reply more than 'Yes' or 'No' to a question, although there may be instances when this simple answer is appropriate.

▶ In some cases your evidence may include positive points about a parent or other adult. Express these as honestly as any negative evidence.

▶ Part of your legitimate evidence may be second-hand, in that you were told something by another person. Express this accurately with, 'Mrs Jones asked to speak with me on the 25th May. She told me she had seen Selina's mother hit the child and Selena had fallen against the concrete post.' You know what you were told, but you do not know from your own direct observation that Selena was hit by her mother.

▶ You may be asked to express an opinion based on your knowledge of the child or of children in general. Support your opinion with 'because ...' or 'my experience has been ...' Do not go beyond issues on which you can reasonably express an opinion. Other people in court will not necessarily be experienced with children, so be ready to explain any specialist terms or preferably use ordinary language. The local authority lawyer should be ready to help you prepare in this way.

▶ If you do not know the answer to a question, then it is better to say, 'I don't know' or perhaps 'I wasn't able to hear what Samantha's father said to her. I could see that Samantha was crying and pulling away from her father.'

In criminal proceedings, witnesses are first questioned by the prosecution lawyer. There should be no surprises in this part of your evidence, since your answers are part of the local authority or the police case. You will then be cross-examined by the defence lawyer. In civil proceedings the parents' lawyer may ask you questions.

The job of defence lawyers is to defend their client, so their responsibility is to cast doubt on the evidence. Lawyers use a number of adversarial tactics in order to achieve this aim. The end result for witnesses can be anything from slightly to highly uncomfortable. Defence lawyers are not being personally unpleasant when they publicly doubt your observations or experience; they are simply doing their job. Your role is to remain focused and calm.

▶ Avoid getting either annoyed or distressed. Do not relax, even if the approach is initially friendly. You are not having a conversation together; the defence lawyer is cross-questioning you on behalf of the accused.

▶ Take no notice of theatrical tactics used by some lawyers, such as looking contemptuously at notes and throwing them onto the table. Ignore doubtful expressions, shrugs or other dismissive body language and concentrate on the questions.

▶ Answer only the question that is asked and reply with what you can contribute from your direct observations and professional experience. If you are asked questions to which you cannot honestly give an answer or opinion, then do not guess. For instance, you might be asked, 'What did Steven's uncle think about the child's claims?' and you may have to reply, 'I don't know. Mr O'Hare didn't say anything to me'.

▶ If you are asked the same or very similar questions again, do not feel provoked into giving an extended or different answer – as if you were wrong the first time. If a lawyer uses this tactic, you could say courteously, 'I have already answered that question'. The magistrate, judge or the prosecution lawyer should also step in to prevent your being badgered.

▶ Take each question on its own and do not be afraid to think for a moment before replying. You may experience the defence tactic of asking you a series of quick questions to which you can honestly reply 'Yes', followed by a question to which your answer should be 'No', but the lawyer hopes to establish a pattern of your agreement.

If you are called as a witness, it is unlikely that all the practical issues about evidence outlined in this section will arise. But some of them will be part of your court experience. Be prepared and remember that your time in court is a particular kind of exchange. Concentrate on the task in hand and do not relax until you have left the witness box.

This section assumes you will be called as a witness for the prosecution. It is possible the defence team may call you. Most of the practical points are still relevant; certainly do not be tempted to go beyond what you know, however much you like a parent.

Children as witnesses

During the 1990s attitudes and procedures changed somewhat about the possibility of children as witnesses in abuse cases within criminal proceedings. Children are in a particularly vulnerable position over allegations of sexual abuse as the child's evidence may be the main or only strand of the prosecution's case. The evidence of children has become more acceptable, partly as a general recognition in child protection that children can understand the difference between truth and lies. However, prosecutions are often not taken ahead when the children are young, especially the under-7s. If the alleged abuser pleads 'guilty', then children do not have to go to court. But if he or she pleads 'not guilty', then children's evidence has to be heard in court and they have to undergo cross-examination.

Apart from considerations of the weight of the evidence, police and social workers are also concerned about a child's well-being. They have to make a balanced decision about the likely distress for a child of being a witness, against a wish to see an alleged abuser appropriately punished in law. The court process in a prosecution is confrontational and can be distressing for any witness, let alone young children. The defendant must be presumed innocent until proven guilty and it is the job of the defence lawyer to question and undermine the evidence against their client.

There are strict guidelines that govern how children and young teenagers give evidence in any court case, not only one about child protection. The aim is to reduce the potential distress for children, as well as to ensure a good quality in the evidence.

▶ Children can be interviewed for their evidence before the court hearing. The child is interviewed in a special police suite that looks like a living room and the whole interview is video recorded.

▶ No such interview should be longer than an hour. Children can be interviewed more than once, in separate sessions, but not many times.

▶ Children must not be prepared for the interview and there must be no leading questions from the adult. In other words, there must be reassurance that children's evidence has not been shaped by adult questioning.

▶ A video link between the court room and a separate room can be used so that children do not have to be in court, and they do not have to face their alleged abuser. Alternatively, some courtrooms have a screen that shields the child or young person from the majority of the court.

▶ Children will still be cross-examined by the defence lawyer, via the video link, and have to answer questions about their evidence. Particularly in sexual abuse cases, children and young people can find this experience embarrassing and intimidating. The main thrust of the defence is also likely to be that the child witness is lying or, at the very least, confused and mistaken.

▶ Police officers and social workers have to weigh up whether individual children and young people will be able to cope with cross-examination and their possible distress at having their word doubted in public. The non-abusing parents also have to consider these difficult issues on their child's behalf.

The social worker and police child protection specialist will prepare a child for the experience of being in court (but not for the interview). As a practitioner closely involved with the family, you could also have an important role in supporting the child and parent and helping them to have realistic expectations of what may happen. The more you understand what is likely to happen, the better you can prepare the child, as well as offering support after an unpleasant court experience. You may need to work hard to reassure the child or young person that you believe them and rebuild their confidence. It is worth knowing that in many areas there will be a unit or service, linked with child protection, that helps to prepare young witnesses. The NSPCC has published a set of leaflets suitable for use with

5–17 year olds called *The Young Witness Pack* (available from NSPCC publications on 020 7825 2775). You could find these useful if you support children in this way.

Scenarios

The following scenarios raise issues about children's play, conversation and leisure activities. If you were involved as a practitioner or asked for your advice, consider what would be the most positive approach. You can consider the following questions, on your own or with colleagues or fellow students:

1 What might you say or do with this child or others who are watching?
2 What kind of brief notes could be appropriate?
3 What might you pass on to the parent(s) or senior practitioner?

You will find a short commentary on these scenarios from page 231.

Kitty

Kitty is four years old. There is very strong suspicion that she was sexually abused by her grandfather when he cared for her on a regular basis. The evidence was not certain, but Kitty's mother was worried enough to agree to ban the grandfather from their home. Kitty has said very little in the nursery but, when she is painting or drawing, sometimes she draws a figure on the paper then scribbles or paints all over it. Today she whispers to you, 'No more Grandad'.

Marsha

The local child protection team is making initial inquiries about Marsha's family because of concerns that their mother is hitting Marsha and the young baby in the family. Marsha is usually very quiet in the playgroup but today you hear her shouting in the home corner. When you go closer, you can see her violently shaking the baby doll and calling out 'Be quiet! Be quiet! I'll give you such a one!' Another child in the home corner is looking at Marsha with disapproval and says, 'You know you shouldn't shake the baby. You'll make him cry.'

Joan

Joan, a practitioner in your children's centre, has been suspended following complaints of her bad practice. There are claims that Joan regularly humiliated and threatened children, and used unacceptable punishments, including shutting one child in a cupboard and making another child stand out in the rain. This afternoon you have watched a group of children play out what seem to be some of their experiences with this practitioner. The child who is playing Joan is shouting insults at the others and threatening, 'It'll be the wooden spoon for you!' The game comes to a close when the other children all leap on 'Joan' and shout, 'You're going to prison now'. A letter was sent to the parents explaining in brief that the member of staff had been suspended, pending an investigation, but there has been no conversation with the children.

Fazila

You are playing tea parties with four year old Fazila who appears to enjoy making tea and laying out the table. Fazila lines up the dolls who are joining you both for tea. But she puts one doll at some distance from the others. You ask if this doll is coming to the tea party and Fazila replies, 'She's a smelly-poo. Nobody likes her.' You have been working with Fazila's mother to try to improve the child's care, but her clothes are still changed infrequently and some days Fazila has a definite unwashed smell about her.

Helena

You run a holiday support group for carers of children with disability. Five year old Helena has recently started to attend with her childminder. Helena has mild learning and physical disabilities and her family is still distressed that their daughter is not 'normal' and seem to have found it hard to place boundaries on her behaviour. Helena's childminder follows the family line that 'the poor little mite' cannot be expected to behave like other children. Helena has a soft voice and sweet smile, but you are beginning to think that she deliberately hurts the other children under cover of giving them a cuddle or joining in their play. A couple of incidents also make you consider that Helena is adept at setting up other children, so they break the group rules and get into trouble. You want to address the situation, without over-reacting and to be realistic about the ways in which Helena's disability may limit her understanding.

Sammy

This morning break, in the playground of the school where you work, you watched a vigorous physical game between the eight-year-olds that gradually began to concern you. The game involved a lot of shrieking and chasing in which the boys and girls were equally active. But one small group of boys, which appeared to be led by Sammy, seemed to push the game beyond the limits that some of the girls wanted. A couple of girls were pushed against the fence and kissed, although they were shouting, 'Stop it!' You cannot be sure, but it looked also as if Sammy was trying to put his hand up one girl's skirt. Sammy is a child who has concerned you because of the sexually explicit jokes that he makes sometimes.

Ansel

Your class of nine-year-olds starts each morning with a circle time in which children can 'show and tell' any item of interest from their own lives. Today, Ansel got to his feet and told the group that his Mum had gone to a clinic and explained it by, 'You know, because she drinks so much'. Ansel continued in a matter-of-fact tone, 'But Dad says it's a waste of time, 'cos she's such a boozer.' The other children look mildly surprised but interested. You know that Ansel's mother does have a serious problem with alcohol and can be violent when drunk. It seems fair that Ansel should share something of importance to him, but you are slightly concerned about his mother's reaction if she hears about the announcement.

Kimberley

You are the group leader for the nine- and ten-year-olds in your after school club. You have very clear rules about use of the computer and the internet in club time. This afternoon you have had a group discussion about wise rules for the internet to raise the possible risks of the chatrooms that you know the children use when they are at home. Kimberley asks to speak with you after the discussion ends and says she is worried about her friend. Kimberley explains that this friend has met someone on line and is enthusiastic about meeting him. You run past Kimberley whether the 'friend' is really her and the reply leaves you sure that it is in fact someone else. However, Kimberley is being pressed by the other girl to be her companion when she goes to meet her on-line contact.

Good practice with children

There are many aspects of good practice with children and their families that will support your approach to child protection. These ways of working will be positive for children and should be in place regardless of whether your setting ever has concerns over abuse. Good practice in observation and record keeping is discussed in Chapter 4 and partnership with parents is raised in many places in the book. The good practice issues described in this chapter will help children develop respect for themselves and build an image of how adults ought to behave.

The physical care of children

The value of good physical care

Physical care is an important means of communication with young children and can be a powerful vehicle for their learning about adults and themselves. It is seriously unfortunate that tradition in early years has undervalued the contribution of care, seeing it as the poor relation to education. In many ways this attitude still prevails and can be a major stumbling block to quality in early years settings.

Appropriate physical care routines give children an experience of individual attention and appropriate, affectionate touch. A good experience of physical care can help children to build a positive image of how adults behave properly towards children. It is important to treat babies and young children with respect in their physical care. Young children and babies care about how they are handled and they notice the difference.

SAY WHAT YOU ARE DOING

Babies and toddlers should be given time to adjust and not simply lifted up swiftly or bundled off to be changed or fed at an adult's whim. It only takes additional seconds to smile or say 'hello' to a baby or toddler and perhaps to follow up with 'Josh, it's time to change you' or 'Hello, Molly. How about cheese and mash for lunch?' This effort is time and attention very well spent, since the young child feels involved, rather than a small, immobile person to whom other people do things when it suits them.

Babies and toddlers should not be treated like a bag of dirty washing or a body to be fed. Thoughtless routines, or a setting that undervalues care, can effectively put babies and toddlers on a conveyer belt between adults who are more interested in talking to each other than to the children. Practitioners may not intend to distress the young children but this can be the result.

PERSONAL COMMUNICATION

Changing time for a baby or toddler should be a personal time when the adult talks with very young children and listens to what they have to say in reply, even if there are no real words yet. The early years practitioner (parent or any other carer) can tune into the baby's mood, offering a song or a verbal ritual that the baby comes to recognise (perhaps tuneful patterns such as 'Hup, one, two, three!'). Adults can acknowledge a baby's fretful mood by talking reassuringly to a baby who does not feel like being changed.

Individual practitioners, such as childminders, nannies and foster carers should develop a close relationship with the children in their care and will undertake those children's personal care needs. Daily or residential group settings need to be organised so that children, and young people who still have need of intimate care, can feel that they are treated in a respectful and personal way.

A key person or worker system in early years settings means that young children make a personal relationship with one particular adult. This relationship then extends, as children feel emotionally secure, to one or two other team members. Disabled older children and young people, in daily, respite or residential settings, also need the continuity of a key person/worker. Children can learn the ways of this individual adult and the adult carer can tune into the temperament and likes of this child or young person.

Young children, and older disabled children, should not build up a belief that any adult can appear and deal with their intimate physical needs, regardless of whether the child likes them or knows the adult at all well. Residential settings sometimes have serious issues over shift patterns or a high dependence on agency staff. Even when every adult follows good practice in a child's care, that child or young person still experiences being handled in a very personal way by a long list of different people.

SHARE THE CARE WITH CHILDREN

Toddlers want to help with their dressing and mealtimes. Again, a timing of the care routines adjusted to the children, rather than adult convenience, will support young children to feel competent and yet able to ask for help. Young children need to feel that their growing abilities are respected and appreciated, but that being able to do something for yourself does not mean that adult support is withdrawn.

Tell children what you are doing and, where appropriate, ask if they want some help rather than pushing assistance upon them. Show them how to care for themselves and encourage them in all their efforts. Avoid swooping in without words to wipe a nose or a bottom, or to push a child's arms into her coat when she is almost there through her own ability.

SHOW RESPECT FOR YOUNG CHILDREN

Young children need a great deal of physically intimate care and attention but this can be offered in atmosphere of respect. The good practice described in this section applies to all children, regardless of their experiences. Yet also this practice helps children who have had negative experiences to learn how a respectful and responsive adult should behave.

Some young children are happy to sit on a pot, or on the toilet with the door open, and hold a conversation with an adult or their friends. Other children, sometimes from a young age, want more privacy. Their wish should be respected and can be met along with any concerns about safety. For instance, in your group setting the judgement may be that it is unsafe to have locks on the toilet doors. But you can still establish a tradition of respectful behaviour, that children can shut the doors and neither adults nor other children should go barging in without knocking.

Children in primary school and out-of-school settings will have toileting accidents. The youngest children may still misjudge their need to go, or perhaps feel embarrassed about asking. Upset stomachs can throw the ability of older children and some disabled children will continue to need help and support. Good practice is to deal respectfully and discretely with any incident, to offer help to children as they wish and support them as appropriate to deal with cleaning themselves and changing clothes.

Children are sometimes content to strip down to their underwear for games or dance in the early years of school. But some children are made very uncomfortable by this requirement and there should always be an alternative offered to parents before children are ever faced with the situation. Loose fitting clothing that allows children to move about will often be preferable to some children or families.

Children may simply not want to run about in their knickers and vest. And adults spend energy under other circumstances in explaining to young children that you do not flip up your skirt or pull your trousers down in public! Children who have health conditions that affect their skin, such as eczema, can be very self-conscious about exposing their limbs. They may fear, with some justification, that other children will tease them. Some families will have religious reasons for not wanting their children to undress for games.

DISABLED CHILDREN

All the above points are also important in the care of disabled children. They may be unable to deal with their own needs at an age when their peers are managing with little or no help. Physical limitations may hinder a child's persistent efforts to take on her own care or mean that she needs plenty of time and therefore patience and appreciation from her carer. Children with severe learning disabilities may take time to understand what they need to do, or to follow a sequence in their own physical care.

Any daily or residential setting with disabled children needs high standards in care and the behaviour of the adult carers. Otherwise children can be at a greater risk of abuse because they have built an image of themselves as people to whom a range of adults do physically intimate procedures, whether the child wants it or not. (See also page 37.)

Scenario

Even very young children have a sense of bodily dignity and can be distressed and outraged by careless treatment. One example was recounted to me by the mother of two-year-old Alice. The little girl had a persistent attack of vaginal thrush and her mother took Alice to the local health clinic. They were left to wait a considerable time in an examining room and then a male doctor, whom they had not met before, came in at speed. He approached Alice, who was lying on the bed, without any words, pulled down her knickers and pushed her legs apart to look at the inflamed area. With a few words to Alice's mother the doctor confirmed it was thrush, wrote a prescription and left. Alice was in tears and spoke over the following days about 'the nasty man'.

Alice's mother comforted her at the time and realised that Alice's upset was spreading to any male doctor. On their next visit to the clinic, when Alice was unwell, the usual male doctor in the practice was seeing patients. Alice's mother explained the situation and said that Alice was clear that she wanted to be examined by a 'lady'. Fortunately this doctor took the view that Alice's preference was understandable, that he would respect a woman's wish to see a female doctor and Alice's views counted just as much. He phoned through to a female colleague who examined Alice.

QUESTIONS

1 It was fortunate that Alice's next trip to the health clinic was so much better handled. What do you think could have been the consequences for Alice's feelings if she had experienced disrespect yet again?
2 Collect examples of good practice in treatment of young children. In what ways do respectful adults behave towards children during their health care or when the child's experience could be embarrassing, uncomfortable or painful?

Affection and physical contact

Physical – not sexual – contact

Children are very physical beings. They are tactile and learn a great deal through their senses. But there is a difference between physicality and sexuality. The confusion between these two concepts arises mainly from the wide influence of Sigmund Freud's claims about the sexual basis to children's development (through a young child's supposedly powerful feelings of attraction to the opposite-sexed parent and jealousy of the same-sexed parent). But infantile sexuality is an idea, it is not a fact and several respected theorists following Freud in the psychodynamic tradition disagreed strongly with his emphasis on sexuality in childhood. Psychologists outside this theoretical tradition do not support any notion that young children are sexual in the normal meaning of the word.

Many young children are temporarily interested in their own or their peers' private parts but this does not make them sexual in the adult sense. Their curiosity has to be seen in the context of their general fascination with the unknown or unexplained – especially if adults indicate that they do not want children to explore in this way. In a family home, children spend a lot of time trying to post small objects into the video, emptying out drawers and waste bins or playing with saucepans. Such behaviour is not proof that the children are obsessed with rubbish or metal objects. You would make sense of children's behaviour within the context of what was usual for their age (see also page 28).

Children's emotional needs

Children need warmth, expressed affection and physical closeness. There is an enormous gap between responding to children's need for closeness and wishing to abuse them. There has been such publicity about sexual abuse that some parents and practitioners have become daunted, concerned that their appropriate affection for children is open to misinterpretation. Yet the majority of adults do not want and will never want to abuse children sexually. It will be nothing short of a tragedy for children if their need for physical closeness and communication is denied, because adults fear they may be accused of wrongdoing.

Children need experience of touch, of respectful contact. Positive experiences form a psychologically healthy framework in which to judge adult behaviour, or the actions of older children and teenagers. Children need to be able to make some sense of people who are not behaving properly towards them, who require affection or who are imposing their own views and needs on the children. Children have to build from their own experience the confidence that 'this doesn't feel right' or 'I don't want this and I can say "no"'.

Children with no experience of appropriate, close physical affection can be dangerously vulnerable to adults who wish to abuse them sexually (and often use as an excuse the claim that children have a sexual nature). Emotionally deprived children are at risk for two reasons:

▶ They can be desperate for affection and are willing to accept it from any adult who appears to like them and be willing to pay them some attention.
▶ They have no comparison point for judging the behaviour of an adult who starts to impose upon them.

The points in this chapter apply to all practitioners – both female and male. Children will not be effectively protected if they are kept apart from men, if the male practitioners of a team are excluded from the more personal care routines or seriously discouraged from normal close contact with children. Children need experience of appropriate caring behaviour from both sexes. All settings need to have staff discussions about this issue and to avoid any naïve reliance on restrictions of the male practitioners in the team. (See also page 80.)

All staff should be guided by children in expressions of affection. It is inappropriate for adults to demand expressions of affection or particular kinds of expression, such as being kissed or hugged goodbye if a child does not spontaneously offer. Nor is it reasonable for adults to want affection from a baby or child in order to cheer themselves up.

Young children vary: some like to sit close, to hold hands or to sit on an adult's lap, but others are more reserved. There is not necessarily any cause to worry about the less demonstrative children. They may be less overtly affectionate by temperament or their family style may be warm, but not physically demonstrative. You would not be concerned about reserved children unless other behaviour from them made you wonder if they were wary of adults to the point of being afraid. In a similar way you would not worry about very affectionate children, unless they were indiscriminate in their affections. You might also worry about some particular expressions of affection, for instance if a child wanted to open-mouth kiss or rub against practitioners' private parts.

You should make sense of children's behaviour on the basis of their age and ability. Some older children with learning disabilities may behave more like a much younger child. You would interpret their behaviour rather differently from their peers, as well as supporting a child, where necessary, to learn steadily more age-appropriate behaviour.

Young children need the reassurance of physical contact and touch. They do not lose this emotional need as they grow older, although they may be less demonstrative. Children also need cuddles and affectionate touch when they are hurt or frightened. Some schools have developed no-touch guidelines, mainly as a result of anxiety about allegations of abuse, based either on misunderstood physical contact or malicious intent by a child, young person or parent.

Guidelines that seriously restrict physical contact are not appropriate for children in the early years of primary school, and there are many four-year-olds in school throughout the UK now. If you are part of a school or out-of-school setting, then you can have sensible team discussions about how you offer comfort and physical reassurance to children. But keeping a physical distance between you and the children communicates emotional distance to them and lack of caring. A child, who is distressed or has had an accident, will often want physical comfort. If an adult refuses to give this care, then children will feel rejected, they can only take it personally.

If you work in a daily or residential group setting, then you may have written guidelines about physical contact. Any guidelines and how they are put into daily practice need to create an appropriate balance between the well being and protection of children and the protection of adults. Teams need to have a thorough discussion of how any guidelines work, or fail to work, towards this objective. Some of the key issues in work with older children and young people include:

▶ Practitioners need to be able to offer comfort to a distressed child or young person. Children's emotional well being will be under threat if adults are denied any options for light and respectful touch. A team discussion needs to cover, and cover again when necessary, options such as a light touch to the hand or shoulder or the kind of comfort that can be offered by sitting next to a child and putting an arm round the shoulder.
▶ Under usual circumstances in school and out-of-school settings, it would not be appropriate to have regular, very close physical contact with individual children and, of course, appropriate contact should not be offered only to children who are liked or well behaved.
▶ Teams will have to address the gender issues and the unjust assumption that the actions of males are automatically more suspect than females. In 2003 the government in England plans to launch a major campaign to get more men into early years, primary school and out-of-school work. However, such a campaign will fail to get off the ground unless the unreasonable suspicions about men are effectively tackled.
▶ Physical contact will be necessary for safety when adults are supervising some physical activities and games. Respectful ground rules are established when adults say what they are going to do, in order to help or to demonstrate. There should be no need to touch a child or young person in intimate areas of the body. In any kind of contact sport with younger children, adults need to be well aware of their greater size and strength.
▶ All settings should have clear guidelines about acceptable physical restraint: what can be done, under what circumstances and how actions should be recorded after an incident.

Children's curiosity and comments

An appropriate adult role needs to be based on knowledge of children's usual development:

▶ Be ready to answer children's questions about how bodies work. Have simple, honest answers and see if the child has further questions this time. No child wants to hear absolutely everything you know about digestion or reproduction in response to their first question. Some children do not ask many questions of this kind; some are fascinated.

▶ Caring adults have a responsibility to help children learn about appropriate boundaries for behaviour. You will be communicating to children what is usual public behaviour and what should be more private.

▶ You will also, where necessary, be explaining to children about people's private areas of their body and their right to refuse being touched or examined where they do not wish. Most children are able to learn the distinctions and their curious explorations do not get to extreme levels.

If you work with older, or very articulate, children, there may be questions that you feel parents should handle.

▶ Perhaps a child has heard an item of news about a sexual scandal and asks you detailed questions. You could say, 'That's a good question, but I think your parents should answer that'. If the child reasonably asks, 'Why?', you can say that, 'Mums and Dads often have strong feelings about what their children should be told on this subject. It's not for me to decide what to tell you.' Make sure that you speak with the child's parents later that day. Reassure them that you feel their son or daughter asked a fair question, but one that they should answer in their own way.

▶ It is courteous practice for any practitioner to raise the issues with parents of how you answer questions about which parents might have definite views, for instance about birth and babies for younger children and death and bereavement for any children who raise that topic. You can tell a parent how you answered a question on this occasion and whether they would rather you handled the subject differently next time.

▶ Older children within primary school and out-of-school care may also make comments or use language that they have heard from the television, some music or from other children in the playground. There may be some offensive terms that you say are not to be used in your setting at all, because they are rude, cruel or some other explanation that addresses feelings. Some comments from children may be better addressed with a friendly question like, 'Do you know what that means?' or 'I'm not happy about the attitudes in that song; what do you think?'

Communication with children

Children are supported by positive experiences of adults who listen to their views, questions and worries. Children who feel they can turn to an adult who will take them seriously are far more likely to speak up about an experience that is causing them concern or unease – not necessarily actually abusive. Children who have experienced respectful communication from adults are also likely to believe that what they feel and think matters and should not be ignored by any adults for their own ends.

Good habits in communication

Children will be helped in your setting by adults who give children time and attention.

- ▶ Make a habit of listening to what children want to say to you and watch what their body language tells you as loudly as their spoken words.
- ▶ Avoid assuming that, as an adult, you know what a child is thinking or should be thinking or feeling. Give children the time to ask them and listen fully to their replies.
- ▶ Be ready to take children seriously – their feeling, worries, confusions, or dislikes about people. You are not agreeing that their fears are necessarily justified, nor should you ever feed their worries. But you take children's perspective with seriousness, reassure them where appropriate and take further action or investigation if that seems necessary.
- ▶ Respect children's concerns and physical feelings. Children feel dismissed and belittled by remarks such as, 'You don't really feel like that' or 'You're making a fuss, that doesn't hurt'.
- ▶ Help children to learn respectful communication with each other: listening, not interrupting and taking someone else's view into account.
- ▶ Answer children's questions honestly, even if you find some topics slightly embarrassing to answer (see also the previous section).

Communication will be less straightforward with some children. You may work with some children, and parents, with whom you do not share a fluent language. You will be working to support their learning of English, since this language is the most useful shared language in the UK. However, there will be a period in which you will need to use what words you both understand and be generous with gesture. You may sometimes need to say to a parent or supportive older sibling that the younger one was trying to tell you something and you are very sorry that you did not fully understand.

You will also need to use all forms of possible communication with children and young people whose disabilities affect their ability to express themselves – see the discussion on page 108.

Dealing with emotions

Adult reactions

Children are also learning a great deal about feelings: their own, the feelings of others and what are the general ground rules about how you deal with feelings. Even if adults do not believe that they are giving specific messages about emotions, their views emerge through their behaviour. Perhaps a practitioner (or parent) reacts differently when a girl is in tears than to a boy of the same age who is crying. A brusque reaction, or even a preference for jollying children out of deep feelings, can tell children that this adult, and perhaps others too, do not want to hear and see that they are upset, frightened or worried.

Some adults – practitioners and parents – seem to be very resistant to accepting that young children have strong feelings: that they can be emotionally hurt by how they are treated and do not just snap out of sadness or forget all about unhappy events. This reluctance might be due to the following:

▶ Sometimes adults resist taking a child's perspective in many different ways. The adult's judgement about a situation prevails so that they say, 'That's not worth making a fuss about' or even 'You're not hurt that badly'. The same, insensitive adults sometimes make offhand remarks about children in their hearing, as if the children will not overhear or will not care about comments that would annoy the adults themselves.
▶ Possibly, some adults find it less trouble to believe that young children are incapable of serious distress, that they 'don't really notice' or that 'young children soon get over upsets'.
▶ The advantage to adults of this convenient, and inaccurate view, is that they can avoid any feelings of responsibility to support distressed children. Children 'get over' upsets when adults offer swift and appropriate support rather than pretend that nothing much has happened.
▶ Adults may also try to protect themselves against their own possible distress when children are unhappy. This explanation may underlie the view that children were not 'really upset' at the beginning of the session, because they cheered up later. Some adults also challenge the genuineness of children's upset on the grounds that there are no 'real tears'.

Positive support for children

A far more positive approach is to accept children's feelings as they express to you. You need to tune in to the seriousness as expressed by children or young people – neither belittling their strong feelings nor making more of an incident than they want. You can support children in recognising and dealing with their feelings through how you talk and listen with them.

You can also show children ways of expressing feelings by how you handle your own emotions – in words and actions. For instance:

▶ You might agree with children – 'I'm sad too about Minnie (the nursery mouse who died). I miss her little face in the morning.' Or you might admit that you too are touched by children's film or video – 'Yes, I know it's just a story. But that doesn't stop me feeling a bit sad'.
▶ You can show feelings of happiness and elation in shared activities with children – 'We did it! We made it work. I'm so proud of us all.'
▶ Sometimes the emotion may be more that of frustration or disappointment – 'That is so annoying. There's something the matter with this glue. Let me see if I've got something that will work.'
▶ You will also get opportunities to show children assertive behaviour rather than aggressive – 'Yes, I thought that man in the market was very rude to us. I told him so, but I wasn't going to shout the way that he did.'
▶ Older children and young teenagers may lead a conversation by asking you questions about 'what's going on?', 'why do people behave like that?' or 'are you worried about … ?'

These kinds of comments and short conversations build a confidence for children and young people that caring adults will share feelings and protect them, but with explanations. Opportunities to explore feelings can also arise through children's play and their interest in stories. For instance:

▶ Feelings and dilemmas often feature in books that you read to a small group or in story telling. The worry or fear experienced by a character in a story can be a good opportunity to discuss feelings with children. You might talk a little about what the children think a character may be feeling, or what they might feel in the same situation. A happy resolution to the story might lead to discussion from the children about what makes them happy or excited.
▶ Older children may raise issues for discussion from books they now read independently or from television programmes and films. Children who have been encouraged to express views can be articulate about different values and the rights and wrongs of a situation.

▶ In early years settings children's pretend play can be a rich vehicle for emotions. Play in the home corner or with dolls can be a way to explore scenarios as well as try out skills that a child might not be allowed to practise in a real kitchen or with a real baby. Outdoor play may be an ideal vehicle for the livelier pretend play that encompasses superheroes and the struggle between good and evil in children's terms. Children in school can use their break time in the playground for similar games on occasion.

▶ Children's mixed feelings can emerge through play with puppets or dolls and can provide a relief for frustrations in their lives, not necessarily abusive experiences. Children may choose to speak through a puppet to express feelings or concerns that are easier to voice through this medium.

SUPPORT THROUGH GROUP WORK

Very young children need individual attention and will not respond well to being treated as one of a group. With support, three- and four-year-olds have become more able to operate both as an individual and a member of their nursery or pre-school group. Group work should never displace the opportunities for personal conversation, but sensitive adults can raise issues and follow children's concerns in small groups, like circle time. This type of activity only works if the adult helps to establish ground rules about listening and respect for the views of others – rules that apply to the adults just as much as the children.

A regular circle time with a small group can be a chance for individual children, if they wish, to share something that has happened in their life. On occasion children may tell about events that provoke sympathy, for instance, that Granma has gone into hospital or that their rabbit has died. At other times, children may share happy events, for instance, that they have a new baby sister and Mum lets them help. When children feel emotionally secure and confident in the adult, then they may well raise matters of concern to them, that have arisen through their play, especially pretend play.

Confident four- and five-year-olds may sometimes share very intimate family matters. Younger children are learning the boundaries between personal and public and their circle time feels personal to them. Care is needed by adults to acknowledge a child's comment but sometimes to limit courteously any more details. You might follow up through an individual conversation with a child, explaining that you appreciate how upsetting it was to hear Mummy and Daddy having a row, but that the parents will probably be embarrassed if everyone in nursery knows about the row in detail.

School-age children can be adept at group discussion, in situations like a class meeting, school council or group meetings in an after school club. Much depends on the children's experience and the skills of the adult facilitating the discussion. Children and young people soon realise if a group meeting is not a genuine discussion but rather a chance for the adult(s) to tell children what they should think or do.

When children have experienced adult support for their own concerns, they have emotional resources to spare for other people, including their peers. Older children and young teenagers can show empathy for others and be ready to behave in a thoughtful way to peers who need company or emotional support. Schools, that have an effective positive behaviour policy, have sometimes mobilised the skills of the children and young people. Primary school children have been active in playground friendship squads, mentoring of younger children and conflict resolution. Such schemes have worked because the children steadily learn these skills through the personal and social part of the curriculum and the school staff set a good example. Peer support schemes can work well in secondary school and within residential care, so long as young people are given support in the necessary skills and there is proper discussion about the boundaries to any scheme.

ACTIVITY

Gather ideas and examples of how you can support children's feelings in a positive way in your setting or through your work as an individual practitioner, such as a childminder.

1 Note down examples of play or small group discussion. What have you done within the last fortnight with the children? What emerged from the play or the group conversation? What seemed to interest the children most?
2 Look out honestly for the opportunities that you provide for children to talk with you one-to-one. Perhaps keep a note over a fortnight of conversations that you have with children, when the child has wanted to share something with you. How far are you able, honestly, to give the time individual children would like? Are there any implications for how you organise the day, or session, or make yourself available to the children?

A positive policy for dealing with behaviour

Children and young people need experience of adults who handle their behaviour in a positive way, without using threats, verbal humiliation or physical forms of intimidation or punishment. Your setting should have a clear policy on how you deal with children's behaviour and the ideas and approaches should be shared with parents. Some families will be pleased to hear that you act in the same way that they do at home. Others may be confused and need reassurance that removing physical forms of punishment definitely does not mean that you let the children run wild.

A positive approach to children

The main themes of a positive approach are as follows:

▶ You should look at situations from children's perspective – through their eyes. Children are helped to behave well and to deal with their feelings or frustrations by adults who allow for children's understanding and do not simply impose adult views.

▶ Practitioners, or parents, need to be clear about what they want children to do and not just what they do not want. You can communicate and explain clear ground rules to children, phrased as a 'Please do ...' and not as a list of 'don't's.

▶ Follow your own ground rules and show positive behaviour yourself. Children are not impressed by an approach of 'Never mind how I behave. Just do what I tell you!' Children are helped and inspired by adults who model what they would like children to do: helping others, saying 'sorry' and dealing with frustrations in ways that do not dump on other people. All adults need to set a good example.

▶ Encourage and show pleasure in the behaviour that you want from children. Notice by smiles and words when they have made an effort. You do not have to reward children with treats or lavish praise. In fact, overdoing reward can backfire, because children come to believe that they should be rewarded with sweets or privileges.

▶ Be generous with your time and energy in giving children encouragement for what has been well done. Avoid putting most of your efforts into catching children out in wrong-doing. Try at least to double the amount of encouraging remarks and make any potentially critical comments emerge constructively.

▶ When it is possible, offer children alternatives rather than a straight 'you can't do that'. Be ready to ignore minor misdemeanours, if possible, to avoid a situation in which you seem always to be nagging a particular child. Some selective ignoring, like compromise, is a strong option if you chose to offer it, rather than giving in because you do not currently feel like standing firm on a ground rule that should be held.

▶ Keep children's troublesome or disruptive behaviour separate from them as individuals. Think this distinction in your own mind and be prepared to say it out loud – 'I like you, Ramona. I don't like what you're doing to Freddie.'

▶ Avoid labels for children, whether these are rude, like 'You're a stupid/selfish/naughty child' or they appear to be compliments, like 'What a good little girl'. A positive approach focuses on the child's behaviour at the time, rather than implying that this occasion sums up her entire personality or competence.

▶ Never say, 'I won't like you any more if ...' Children or young people should never come to believe that a trusted adult's affection can change from moment to moment, depending on how children have behaved.

All adults have to weigh up when and how they need to intervene physically to keep children safe.

▶ Sometimes young children need to be physically contained within your arms or removed from other children whom they are hurting.

▶ It is crucial that such actions are calm and adult behaviour and words do not raise the emotional temperature. You would always first try non-interventionist methods to calm a situation.

▶ Children should never be dragged, handled roughly, nor hurt through the physical containment and you should accompany your physical actions with calming words.

▶ In such circumstances, adults are using their greater strength appropriately to keep children safe and help them to calm down. It can be a physical way of reassuring children that you will hold to boundaries when the children have gone beyond their own ability to stop themselves.

▶ If you work with older children and young teenagers, then physical containment raises other issues, not least your own physical safety. Your setting should have clear guidelines about how you can hold and restrain children who are out of control. If containment is a regular event for your setting, then everyone should have had specific training in appropriate techniques of restraint.

A positive approach to children's behaviour is underpinned by a set of values that see adults as having responsibilities towards children as well as rights. A great deal of practice and observation of children in homes and group settings confirms that the positive, rather than the punitive approach works well and helps children develop towards individuals who feel able to guide their own behaviour.

The case against hitting children

If you listen to discussions between adults about children and discipline (in everyday conversation or on the radio or television), you will almost certainly hear adults who believe that it is fine to hit children or are puzzled about what else to do. Some adults express what can only be described as enthusiasm about this kind of punishment and persistently link the right to hit children with the need for discipline. Supporters tend to use the word 'smack' rather than hit, perhaps to avoid facing the contradiction that they are proposing actions against the smaller and younger members of society that would be condemned if used against fellow-adults.

There has been a long tradition within the UK, and in other countries around the world, of adults' right to hit children. Beliefs run deep within cultures and are sometimes justified on a religious basis. There is now a strong counter-tradition within work with children, but it is useful for you to understand the deep roots of some of the opposing views.

The main themes in opposition to hitting children are as follows:

- ► There is a moral stance that it is wrong to hit children. UK society does not as a whole approve of adults settling disputes and imposing their wishes through hitting other people. It is unacceptable to treat young children in this way.
- ► There are many alternatives to hitting when adults need to deal with children's behaviour. Hitting, like any emphasis on punishment, is a negative focus – 'don't' and 'No!' – rather than on what you want the child to do.
- ► Hitting is far too often a reflection of adults' moods: that they have had enough for today or are embarrassed by a child's public misbehaviour. Children can be given an inconsistent picture by adults who are sometimes cross and hit out, but on other occasions, very similar as far as the child is concerned, the adult uses other methods.
- ► Children do not like being hit – although children who are regularly hit may develop a protective shell to give the impression that they do not care. Children tend to focus on the shock and distress of the slap, fierce shove or shake and any lesson about their own behaviour is lost in their reaction to the adult behaviour.
- ► Hitting gives children the clear message that physical means are an acceptable way to settle arguments or express anger and frustration. They often use this method themselves, either with other children or they hit the adult back in retaliation. Adults are setting a very bad example through their behaviour.
- ► Supporters of hitting use bizarre phrases like 'a gentle smack' or 'loving

discipline'. But hitting children is rarely calm and you need to challenge the dubious reasoning underlying any claim that it can be an expression of affection.

▶ Parents who hit face the difficult problem of what to do if a light 'smack' or 'tap' does nothing to stop children, or they soon return to the forbidden activity. Parents are tempted to hit harder and longer and they seriously risk losing control.

Adults, as parents and practitioners, need to consider their attitudes as well as their actions. Childhood experiences can muddle adult thinking, as people may struggle to reconcile the fact that parents, whom they love, raised them in a time when it was socially more acceptable to hit children. Times have changed and some adults have to address their feelings of 'my parents smacked me and it didn't do me any harm!' The questions have to be, 'What good did it do you?' and 'Was there no other way that you could learn how to behave?'

THE LAW AND HITTING CHILDREN

The legal situation about hitting children has changed steadily over the last couple of decades, but the national governments within the UK have still not simply brought children under the same legal protection against assault as the law gives to adults. Many other European countries have taken this step, in order to treat children as citizens with rights. As well as changes in law, there have been parent education campaigns to create a climate in which adults make the effort to guide children's behaviour in more respectful ways.

Educational and child protection legislation throughout the UK has now removed the option of using corporal punishment (hitting and other forms of direct physical discipline) on children in public establishments: early years settings, any state or independent schools, foster care and residential children's homes. Where there is any room for doubt in group settings, the good practice guidelines and staff job descriptions make it clear that physical punishment is never an acceptable option.

An anomaly remains because law in each of the four nations comprising the UK still allows parents to hit their children, under case law that allows these adults to inflict what is described as 'reasonable chastisement'. In England, the national care standards extended that right to childminders, who have parents' written permission to hit their children. Professional standards for childminding are opposed to this right and an energetic lobbying campaign may yet reverse the situation.

There have been significant campaigns aiming to bring all children under the same legal protection as adults but at the time of writing (2003) no part of the UK has taken this step. The loophole for parents arises from a case as long ago as 1860 when a thirteen-year-old died as the direct result of a beating by teachers at his school. The judge presiding over that case was making the point that killing children was beyond reasonable. Parents who are judged to have overstepped the boundary of acceptable punishment may be prosecuted for wilful assault and causing unnecessary suffering under the Children and Young Persons Acts (1933 for England and Wales, 1937 for Scotland and 1950 for Northern Ireland). The burden of proof remains with the prosecution to establish beyond reasonable doubt that a parent's actions went beyond the limits of lawful punishment of their child or young person. Many parents have been excused legally for repeated attacks on their children, including using implements, on the grounds that the adult behaviour fell within reasonable chastisement.

In 1991 the UK central government signed the United Nations Convention on the Rights of the Child 1989. Several of the articles within the Convention aim to secure children's rights to be protected from physical or mental violence. The UN Committee on the Rights of the Child (which monitors the Convention) has recommended prohibiting physical punishment in families and the active change of social attitudes that support it. The UK government was challenged, after a case went to the European Court of Human Rights, that children were not properly protected under current law. There have been consultations around the UK, but genuine change has not followed.

A PERSONAL EXAMPLE

My parents disapproved of hitting children; they regarded it as a serious misuse of adult strength. So, it came as a shock to me when my first teacher in primary school (1950s) not only yelled at us, but regularly hit children over the knuckles or on the open palm with a large wooden ruler. I was only ever on the receiving end of this woman's cruel words. But I will never forget watching her hit other five-year-olds, sometimes just for simple mistakes and in the case of a friend of mine for wishing to write with his left hand.

In my secondary school (1960s), the religious education teacher had unpredictable outbursts of temper that sometimes led to his hitting pupils very hard round the head. There were many such incidents during my seven years at the school, some bad enough that parents came to complain to the headmaster. As pupils we finally recognised that this man was never going to be sacked. I later discovered that parents who came to complain were pressed to consider the damage to the school resulting from an assault charge. The man's conduct was further excused on the grounds that he had allegedly been shell-shocked during the second world war over twenty years previously.

Both my first primary school teacher and the religious education teacher were disliked by the pupils. Neither teacher was respected. They provoked feelings of unease or fear in us because of their unpredictability. But their behaviour was tolerated within schools which also had considerate, excellent teachers who did not resort to physical attack, either as a form of punishment or in reaction to some internal fury. As pupils, we reached the conclusion that these teachers fell within what adults regarded as normal behaviour towards children or young people, an extreme end perhaps but acceptable nonetheless.

ACTIVITY

Readers will vary in age and some will have no experience of institutions, such as schools, in which physical punishment of pupils was a real possibility. I am of the generation that watched children beaten in public. In my primary school, a church school, children were hit by the headmaster with a slipper during morning assembly. Such experiences certainly shaped my view of adults in authority and of the position of children. Admittedly views vary, some adults still believe that such attacks acted as a deterrent. In fact records of the time show that in secondary and primary school the same children, most usually boys, were beaten many times, with no observable change in their behaviour.

1 If you have childhood memories like my own, you could consider what images they left of adult behaviour.
2 If you have no direct experience of this kind, then you could talk with older colleagues or members of your family about their experiences.
3 How did they feel about adults who used physical punishments or threats?
4 What do the memories tell you about a different social era?

Bullying by children and young people

Behaviour that would be called bullying includes:

▶ Physical attack or intimidation through the threat of attack
▶ Taking another child or young person's possessions or ruining them
▶ Persistent verbal and emotional cruelty to peers, including direct offensiveness and spreading rumours through word or text messaging
▶ Physical and verbal harassment with sexual overtones.

Bullying is a type of aggressive behaviour and children and young people can be seriously distressed by such treatment. Attacks do not have to be physical in order to undermine children or young people. They can be very affected by persistent verbal harassment and ridicule, even to the point of self harm.

Schools, out-of-school and residential settings would normally use the good practice framework related to bullying in order to deal with intimidatory behaviour between children or young people, that would be judged abusive if an adult were involved. When bullying includes a sexual element, then policy and practice need to recognise that this behaviour is outside developmental norms. However, it would be usual to treat young sexual abusers as both bully/abuser and potential abuse victim.

SIGNS OF POSSIBLE BULLYING

You need to be attentive to changes in a child or young person, without of course assuming that any change is evidence of bullying. You will notice that many of the signs of ill treatment by bullying are similar to those that could flag up possible abuse or neglect by adults. The common factor is that a child or young person is being ill-treated and needs appropriate protection:

▶ Children and young people may tell a trusted adult directly that they are being bullied. Alternatively they may try to let you know in a more roundabout way, for instance by saying they do not like school or club any more or do not want to attend a leisure or sporting activity that they previously enjoyed.
▶ Children and young people may have unexplained injuries, their clothes may be torn or dirtied or they may inexplicably be missing possessions or money.
▶ A child or young person's behaviour may change, such as a loss of confidence or fear of particular children. Children may regress in development, for instance bedwetting.
▶ Children or young people may show serious over-concern about their hygiene or weight, because they have been targeted and called 'dirty', 'smelly' or 'fatty'.

▶ Children on the receiving end of bullying can show the effects in their physical and emotional health. They may appear depressed, express feelings of hopelessness and in extreme cases resort to self harm, even suicide.

WHY DO CHILDREN AND YOUNG PEOPLE BULLY?

The work of Kidscape has demonstrated that there are different reasons underlying bullying. Adults who genuinely want to help need to keep an open mind about what is happening and why. Reasons are not excuses, but a better grasp of what is probably going on in the mind of a bully can direct adults towards more effective help.

▶ Some children and young people bully because they have no conception that they should limit their demands. As Michele Elliot has pointed out, such children can be the original 'spoiled brat' who use harassment and attack to get what they want.

▶ Children and young people, who have not been indulged by their families, may have learned through life experience that intimidation of others makes them feel good and is a quick route to getting what they want.

▶ Some bullies are essentially 'victims-turned-bullies'. They may have experienced bullying when they were younger or smaller, nobody helped them and they feel it is now payback time.

▶ Children and young people who have been abused in different ways, including sexually, may have little idea how to relate to peers other than through bullying or abusive behaviour.

▶ Some children or young people have very poor self image and confidence, despite the appearance of being strong and forceful. They have learned to use bullying, physical or verbal, to boost themselves and feel powerful.

▶ Some bullies are part of a group that intimidates others. The less enthusiastic children or young people feel reluctant to object. The activity is part of the group identity and they will have to find new friends if they refuse to be part of bullying. They may also fear, on the basis of sound experience, that refusal will lead to their becoming the new targets.

THE ROLE OF ADULTS IN HELPING

All practitioners working with children and young people need to create a supportive and telling atmosphere, whether within a daily or residential group setting or in a family home as a childminder, nanny or foster carer. Children and young people who are being bullied need a sense of reassurance that adults in whom they confide will take them seriously and help them resolve the situation. They want to have adults understand the situation from their perspective, and they do not want adults to take thoughtless action that only makes matter worse.

Adults need to offer the following good practice in communication:

▶ Give time and attention in general for the children and young people. They will not confide in adults who do not have time to listen or show empathy for the perspective of children and young people.

▶ Listen carefully to what is said by the children or young people on the receiving end. Take what they say seriously; it has upset or frightened them, even if at first hearing the events seem minor to you.

▶ A child who has been bullied may not want you to tackle the children who have done the bullying. It is important to listen and certainly not to take sudden action. But you may need to explain your responsibilities to keep people safe, which means that you cannot simply ignore what has happened.

▶ If the bullying is happening within your setting or family home, then find an appropriate opportunity for a calm but firm conversation with the child or young person, or group, who are accused.

▶ It is very important to avoid adult behaviour that is bullying in its turn. You need to check out what has happened and listen to what the accused children and young people have to say.

▶ Be ready to challenge children or young people who claim, 'He said we could have his bag' or 'It's just a joke!' You need to communicate very clearly that real jokes are shared by everyone involved. The bullies did not stop when it was very clear that the child or young person they were harassing was upset and frightened. So this was not a piece of fun at all.

▶ Come to as clear view as you can of what happened. Impose consequences where appropriate, that may include an apology, (but there is no point in insisting on a 'sorry' that will be inauthentic) and the return of anything taken.

You need to consider, with your colleagues in group settings, what further action needs to be taken beyond this incident.

▶ Children and young people who have been bullied need support as appropriate. Affirm that they were right to tell and work to boost their self confidence or skills of assertiveness if this might help.

▶ Consider the possible reasons for the bullying behaviour and what you could do to re-direct the children or young people. In some cases they may need continuing support in order to meet their legitimate emotional needs in less harmful ways.

▶ Less keen participants within a bullying group may need help to establish other friendships.

▶ In some cases there may be more general discussions that need to happen in order to mobilise the power of bystanders, exploring how they felt unable or unwilling to tell or help.

▶ Does this incident raise more general good practice issues in your group setting? For example, have children or young people let you know that there are times of the day, parts of the building or outdoor space that need better or different adult supervision?

▶ Do you all need some new ground rules, discussed and agreed with the children and young people themselves? Such rules may need to cover children's right to defend themselves and how. You may well say that hitting must not be children's first reaction but then they do need to feel they can shout at a peer who is harassing them.

In settings with a strong and positive approach to behaviour, it can be possible to work alongside the children and young people through the power of group discussion, meetings or an effective school council. Children cannot be expected to tackle and resolve bullying on their own; adults have serious responsibilities. However, supported group work can create an atmosphere in which it is clear to everyone that bullying is unacceptable behaviour from anyone: child, young person or adult.

Guided group discussion can highlight the feelings of the bullied child or young person in a way that the bully will find harder to ignore (bullies often operate by de-humanising their victims) and support can be given to those bullied. Children or young people who have bullied should also have a chance to speak up and be heard, so that the group can understand what may be going on in their mind. Group meetings should be supportive of changes in the behaviour of a child or young person who previously bullied others.

Learning about personal safety

Responsible adults can support all children and young people to learn about how to keep themselves safe. Kidscape has been prominent in offering balanced advice in this area. This section is written for practitioners, but the ideas and advice are equally relevant for parents supporting their own children.

▶ A key point is neither to wait until something happens, nor to focus only on those children and young people whom you believe to be more at risk. Learning how to keep themselves safe, and being confident about what to do in doubtful or frightening situations, is part of growing up through childhood. Helping children learn about personal safety is a continuing process over the years, certainly not something that is 'done' after a couple of conversations or a special session at school.

▶ Support for personal safety needs to be balanced. Children are not effectively protected by an over-emphasis on stranger danger, because most sources of risk will arise from people they know. Likewise, safety messages need to be considerate; children can be unnerved when they gain the idea that danger lurks behind every bush and corner.

▶ An equally unfortunate consequence of the focus on stranger danger is that it has made some people, especially men, wary about offering help to an unknown child or young person who seems to be lost or in distress. Caring adults need to consider how they offer help, but children are at unnecessary additional risk if potential help walks away for fear of being misunderstood.

PARTNERSHIP WITH PARENTS

Early years, school and out-of-school practitioners can be helpful adults to a child or young person: what you say and do, your willingness to listen to any of their concerns and the positive role model that you show in dealing with uncertain or worrying situations. Practitioners who work as foster and residential carers are sometimes supporting children and young people whose safety has already been compromised.

Supporting children in personal safety is a shared responsibility between practitioners and parents. You should talk with parents about this area of work. Like any other aspect of your curriculum or planned activities, parents have the right to be informed and consulted about what you are saying to children and to understand some of the subtle messages that you wish to communicate. For instance, you are not telling their children that it is all right to be rude to adults: strangers or familiar people. You are explaining that adults do not deserve politeness from children if the adults behave in such a way as to upset, worry or frighten children. Some parents may appreciate being part of discussions or want to read any leaflets you use.

POSSIBLE RESOURCES

You have a range of resources to draw on:

▶ Stories, told from books or played out with dolls or puppets, may be a way of communicating simple points to young children. Activities that use children's imagination can develop into 'what if..' scenarios that explore possibilities through discussion or supported role play.

▶ Videos, books and leaflets can be useful with older children but they do not do the work for you. Videos or helpful leaflets need to be accompanied by conversation at the time and at any point later that children or young people want to talk.

▶ Sometimes news items or themes in a television programme naturally provoke a conversation in which safety can be a topic.

▶ Exploration can be through supported group work (see also page 190) as well as being responsive to questions and comments from children and young people.

Resources like books or videos do not substitute for attentive and personal conversations with children. They learn best through talking and listening with a caring adult whom they trust: one who will answer questions now and sensitively return to the key ideas at appropriate opportunities in the future. Older children and teenagers are also able to talk in group discussions or meetings where they feel safe and supported by familiar adults.

Children's awareness of the news

Older children and young people are aware of distressing events covered by the news media on television and in the newspapers. Events, such as the murder of Sarah Payne in 2000 and of Holly Wells and Jessica Chapman in 2002, can lead to necessary conversations with children and young people. Adults, parents as well as practitioners, can find the content uncomfortable and wonder how best to deal with questions and anxieties.

When faced with any distressing event, it is best to answer children's questions and respond to their comments as these arise. These two events received saturation news coverage, but they were not the only distressing events over this period that were likely to provoke children's concerns. Similar issues arose about 'what should we say to the children' from the destruction of the twin towers in New York in 2001 and prior to that from distressing images during the outbreak of foot and mouth disease in the UK.

It is important for familiar adults to respond to children through ordinary conversations. Communities, like Soham, who are devastated by loss are often provided with helplines and counsellors from outside the area. Such a facility can be valuable, but many children and teenagers want to talk with the adults they already know, not with strangers, however well trained. Young people often want to talk with their peers, perhaps with a supportive adult nearby. It is important for all caring adults to recognise children's need for a familiar face and voice, rather than become convinced that complex emotional issues are best passed over to the 'experts'. Distressed or confused adults can sometimes feel, 'I'm so worried I shall say the wrong thing', but there is no perfect answer.

▶ Children need adults who will listen and follow their lead. If children voice a question, then they want and deserve an honest answer. An adult reply to some comments can be, 'What makes you say that?', in order to help you get a handle on what concerns the child.

▶ Of course, children or young people should not then feel overwhelmed by adult emotions: distress, fear or anger. But they can learn when adults admit, 'I feel sad/confused/upset too', rather than trying somehow to make everything alright for the child.

▶ In terms of personal safety, prominent news items require practitioners and parents to admit that some adults intentionally harm children. But a honest message is that most adults are kind and caring. See also the section on stranger danger on page 208.

▶ Adults are concerned sometimes that honest conversation undermines the 'innocence' of childhood. But of course children are not innocent in the sentimental way that some media discussion likes to promote. Children are ignorant in the most positive sense of the word; there is so much they do not know. Children are learning about the world and they need an accurate framework in which to make sense of events.

Build children's confidence

Personal safety is supported by children's sense of self-confidence and a conviction of their own self-worth, their right to feel and be safe.

▶ Children learn these feelings through experience, including affectionate and trusting relationships, and respect shown for their feelings (see page 188). Children and young people then become sure they are worthy and will probably talk with you if they are worried.

▶ Make it easy for children to tell and deal with anyone in your team who undermines that process. For example, a primary school safety or bullying discussion can stress the importance of 'telling' rather than keeping quiet about unhappy experiences. However, this message is undermined if children later find their attempts to speak up about playground troubles are dismissed by a teacher or playground supervisor as 'telling tales'. Adults who feel inadequate about how to help resolve a problem may dismiss the children with comments like, 'you can sort that out yourself, don't bother me.'

▶ A guideline about 'telling' must not be applied in any way that puts further pressure on children or makes them feel responsible through their silence. Circumstances, such as peer group pressure and loyalty, can combine to make it very difficult for some children to tell about playground troubles or bullying. It can be even harder to tell about abusive experiences (see page 198). When children or young people finally manage to speak out, they should never be given the message of 'why didn't you say earlier?'

▶ Children need to develop trust in their own feelings about appropriate behaviour. This confidence develops on a basis of good experiences with adults who have shown respect about touch and physical care routines (see pages 178 and 184). Older children can then have developed a strong sense of when someone is overstepping an appropriate boundary.

▶ Affirm children and young people when you listen to their intuitions or 'gut' feelings about people. You would not encourage unreasonable criticisms of people as 'nasty' or views that seem, after some talking and listening, to be based in unsupported prejudice. But most children's views that somebody is 'creepy' are based in their observations.

▶ You can have an open-ended conversation that explores 'What makes you say that?' or 'What does he do that you find "creepy"?'. Sometimes the explanation will be innocent; perhaps a child has not understood that her uncle leans close because he is hard of hearing. But there are still alternative ways to solve this problem that avoid the uncle sitting closer than the child wishes. On other occasions you may hear about aspects of the adult's or young person's behaviour that leave you feeling uneasy and you will explore what might be done.

Rules with attention to children's rights

You need to establish guiding rules about behaviour in ways that do not put children at risk. For example:

▶ Children should not be told that they must be polite to all adults at all times, nor given the idea that adults are always in the right. You can encourage courtesy and still help children to understand that some behaviour from adults is inappropriate and removes any adult right to expect politeness from children.

▶ Children, who are encouraged as a general rule to follow adult requests, need to understand that they do not have to obey all adults, especially when what is asked seems wrong or makes the child very uncomfortable. Children can learn their right to say 'No' and to tell a trusted adult about experiences that they do not like.

You should encourage children to deal non-aggressively with their peers, to speak up rather than hit out in anger and to get help from adults if matters are getting out of hand. Children and young people are supported when adults understand and coach them in the skills of problem solving and non-aggressive conflict resolution.

▶ But children are not well protected by an absolute rule of, 'Never yell at people or hit them'. Schools and other group settings need effective behaviour policy and practice that does not leave the less aggressive children at risk of bullying.

▶ Adults are responsible for creating a situation, in schools and other group settings, that enables children to follow the rules that the adults have set. For instance, it is unacceptable for the staff of a school or a after-school club to say 'there's no hitting here', unless the adults step in effectively when some children use physical means to get their own way. Without adult support, the better behaved children may resist hitting back, or get into trouble when they defend themselves. Yet the lesson they are learning is that the strong win out and adults are unfair.

▶ With greater independence, older children and young people start to face situations when talking is not going to help and there is no friendly adult upon whom to call. Children have the right to defend themselves out in their neighbourhood from bullying peers, intimidating older children or adults. An effective defence will sometimes include yelling, shoving and hitting out at somebody who will not let the child get away through less noisy or physical ways.

▶ Such choices need discussion with children. You can teach children to yell, push and struggle if they are attacked or grabbed, but do not encourage them in unrealistic estimates of their own physical strength. There is a time to run away, as fast as possible.

Rules and responsibilities for adults

Children will be learning about ground rules for their own behaviour: what is expected, what is not allowed. But they also need to learn that adults cannot simply do as they like; there are ground rules that apply to adults as well. You can help children and young people by explaining these points – not all at the same time of course! Look for opportunities in ordinary conversation, about television programmes or events you observe on the street.

Children can be reassured when caring adults explain that unknown adults are the ones in the wrong, when they put children in an awkward position. Examples of unacceptable adult behaviour could be:

▶ Striking up a conversation with a child who is alone, asking a child for help or pressing a child to 'come and look at' something.

▶ Sensible and okay unknown adults do not insist on helping children who have said they are 'fine' or offering presents and sweets when the child is uncomfortable about this attention.

▶ Adults or young people familiar to a child have no business ill-treating children nor pressing them to keep uncomfortable secrets.
▶ They should not try to come between a child or young person and their family. Children are right to be wary of an adult who encourages them to do something that their family would not like.

It is not a child's responsibility to sort out the 'bad' strangers or less known acquaintances from the 'safe' ones. On the contrary, it is the responsibility of all adults to behave properly towards children.

▶ Adults or young people have no right to use their greater physical, intellectual or emotional powers to coerce children.
▶ Rules for proper adult behaviour hold regardless of whether the children were involved in any misbehaviour, for instance, having wandered off from their school group on a trip, or ignored a family rule like 'don't talk to strangers'.
▶ Rules for adults still apply even if children have accepted sweets or gifts from the adult or young person. In fact the older person is in the wrong for having put the pressure on the younger or more vulnerable person.

Learning safe and appropriate behaviour

Children learn in an atmosphere of respect and trust and one in which their concerns are taken seriously and not dismissed as 'silly'. Adult behaviour is crucial here, including behaving in line with what you say.

▶ Help children to make decisions and choices, even when it is not easy to weigh up the options. Look for everyday opportunities to offer children choices and to follow their wishes. Listen if they do not want to do something and understand why, even if on this occasion it has to happen.
▶ Children who are treated with respect, learn about boundaries to personal space and their rights over their own bodies, including a right to say, 'No'.
▶ You may talk about 'good' and 'bad' touches, what makes children uncomfortable, 'happy' sitting distances and 'private' areas of their body.
▶ From a very young age, children can learn about bodily respect. Good practice in their physical care as babies and toddlers shows that the carer respects them, not treating the baby like a bundle of mucky washing.
▶ Continued respectful physical care, with an appreciation of privacy is crucial for older children, including those with disabilities that mean they will need further help, perhaps always.
▶ Care over first aid, trips to the dentist and health needs are further opportunities to build children's confidence and bodily awareness. Any health

professional should talk with children, say what they are about to do and definitely not claim 'It doesn't hurt' when it clearly does.

▶ Children sometimes dislike attention that is not abusive but they find intrusive, such as Auntie who insists on kissing them full on the lips. Children's preferences should be respected (find another way for Auntie to greet the child), otherwise you build the belief that adults can impose.

▶ Look out for normal, everyday opportunities to let children learn the names for parts of their body. Give simple and honest answers to their questions about bodily functions or where babies come from.

▶ Respect children's wish for privacy, especially likely as they get older and help them to respect the privacy of others.

▶ Older children can follow the idea of 'good' and 'bad' secrets. 'Good' secrets, perhaps better called 'surprises', are enjoyable because they will give pleasure to someone else ('What we've bought Marsha for her birthday'). 'Bad' secrets make children feel uncomfortable or unhappy. They feel they should say something but an adult, or young person, is pressing them to remain silent against their wishes.

▶ Older children and young people also need the message that it is wise, and a sign of strength not weakness, to cease contact with someone whose behaviour is dubious. Older children sometimes feel that they can handle an adult or teenager whose actions have crossed the boundary toward sexual abuse, especially if that person appears mainly 'nice'. They may not realise that abusers, like paedophiles, will increase the pressure until it is very hard to get away from the situation and harder to tell.

GIVE REALISTIC AND ACCURATE MESSAGES

Responsible adults need to be thoughtful and realistic in any work on helping children to keep themselves safe. Your aim is to help children to develop a protective caution, without making them think that there is danger lurking behind every bush.

▶ Avoid the trap that strangers are the main source of danger to children. Any discussion or leaflet that focuses mainly on 'stranger danger' or not talking to strangers is likely to mislead children. Children are most at risk from adults with whom they are already acquainted – either well-known as family or friends or a recognisable local person. Children need to be alerted to adult behaviour and to be wary of adults, familiar or strangers, who behave in a way that makes the children uneasy or upset.

▶ Avoid talking as if distress or danger only comes from adults. Children need the confidence to speak up about another child or young person who is ill-treating them at home, in the local neighbourhood or within any group setting.

▶ Help children to realise that abusers, for instance paedophiles, look normal, 'just like anybody else'. They do not have dark overcoats and menacing expressions! Children and young people need to go by people's behaviour and whether this seems right, now or later on.

When children or young people go missing, the news media tends to focus on abduction by strangers, with the misleading discussion that 'nowhere is safe nowadays'. It needs to be said to adults, as well as to children, that murders of children are rare, although any death of a child is one too many, and abductions by complete strangers are even rarer. When children do not survive their childhood, it is far more likely that they have died from accidents, road or domestic, or the diseases that, despite medical advances, still sometimes kill children. To acknowledge these facts does not reduce the tragic nature of the families' loss in Soham or the parents of Sarah Payne. But there are serious consequences for children, when familiar adults try to build rules for everyday life on the basis of rare events.

All readers will have heard of the murder of Sarah Payne in summer 2000, but who knows the names of Daniella Hurst or of Keiran and Jade Austin? Yet, these children died within the same fortnight, murdered in each case by their own father. From June to November 2000, around fifty children in the UK died under circumstances which required special investigation. In most cases, where there was a basis for criminal prosecution, the violence had been perpetrated by people well known to the children, most often within their own family.

Of course children would not be supported by safety campaigns to make everyone afraid of their own fathers, or anyone else in their family. The vast majority of parents and practitioners will protect children. Some adults have put themselves in grave danger to keep the children safe. Most strangers who harm children are behind the wheel of a vehicle, and many of them have made strenuous efforts to avoid the child who ran out from between parked cars or who wobbled in front of them on a bicycle. The real dangers to child pedestrians and bike riders are met by steadily teaching children about road safety. The genuine dangers to children from people are best met by steadily coaching them in personal safety and life skills.

Children should never be left with the impression that they are totally responsible for protecting themselves. Adults carry the main responsibility: both in protecting children and in behaving in a safe and proper way. Children need to feel that they can make some decisions and keep themselves safe, but not that this ability is a burden. Some children have done their level best to protect themselves, have said 'No' to an abuser and tried to tell, yet have still experienced abuse. They should never be left with any sense that they failed; the failure and the responsibility rests with the abuser.

Safe behaviour on the internet

The development of the internet has raised a whole new area of personal safety for older children and young people who spend time in the chatrooms. Again the safe behaviour messages need to be given consistently from all adults involved with children and any guidance in school or out-of-school settings needs to be undertaken within communication and partnership with parents and other family carers. The main messages to get across to children and young people are:

▶ Be cautious about people you 'meet' within an internet chatroom. What people type in is not always the truth and often the fiction is about fun. But some adults enter chatrooms, where there will be children and young people, with the intention to trick and distress.
▶ Be wary about rude, unpleasant or suggestive messages. Do not respond at all, pull out of the exchange and let an adult know what has happened.
▶ Never pass on personal details such as your home address, telephone, name of your school or other setting, nor your picture. Check any exchange of information with a trusted adult before you send anything.
▶ Never arrange to meet someone you have met online unless you go to a public place and are accompanied by an adult like your parent.

High risk children and young people

Some children and young people can be especially vulnerable. Children of refugee and asylum-seeker families can need high levels of support and some may have witnessed extremely distressing events. Unaccompanied asylum-seeking children have automatic looked after status and are therefore the responsibility of the local authority.

Older children and young people who have experienced years of disruption and lack of care from adults can develop an outlook bordering on self harm. They may deliberately seek out dangerous situations and persist in making contact with other people whose aim is to abuse them. Practitioners who work in specialist daily settings, residential and foster carers can find themselves trying to protect children and young people from the consequences of their own behaviour. There are several key strands in how you work with these children and young people:

▶ As hard as it can be, persist in your attempts to boost their sense of self esteem, that they are people who are worth protecting and that key adults in their life care and worry about them.
▶ Look for all possible ways to replace the social contact, personal identity or excitement that is being fed through risky behaviour.
▶ Use the authority that you have to create boundaries for acceptable behaviour and address the problems that seem to fuel children or young people's tendency to put themselves at risk.

CHILDREN AND YOUNG PEOPLE WHO GO MISSING

Older children and young people can put themselves at risk by running away from the family home, foster or residential care. Projects that have looked at patterns for children and young people who run have identified different reasons for running. Some children are escaping as a result of distress and unsolved problems – sometimes an experience of abuse or bullying. Some children have not run out of choice but have effectively been thrown out by their family. Some children run for excitement and sometimes to reach a place or people with whom they feel happy. There is not a close relationship between level of risk and how far children run. A child or young person may stay in the immediate neighbourhood but go to the home of a known abuser. Children who run further afield may be safe with friends or acquaintances. Most runaways do not appear to go far and many return to their family or care home of their own accord.

Running away should always be noticed and not treated as something all teenagers do – many teenagers never run – nor allowed to become 'just an occupational hazard' in settings that care for vulnerable children. Truanting from school should also be taken seriously. Children and young people who truant are often becoming enmeshed in a social network that divides them ever more from their peers in school and raises the possibilities of further trouble.

It would be important for any family to consider why their child or young person felt compelled to run away. Residential settings, boarding schools as well as homes for looked-after children and young people, need to take a serious look at patterns of running. It is appropriate to treat runaways as a potential child protection issue, which may also raise problems about life in this group setting, and not exclusively as 'bad' behaviour from children. The police should immediately be involved in seeking a missing child or young person when they are on the child protection register.

▶ A positive approach to handling behaviour in a residential school or home unit can create a better atmosphere in which troubles do not escalate and children do not have to run in order to get attention or solve their problems.

▶ Good relations with other agencies, including the police, can build a response that acknowledges the seriousness of the situation, without being punitive and labelling runaways as deviant.

▶ Children or young people should ideally be collected or welcomed back if they return of their own accord. They should be encouraged to phone in, with the understanding that adults care about them, worry and need to know if they are delayed.

▶ On children's return, there needs to be a discussion about what has happened, although it will be a delicate balance between addressing the serious issues and avoidance of nagging or a row.

CHILDREN ABUSED THROUGH PROSTITUTION

Some older children and young people can be pulled into prostitution as a means to find an income as runaways. But teenagers do not have to run away to be at risk from an exploitative and sexually abusive relationship, perhaps where sexual favours are linked with the provision of drink, drugs or consumer goods. Some adults groom vulnerable young teenagers towards accepting being abused through prostitution, as part of an allegedly loving relationship with the pimp. Some children and young teenagers are prostituted by their own families.

Young people of 15 or 16 years can be cautioned and convicted as prostitutes. But, in recent years the police response has changed significantly towards seeing such young people as being at risk and in need of protection, not as deserving a punitive, criminal approach. Early intervention is crucial and good practice is supported by being alert to the difficulties that young people can face in trying to make a change in their life. Supportive adults need to recognise that children and young people abused through prostitution often have rock bottom self esteem, are frightened of violence from their abusers and may also have problems of drug dependency.

Security to protect children and adults

Balancing access and security

Any early years team needs to be highly aware of young children's safety, that they cannot walk or crawl off the premises and nobody realises. Group settings for older children need to be sufficiently secure that children cannot simply leave, or be removed, without an adult realising very swiftly.

In the second half of the 1990s, several frightening, and sometimes tragic, incidents also raised awareness that some mentally disturbed individuals may target settings with children. Nurseries, pre-schools or primary schools cannot turn themselves into fortresses and it is important to realise that incidents such as the murders at Dunblane primary school are very rare. The realistic, everyday balance that has to be found is between access and sufficient security.

You want to welcome parents and children into the building, yet avoid making it easy for people, who have no business in your setting, simply to wander in.

▶ Explain how you handle security to parents when they first come with their child. Communicate clearly to adults that security is a shared responsibility and bring older children into that understanding, without making them scared.
▶ You need appropriate front and back door security and for any yard or garden gates. Stress to parents that care over latching gates and closing doors properly is for the safety of their young children.
▶ Larger settings such as schools have to address whether there are times of the day when only one entrance is accessible, so that arrivals and leaving can be monitored. Visitors will need to sign in and be given identity badges.
▶ Early years settings need to manage the personal aspects of transition times, because children must pass explicitly from the responsibility of a parent to the practitioner and then the reverse. Older children and teenagers will increasingly manage their movements independently.
▶ At busy times of the day or session, you may need a system in which somebody is always by the door – to greet parents and children, or to say goodbye and courteously to check unknown visitors at these times.
▶ At times of the day when there is less coming and going, the door may be locked and either someone goes to answer a knock or bell, or an entry phone system is in operation.
▶ Any door handles should be out of the reach of younger children. If you work with older children, for instance in an after-school club, then it is time to

teach them about safe behaviour at the door: checking who is there, fetching a practitioner and not simply opening the door to anyone.

Close circuit television (CCTV)

CCTV is now prominent in many of our buildings and urban streets. Some group settings like nurseries and schools also consider whether to install CCTV to address the additional protection of children. CCTV is not an inevitable step for protection and the system does not replace attentive adults with eyes and ears fully alert. CCTV might be a serious consideration if your setting is in a neighbourhood where it is not unusual for strange adults, perhaps the worse for drink or mentally unstable, to wander into buildings. Alternatively you may be in an area with a high burglary rate and the setting and its equipment need to be protected.

The choices in CCTV are basically between a high profile, visually obvious system or a more covert arrangement in which cameras are hidden in normal equipment such as junction boxes or clocks. The overt system can be effective in deterring intruders, or thieves, but can be put out of action fairly easily, for instance by spraying the lenses of the camera, because the equipment is obvious. If your setting needs some form of CCTV, then you should get professional advice about the different systems, check your budget and make sure that any system could easily be upgraded or extended if necessary.

The CCTV cameras for security are likely to be positioned close to the entrances to your buildings and not in all the group rooms. There has been discussion in the press about wealthy families installing CCTV in ordinary homes to monitor their nanny and it has been suggested that such a system could deter potential abuse by staff in early years settings. CCTV is not an effective way to deal with child protection issues and using such a system raises other problems:

▶ Cameras in every room do not offer a guaranteed way of catching abusive staff. The few practitioners who wish to abuse children will avoid the cameras or take children out of the setting to abuse them.
▶ A CCTV system would most likely create an atmosphere of distrust and lack of co-operation from a staff team. The sense of being spied upon is insulting to the majority of staff who aim for good practice.
▶ Cameras in bathrooms and toilets would be a serious breach of privacy for adults or children.

Centre managers and senior practitioners should be sufficiently visible and present in all parts of the setting that they hear or see poor practice. They certainly should not be depending on CCTV. Good practice should be established and maintained in any setting in the ways discussed in this and other chapters of the book.

A few early years settings have also established CCTV that is linked to the nursery website on the internet. These systems are marketed to nurseries as a way to reassure parents that their children are safe. Parents also have a password that enables them, or other relatives, to log onto the website and watch their children. The argument is that parents are able to join in their child's day whilst at their own place of work. But this kind of argument is seriously flawed.

▶ Parents are not spending time with their children or being a genuine part of the child's day; they are watching a screen. It is far better for the parent, child and the staff team to have parents create the time to be physically present and experience some of their child's day.

▶ There is nothing in the system to ensure that parents or other relatives only watch their own children, nor that they do not talk about what they see of another child's frustrations or difficulties.

▶ The cameras and access on the website are an infringement of all the children's rights. Just because they are young, children should not be recorded and watched without their informed consent.

▶ Nurseries have been reassured that paedophiles could not hack into the system and watch children for abusive purposes. Unfortunately, this is an empty and misleading promise. Years of computer systems, passwords and other elaborate protection methods have shown that someone with the computer skills and motivation can hack into any system.

Some nurseries, schools and after-school settings have developed their own website. But the best ones do not try to offer some kind of 'you can have it all' to working parents who share the care of their child. If you develop a website, you need very clear guidelines about what material is put on the site and in what ways images of children appear, if at all.

Final thoughts

The ideas in this chapter are part of good practice with all babies and children. They form a framework for respectful behaviour towards children and are important regardless of whether your setting ever has to deal with a child protection case. Friendly and open communication, a positive approach to children's behaviour or helping children learn to keep themselves safe are all significant parts of the work of a early years, school or out-of-school setting. Such approaches will not, unfortunately, guarantee that children in your care are never abused. There is no certain method for total child protection. Yet good practice will increase the chances for children to speak up rather than keep silent and turn to a trusted adult to help them deal with and recover from the experience.

Scenarios

These scenarios raise issues that are not all focussed on individual children or young people. Use the information in each scenario to explore ideas yourself or through a discussion with colleagues or fellow students. You could consider the following questions:

1 What are the main issues raised in this scenario?
2 How might some of the problems or dilemmas have arisen? Some difficulties can have developed from good intentions that have gone awry.
3 What needs to be done or said now and by whom?

You will find a commentary on the scenarios from page 234.

Meadowbank Nursery

A division has developed between staff in a large nursery over approaches to the physical care of babies and toddlers. Two practitioners feel that very young children should be given time and attention for their personal care routines. The other two practitioners who work with the youngest children argue that everyone is supposed to focus on educational activities and that changing and feeding time is 'just care'. A situation has now developed where toddlers vote with their feet and go to the more caring practitioners to be changed and if they want any personal attention. Their colleagues now say that the children are spoiled and should not be able to exercise this kind of choice.

Happy Days Nursery

This private nursery and others within the same chain have promoted access to the nursery website as a way for parents to join in their child's day. The baby room team in Happy Days have reached an uncomfortable position now with one mother who uses the viewing facility a considerable amount. She then phones from her office to direct her toddler's day: that his nap is being allowed to continue for too long or that he is not being given enough attention compared with the other toddlers. Today she has started to comment on the behaviour of other children in the room.

Pike Lane Pre-school

Students on placement at Pike Lane have reported back to their tutor their distress over how the children are treated. Three- and four-year-olds are run through a very structured session in which they have little or no choice about activities and are expected to sit still for a long time. Children who fidget or who try to move across to the 'wrong' activity are told off at length and threatened with losing their short time out in the garden. The students report that children who have toileting accidents are told they are 'dirty' and 'stupid'. The end of session group called circle time is run mainly as a way to highlight which children have failed to behave well today. The students tried to raise their concerns with the pre-school leader and were told firmly that the parents wanted this kind of strong regime, on the educational and discipline front, and so the pre-school was meeting the demands of partnership.

Longmead Primary School

Staff and parents are keen for the children to learn to swim and groups are walked to the nearby leisure centre. Several children say that they do not like the swimming coach, that he is 'horrid' and 'shouts all the time'. There is an incident in which two parents, who are helping with the group, get into an argument with the coach about his insistence that tired children continue to swim widths without stopping. Their concerns are raised in a meeting but the head takes the view that, although the coach can appear sharp and rather impatient, he is successful in getting children to swim. Plans are raised that the eldest children form a swimming team for a gala and that the coach will give them extra tuition. Parents start to say that their children do not want to have extra lessons from this swimming coach.

Breakstone Secondary School

This year the school introduced a new behaviour policy with the strong message that bullying would not be tolerated. Soon after the introduction of the policy, Kelly accused two of her thirteen year old peers of a campaign of verbal bullying against her. The other two girls, who were close friends, agreed they had had a couple of fierce arguments with Kelly, but denied all the accusations of harassment. Kelly's version was believed, the two girls were given written warnings about their behaviour and their timetable was changed so that they were no longer together in class.

A month later Kelly accused one teacher of shoving her against the door. There were witnesses to the alleged assault, Kelly's version was disproved and she had to apologise to the teacher. In the discussion that followed it became clear that Kelly's home circumstances were very disrupted and she seemed desperate for attention for herself. Within the same conversation, she admitted that she had fabricated the allegations against her peers. Kelly was offered support within the school pastoral system, but no further steps were taken about the experience of the two girls she had falsely accused of bullying.

Appendix 1

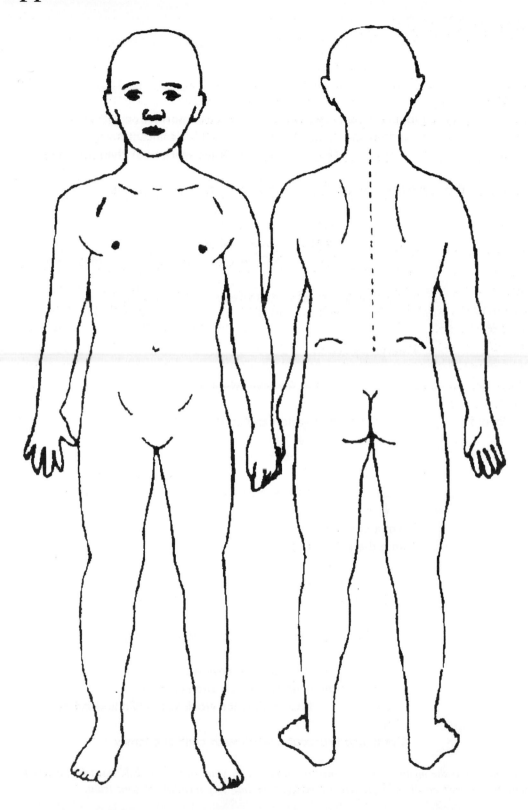

Appendix 2:

Steps in the process of child protection

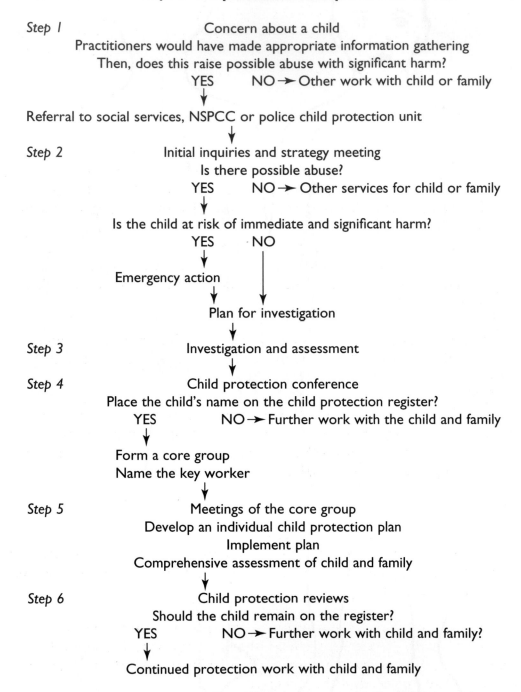

Step 1   Concern about a child

Practitioners would have made appropriate information gathering

Then, does this raise possible abuse with significant harm?

YES   NO → Other work with child or family

Referral to social services, NSPCC or police child protection unit

Step 2   Initial inquiries and strategy meeting

Is there possible abuse?

YES   NO → Other services for child or family

Is the child at risk of immediate and significant harm?

YES   ·NO

Emergency action

Plan for investigation

Step 3   Investigation and assessment

Step 4   Child protection conference

Place the child's name on the child protection register?

YES   NO → Further work with the child and family

Form a core group
Name the key worker

Step 5   Meetings of the core group

Develop an individual child protection plan

Implement plan

Comprehensive assessment of child and family

Step 6   Child protection reviews

Should the child remain on the register?

YES   NO → Further work with child and family?

Continued protection work with child and family

Please note that the organisation that inspects child care in your part of the UK must be informed about any allegations or child protection investigations into any members of your team.

Appendix 3: Commentary on the scenarios

In this section you will find some comments on each of the scenarios given within the book. There is not a set of right answers; these are some key points that need to be raised. You may have explored other important issues not mentioned here. Comments about taking steps within child protection refer to responsibilities described on pages 49 and 69.

Chapter 1

CLEMENT

Young children who have had a caring but restricted early experience can develop quite quickly when their horizons are stretched, but this change cannot be assumed. It is important to monitor Clement and ensure that his development progresses well.

Clement's mother and grandmother sound caring yet seriously anxious. Family support could be a great help to guide them in more positive child care and play for Clement.

Supportive conversations may help determine whether there are genuine dangers within the family home or the local neighbourhood, and what needs to be done.

Staff need to welcome Clement's grandmother but cannot agree to serious restrictions on his movement indoors or out in the garden. A positive approach on partnership means that the staff are careful to explain and show how they keep young children safe.

HEATHER

Heather's conversation and pattern of play are not usual for a four year old girl. The nursery staff should be concerned, although this raises the sensitive issue of what is legitimate concern for professionals and what should remain private family business.

The new member of staff needs to raise her concerns with the head of centre, since her colleague does not seem to take this incident seriously enough. Being the new practitioner can feel awkward, but the pattern of Heather's behaviour needs to be discussed.

Heather's mother may be behaving in an irresponsible way, so that her daughter is inappropriately aware of adult sexual activity. The child also seems to be poorly supervised at home, if her comments about the film are accurate.

Heather may be imitating what she has seen and is not abused herself through direct contact. But it is regarded as abusive to allow children to watch sexual activity, or for adults to behave so that they are highly likely to be observed.

The head of centre or Heather's key worker needs to talk with the mother in a private conversation. Heather's behaviour needs to be described in terms of concern about what she has been seen to recycle in play and certainly not that she is a 'naughty' or 'silly' girl.

Much would then depend on the reaction of Heather's mother and monitoring the child's play and conversation over the following weeks. If her mother recognises that she has been irresponsible and potentially neglectful, then there may be changes for the better. If the situation does not improve, then the centre needs to take advice within a child protection context.

Danny

The information about Danny raises the real possibility that he is neglected and possibly physically abused, by his mother or older siblings.

His older siblings do not cause concern but, in some families, one child is singled out for neglect or abuse.

The nursery class team and the head need to keep descriptive records of Danny's condition each day and be clear with Mrs Sanders that their concerns are very serious and could well be taken further.

The school will need to find out, if they do not already know, whether Danny's father is around and his involvement, and if the family has a social worker. There are five boys in the family but only four in this school. Is the fifth son in another school or has he been taken into care?

Unless there is a significant improvement, the school should consult with the child protection team.

JANICE

The pre-school team are right to be concerned about the changes in Janice's behaviour, since she sounds like a very unhappy child.

The family sounds under heavy stress and Janice's mother is scarcely coping with all the problems. Mrs Matthews' explanation about the constipation is feasible and she is open, and distressed, about having hit Janice.

If this pattern of behaviour is consistent, the pre-school team could feel confident to monitor and support Janice and advise Mrs Matthews on how to contact local sources of family support to relieve the pressures.

CAMERON

It seems likely that something has happened to confuse and distress Cameron. It is tempting to consider his mother's new boyfriend as the source of risk. But Cameron has also recently spent three weeks with some friends of his mother.

Cameron's mother seems unable to consider his emotional needs. So it is possible that he might not confide in her about an abusive experience or might be dismissed if he has spoken.

The school needs to tackle the issues with Cameron's mother. One issue arises from his refusal to go home with the boyfriend and this strong reaction needs to be addressed with Cameron's needs to the forefront.

His comments about people holding his 'willy' need some exploration, if Cameron is comfortable to talk, perhaps with the male teacher. Another possibility would be to ensure that Cameron's class soon has a general session on appropriate touch, raising issues that concern Cameron, but in a way that does not put the spotlight on him.

The school needs to keep descriptive notes of Cameron's words and actions and of conversations with his mother that attempt to explore the situation. Without reasonable reassurance from such conversations, the concerns about Cameron may have to be taken further.

SAJIDA

The after-school club team needs to liase now with Sajida's parents and the school.

It is important of course not to leap to conclusions. Perhaps Amy did 'bang' Sajida, but it was in the course of trying to catch her. However, the child seems to have more accidents at school and home than in the club. This difference between settings raises concerns that Sajida is either poorly supervised elsewhere, or is being directly hurt by somebody.

Sajida has spoken language, but she may need help through signs and images to communicate the details of her accidents.

It is important that nobody comes to a premature conclusion that Amy or Sajida's family have hurt her. But equally, it is time to challenge the simple explanation that Sajida's clumsiness explains a series of accidents.

Abbas

It is appropriate that the school team resist making judgements about Abbas and his family. Ten-year-olds can be very competent and in many cultures older children take safe responsibility for younger siblings.

The staff may feel regret for Abbas that he cannot have an independent social life, but that would not be a basis for intervention.

It would be appropriate to talk with Abbas' parents about the arrangements for Nneka when her brother goes to secondary school. Perhaps there could be a friendly offer to link Nneka up with another family who walk in from the same direction.

The children appear well and healthy. So staff would need some further basis for speaking to the parents about leaving them alone in the evening, if that in fact does happen. There may be other people in the home.

Selena

The teenagers, not only Selena, need to know that an adult is taking the situation seriously. Some of the alleged problems occur in school, so it is appropriate and necessary to explore the claims and address the behaviour.

If Selena's account is accurate, her class teacher was very unhelpful. Such lack of respect for young people's concerns undermines any policy about bullying and the principle of telling. The teacher's behaviour needs to be addressed within the team.

There needs to be some exploration of Ian's alleged behaviour, and whether he has now done the text messaging. Some fifteen-year-olds lack social skills, but his actions have gone beyond awkwardness. Ian seems not to understand 'Stop it' and that he has distressed and scared Selena.

The next steps depend on to what extent Ian responds to clear direction from the adults about acceptable and unacceptable behaviour.

It is likely that Ian's parent(s) should be informed, especially if there is any written agreement about his behaviour from now on. Ian and his family need to understand that, assuming Selena's allegations are all true, then the young man's behaviour could become a police matter if he continues to harass any young woman in this way.

Chapter 3

NATASHA

There is cause for concern about Natasha since the care arrangements seem to be unpredictable and potentially unsafe. All carers within her family need to understand that nursery hours are not elastic and that children must be handed safely to a member of staff.

The information from the nursery handyman raises further concerns. The nursery needs to gain some idea of the reliability of this information before raising anything with Natasha's mother. The lack of supervision, if true, is outside nursery time, but the staff can have the same concern that a neighbour might feel. If Natasha's mother is unresponsive, the nursery could look for a low-key conversation with the local health visitor or social work team.

It is appropriate that the handyman should share information relevant to the children in nursery, but it is inappropriate for him to talk dismissively about 'these people'. Some discussion needs to follow about respect and boundaries.

AARON

The behaviour of this practitioner is unacceptable and needs to be challenged promptly within supervision with a senior member of staff.

If the practitioner feels uncomfortable about Aaron's disability, it is her task to deal with her feelings, not to show distaste and certainly not be offensive in his hearing and to a parent.

A senior practitioner needs to be sure that this person understands why her reaction is emotionally cruel and her comments to the parent are unprofessional. There need to be a clear commitment that she will change her behaviour towards Aaron and in similar circumstances in the future.

ANN-MARIE

Partnership with parents does not mean that settings should agree to or accept any action from parents, however deeply they hold beliefs.

The nursery needs to keep records of what has happened and the reactions of Ann-Marie's parents. The team will be aware that UK law still allows 'reasonable chastisement' of children by their parents. But it is not the nursery's task to try to work out if such an excuse would apply here.

There needs to be a proper meeting with Ann-Marie's parents to express the serious concerns of the nursery and listen to what the parents have to say. Unless concerns are put to rest, it is likely that the nursery will have to take further steps in terms of child protection.

GREG

This student's behaviour is unacceptable and needs to be challenged. She appears to have taken a dislike to Greg and her behaviour is emotionally abusive and offensive. Additionally she seems not to understand good practice about developmental records or the importance of a social mealtime.

It can feel uncomfortable for a practitioner to appear to be reporting on a colleague. But all group settings need an atmosphere in which team members can express concerns to a senior practitioner.

In this case a senior practitioner needs to deal directly with the poor practice and communicate with the student's tutor.

MONICA

It is respectful that practitioners follow the family diet for children in their care. However, partnership with parents has boundaries set by your responsibility for children's well being.

There are health risks when a diet removes many sources of nutrition and young children have different nutritional needs from adults. Babies and toddlers have become very ill and died from extremely restricted diets.

It would be appropriate to attempt another conversation with the mother. But if there is no progress, then it would be necessary to make contact with another professional, most likely the health visitor who is responsible for the baby.

If the mother acts on her threat to find another childminder, it would be appropriate to ensure that the local childminding advisor knows the details of the situation. It is important that this family does not get 'lost'.

KAYLEIGH

It is right to be concerned about Kayleigh and to consider what may happen if nothing is said. Adults can be genuinely concerned about the well being of young people for whom they do not have direct responsibility.

A possibility is to have a quiet word with Kayleigh at the next weekend. Explain what you have seen and your concerns and give her the choice to talk with her father this weekend. Otherwise you will speak with him. It would not be appropriate to keep secrets with Kayleigh about truanting.

CIARAN

Good practice in child protection for any setting needs to show respect for children's choices. All team members should be enabled to deal with possible disclosures so that a child is not 'passed on' from the person to whom they have chosen to speak. It is appropriate that the adult explains to a child or young person when and why the information has to be shared with somebody else.

The teacher with responsibility for child protection needs to deal with the head's demand, explaining how she and you will work together. There needs to be consideration about contact with the parents.

From Ciaran's comments there is concern that he and his sister could be at risk and that steps need to be taken within child protection. But it could be very distressing for Ciaran if the one person in whom he has confided is made inaccessible.

Chapter 4

SERGIO

This kind of behaviour is not usual for a four-year-old and should not simply be dismissed. The team has coped by reducing Sergio's opportunities for inappropriate behaviour, but have not challenged his actions. The team has also generated a spurious cultural explanation that needs challenge.

Without further information, it is not possible to know how Sergio has learned it is acceptable to impose on women in this way. He may have observed inappropriate touching or heard adult conversations that are dismissive of women.

There needs to be firm boundaries set for Sergio's behaviour, with an explanation suitable for a four-year-old. The team needs to monitor that his behaviour does change.

There also needs to be a conversation with his parents about the behaviour, the legitimate concerns that it raises and how the setting is now dealing with Sergio's actions. There will need to be written notes on the meeting and any further action would depend on the parent's reactions.

SALLY

It is good practice to listen to this mother's concerns and ensure that you understand what she is saying, including a bit more detail on what Sally says in her play with dolls.

However, it would not be appropriate at this point either to agree or disagree with the claims, nor to the mother's request. You should thank her for telling you her concerns and that you will talk with your head.

There needs to be an internal discussion about the dynamics of the group room run by Richard and Jessica. Much will depend on whether there have already been concerns about Jessica's style with the children. It will be important to hear Richard's view before he leaves.

It is important that you, or your head, gets back to Sally's mother within no more than a few days. If there is an issue of poor practice, then this problem will not be resolved by moving one child. If you feel reassured that Sally's comments are not imitated from Jessica, then there may be reason to have a further conversation to help her mother consider the possible source.

RORY

Rory's parents are fully responsible for him when he is at home and they have to balance their home and work commitments in a way that keep their son safe and happy. So, it is not for the nursery to be apologetic about their hours.

Rory's mother needs to know that the nursery is responsible for tracking injuries to the children. It is also fair for Rory's key worker to say that toddlers need careful watching and to put the perspective of a young child's needs to be engaged in safe activities.

It may be possible to have a friendly conversation about work-life balance. The family may need a different kind of childcare, probably a live-in nanny, if their work commitments continue at this high level.

If Rory continues to have many accidents at home, it may be necessary to involve the health visitor as a next step.

Owen

It is usual that some parents have baths or showers with their young children. This pattern may seem odd to anyone whose family style was less intimate in this way.

Owen seems perfectly happy and there is nothing in what he says that raises concerns.

Your colleague's reaction does need some exploration in a confidential way. It is possible that her family was more reticent about bathing. But her words and the shudder raise the possibility that she experienced inappropriate or abusive attention around bathing routines as a child.

Yvette

You may disapprove of Yvette's style of dress. But that is not club business unless her clothes are unsafe for play, in which case a conversation with her mother could be about practical play clothes and shoes.

Yvette's comments about Martin would probably not be concerning without the incident with your male colleague. It is important not to link the two strands together by any assumptions about Martin.

A conversation with Yvette's mother could raise in a friendly way that her daughter seems enthused about Martin and imply a question about his place in the family.

It would be wise to be alert to Yvette and notice if her behaviour suggests an inappropriate intimacy with male practitioners or boys in the club. If the same kind of incident is repeated, then the club team will need to consider a further conversation with her mother.

The club team may need to develop clear boundaries that children are welcome to be close, to sit next to practitioners but not on their laps.

WINSTON

Some parents have resorted in desperation to alcohol to deal with night waking children. It is not a safe option, since young children can easily be made ill by alcohol. It is additionally against the law, since they are younger than the legal drinking age.

Winston's mother needs advice for coping with the sleep disruption and empathy for this very tiring period. The nursery may be able to give some suggestions. Alternatively the local clinic and health visitor should offer constructive support on this very common problem with toddlers.

So long as Winston's mother stops using the sherry, then the incident need go no further than support and advice.

OLWYN

It is risky and inappropriate to assume that any out of the ordinary behaviour can be explained away by disability.

Olwyn's behaviour has changed over masturbation and the incident in the toilets raises concerns. You will have talked with Olwyn to try to get an idea of what happened and the next step depends a great deal on what she says. If the boys have been involved in inappropriate activity, then there needs to be a firm conversation with them.

You need to talk with Olwyn's mother about her tendency to masturbate, how you are dealing with this behaviour and some sense of whether the same pattern is occurring at home. You also need to explain the toilets incident and what you have said to Olwyn, even if the details are unclear.

You need to work to get more specific about what feels wrong about the new driver. This unease and your other concerns need to be raised fully in a supervision conversation with someone else in the school: the class teacher, or the teacher with child protection responsibility.

JEROME

The conversation with Jerome raises serious concerns about him and his siblings. They seem to have been lost in the social work focus on his mother.

You can empathise with Jerome's fears but cannot keep quiet for this reason. If you speak with staff member responsible for child protection, he or she should make contact with the family's social worker.

It is not inevitable that the family will be split up but some level of family support is probably needed and it sounds as if the social worker needs to take a whole family view.

It will help Jerome if the school can be flexible on his deadlines and offer as much support as possible for homework.

Chapter 5

THE SCENARIO ON PAGE 166

The situation with the bad practice shown by the supply teacher has been generally well handled.

The children have been reassured and given a clear message about adults' responsibilities to behave properly. They have also experienced that their teacher and head genuinely wanted to hear from them what has happened.

It would have been better for the head teacher to write to the parents of the children in the class. At least some of them will have talked about what happened and the story will travel the local grapevine very fast. Parents should not have to tackle the class teacher or head to find out what occurred, nor should they have to depend on information from their children over such a serious incident.

The head and class teacher would also need to check to what extent other staff had been aware that something was going very wrong in this class. Two days is not long, but it would be too long for staff to assume that serious noise levels were a matter for the supply teacher concerned.

KITTY

Any conversation with Kitty needs to be gentle and avoid leading questions. You could reflect back her comment with a question in your tone or add something like, 'No more Grandad? Is that a good thing, Kitty?' When Kitty scribbles over a figure, you could ask a non-specific question such as, 'Tell me what you've done to your drawing?'

It is important not to assume that all of Kitty's play is related to the alleged abuse and to support her as you would any four-year-old.

It will be appropriate to keep notes of Kitty's progress and careful descriptions of play and conversation. Much of this observation could be shared carefully with her mother.

MARSHA

It would be right to intervene in the play, following the lead of the other child. Marsha could be helped to comfort the baby appropriately and you could make non-critical comments about how careful everyone has to be with babies.

The setting should already be keeping notes since a child protection enquiry is underway. Everyone has to take care not to over-interpret children's play and conversations. But this incident has the look and sound of a child imitating what she has observed.

JOAN

There needs to be a conversation about Joan with the children and observation of their play is a natural opener today.

The group needs to be reassured that Joan's behaviour was wrong and that she will not be allowed back. It may feel right to apologise to the children that nobody has had a 'proper chat' with them about what happened.

Depending on the details and timing of the incidents, it may be that children need a chance to talk about the events. Alternatively, they may deal with their feelings effectively through the play.

Within reason, the children should be allowed to play out their distressing experience. They will then probably move on to other themes. If this shift takes time, then practitioners could look for ways to intervene that could redirect the play, without insisting that the play theme stop altogether.

FAZILA

It should be possible to join in Fazila's play through imagining, 'what can we do?' to make matters better for the doll. If Fazila makes the direct link to her own situation, then you can follow her lead.

Depending on your relationship with Fazila's mother, it may be possible to share this play as a way to highlight her daughter's feelings.

If friendly pressure on Fazila's mother does not seem to work, it may be necessary to speak with the local health visitor.

HELENA

Disabled children can behave in ways that hurt or distress other children, as well as being secretive about their behaviour. A sentimental approach does not help children, nor does a reluctance to address their behaviour out of pity.

It is right to be careful over over-reaction, but observation over the days should give you a firm basis for a conversation with Helena's childminder. You definitely do not want to label the child as a 'bully', but her behaviour may need clear guidance.

SAMMY

The adults need to intervene in a game that has unacceptable elements of pressure and possibly touch. A first step would be to tell children that 'Stop it!' means precisely that and a game is no longer playful if anyone is hurt or distressed.

It is also appropriate to explore with the girls in question. You could ask, 'I was concerned about what was going on by the fence. What exactly happened?' The girls may need to be reassured that they were not responsible for the chasing game going too far.

Depending on what emerges, there may be a need for a whole group discussion about appropriate touch, listening to 'No' and play without pressures.

If Sammy's behaviour has been inappropriate, then a private conversation with him may be necessary. Depending on the seriousness of what has emerged, his parents may also need to be informed.

ANSEL

Practitioners are sometimes taken aback at what children choose to share within a successful and supportive circle time.

It would be appropriate to follow Ansel's comment with something like, 'We all hope it works out well, Ansel.'

Under the circumstances, it seems unwise to approach Ansel's mother and it would not be usual to report back to parents every item their child shared in circle time.

If his mother raises the incident, you could say, 'The children share events of importance and your visit to the clinic is very important for Ansel. But I stop children if they go into detail about family matters.'

KIMBERLEY

You need to tell Kimberley how pleased you are that she has spoken and confirm that she should not be her friend's support.

Kimberley needs to be encouraged to talk with her parents about the situation, with your help if she wants. Her family can then contact the family of the friend who is putting herself at risk.

Chapter 6

MEADOWBANK NURSERY

Good practice with very young children is shown by attention to their personal care and giving time. There is no 'just' about care or personal care routines and young children's learning can only be supported in an emotionally warm atmosphere.

The current situation needs to be resolved on a team basis and with proper leadership from the head of centre. Some discussion might work within a staff meeting but some more detailed in-house training about good practice might be necessary.

Further problems arise if the more caring practitioners do not get support from the head of centre. A possibility is to talk with a local advisor in a diplomatic way, but raising the real concerns.

HAPPY DAYS NURSERY

Partnership with parents means a close liaison over baby and child care. Staff should make efforts to ensure continuity between home and nursery, especially for the care routines. However, parents need to trust the staff in this shared care arrangement and directing operations through the nursery webcam facility is not acceptable.

The key worker, with the head of centre if necessary, needs to talk with the mother about boundaries and trust. A warm welcome can be given for her to spend real time with her child in the nursery or pick him up early on some days.

The nursery may also need to rethink the webcam facility as regards the privacy of all the children.

PIKE LANE PRE-SCHOOL

The students need to be reassured that their concerns are valid; they have observed bad practice and they were right to challenge what they observed.

Their tutor needs to contact the pre-school leader and meet to discuss the concerns. If the students' account is correct, there are serious concerns about practice in this setting. The team has lost sight of the balance between children and partnership with parents. The group is not a suitable work placement for students.

If the tutor meets with the same reaction as the students, then the matter will need to be taken further, most likely through the local advisory team for early years groups.

LONGMEAD PRIMARY SCHOOL

The head should take more seriously the consistent feedback from the children. It is a very negative message to children that their emotional distress about the swimming coach is effectively dismissed. Even if the coach proves to be no more than bad-tempered and insensitive, the children should be supported by the head tackling this bad practice.

The parents' concerns have also been dismissed – a poor approach to partnership. If the head insists on the extra coaching, it is likely that some parents will withdraw their children, out of appropriate concern, and the whole situation will sour school-home relations in a much broader way.

BREAKSTONE SECONDARY SCHOOL

The school team needs to understand much better how an effective behaviour and bullying policy should work in practice.

The first incident with Kelly was poorly handled and it seems likely that a more thorough exploration would have at least queried Kelly's version.

After the second incident with the teacher, the two accused girls will now feel even more badly treated. Young people have a strong sense of justice and these girls deserved a full apology from the staff, let alone from Kelly.

The school team need to appreciate that such mishandling will shape the attitudes of the students as a whole, not only the girls who were unjustly punished. A policy to combat bullying will not work if adults fail to listen or behave like 'bullies' in their turn.

Appendix 4: Further reading

This book has covered a wide range of topics related to child protection and all aspects of the safety of children and young people. This section provides suggestions for resources that you can select in order to find more information and advice. The resources are grouped under two broad headings: resources specifically about child protection and those about good practice with children that supports their development and well-being. I have given website addresses where useful material can be downloaded.

Protection and well-being of children and young people

Arnold, Johann Christoph (2000) *Endangered children: your child in a hostile world* The Plough Publishing House of the Bruderhof Foundation, available from Community Playthings Tel 0800 387 457

Bibby, Andrew and Becker, Saul (2000) *Young carers in their own words* Calouste Gulbenkian Foundation Turnaround Publisher Services Tel: 020 8829 3000

Biehal, Nina and Wade, Jim (2002) *Children who go missing: research, policy and practice* download from www.doh.gov.uk/qualityprotects

Cowley, Liz and Crouch, Maureen (1997) *Managing to change: training materials for staff in centres for young children. Module 5 – Child Protection* National Children's Bureau

Department of Health (1995) *Child protection – messages from research* Studies in Child Protection HMSO

Department of Health (1998) *Caring for children away from home: messages from research* Wiley

Department of Health (2002) *Safeguarding children involved in prostitution* on www.doh.gov.uk/scg/qualitycp.htm

Department of Health, Social Services and Public Safety (2002) *Safer organisations: safer children* can be downloaded from www.dhsspsni.gov.uk

Dorkenoo, Efua (1995) *Cutting the rose: female genital mutilation the practice and its prevention* Minority Rights Publication

Frank, Jenny (1995) *Couldn't care more: a study of young carers and their needs* The Children's Society

Elliott, Michele (1993) *Female sexual abuse of children: the ultimate taboo* Wiley

Gulbenkian Foundation (1995) *Report of the Commission on Children and Violence.* The full report or a summary, *Children and Violence*, are available from Calouste Gulbenkian Foundation, 98 Portland Place, London W1N 4ET

Hewlett, Sylvia Ann (1993) *Child neglect in rich nations* UNICEF

Horwath, Jan and Lawson, Brian (eds) (1996) *Trust betrayed: Munchausen Syndrome by proxy, inter-agency child protection and partnership with families* National Children's Bureau

La Fontaine, J. (1994) *The extent and nature of organised and ritual sexual abuse: research findings.* HMSO.

Lau, Annie, *Cultural perspectives and significant harm: its assessment and treatment* in Adcock, Margaret, White, Richard and Hollows, Anne (1991) *Significant harm: its management and outcome* Significant Publications

National Children's Bureau Highlights – a series of two page briefing papers on many issues affecting children and young people, not exclusively child protection. Contact the NCB Library and Information Service Tel: 020 7843 6008, or look on the website, for a recent listing and costs. The most relevant Highlights include:

No 119 (1993) *Child sexual abuse*

No 139 (1995) *Children and domestic violence*

No 143 (1996) *Children with disabilities and child protection*

No 159 (1998) *Child abuse and child protection in residential care*

No 164 (1998) *Young runaways*

No 166 (1999) *Physical punishment of children in the home*

No 169 (1999) *Family group conferences*

No 190 (2002) *Unaccompanied asylum–seeking children*

No 194 (2002) *Young people abused through prostitution*

NCH *Look beyond the scars: understanding and responding to self-harm* summary and full report, also a leaflet *Self-harm or self-injury: your questions answered*, available on the website www.nch.org.uk/selfharm/

NSPCC Information Briefings will be useful if you want to read further and access a summary of research. The list of briefings includes:

Adult sex offenders

Child neglect

Child protection and education

Children and young people who display harmful sexual behaviour

Disabled children and abuse

Emotional abuse

The links between child abuse and animal abuse

Mentally ill parents and children's welfare

Peer support

Physical abuse

See the contact details on page 244 or download from the section on publications for professionals on the website www.nspcc.org.uk

NSPCC (1995) *The abuse of children in day care settings: conference report of June 1994* NSPCC National Training Centre

NCH Children and Families Project (2001) *Creating a safe place: helping children and families recover from child sexual abuse* Jessica Kingsley

Professional Association of Teachers (1998) *Avoiding allegations of child abuse* Factsheet available from PAT 2 St James' Court, Friar Gate, Derby DE1 1BT Tel: 01332 372337

Scottish Executive (2002) *It's everyone's job to make sure I'm alright: literature review* and (2002) *Vulnerable children: young runaways and children abused through prostitution* from the Stationery Office Bookshop, 71 Lothian Road, Edinburgh EH3 9AZ Tel: 0870 606 5566 or download from the publications section of www.scotland.gov.uk

Sinclair, Ruth and Bullock, Roger (2002) *Learning from past experience: a review of serious case reviews* Department of Health

Tate, Tim (1990) *Child pornography: an investigation* Methuen

Support for children, young people and practitioners

These suggestions cover good practice to support:

▶ Children's emotional well-being, development and general safety
▶ A positive approach to behaviour
▶ Keeping children and young people safe and supporting them as they learn personal safety and skills
▶ Working well with other adults

Adlerian Workshops and Publications – booklets on positive strategies with children and the use of encouragement. 216 Tring Road, Aylesbury, Bucks HP20 1JS Tel: 01296 482148 www.adlerian.com

Anti Bullying Network has a range of leaflets that you can download from their website www.antibullying.net or contact at Moray House Institute of Education, University of Edinburgh, Holyrood Road, Edinburgh EH8 8AQ Tel: 0131 651 6100

Bonel, Paul and Lindon, Jennie (2000) *Playwork: a guide to good practice* Nelson Thornes

Boxall, Marjorie (2002) *Nurture groups in school: principles and practice* Paul Chapman Publishing

Briggs, Freda (1995) *Developing personal safety skills in children with disabilities* Jessica Kingsley

Dorman, Helen and Dorman, Clive (2002) *The social toddler: promoting positive behaviour* The Children's Project

Elliott, Michele (ed) (2002) *Bullying: a practical guide to coping for schools*, 3rd edition, Pearsons

Elliott, Michele (1999) *Feeling happy, feeling safe* Home Office

Elliott, Michelle (2002) *Teenscape: a personal safety programme for teenagers* Department of Health/Kidscape

Fajerman, Lina, Jarrett, Michael and Sutton, Faye (2002) *Children as partners in planning: a training resource to support consultation with children* Save the Children

Fenwick, Elizabeth and Smith, Tony (1993) *Adolescence – the survival guide for parents and teenagers* Dorling Kindersley

Finch, Sue (1998) *'An eye for an eye leaves everyone blind': teaching young children to settle conflicts without violence* National Early Years Network (NEYN publications are now distributed by the National Children's Bureau)

Furedi, Frank (2001) *Paranoid parenting: abandon your anxieties and be a good parent* Penguin

Gottman, John and Declaire, Joan (1997) *The heart of parenting: how to raise an emotionally intelligent child* Bloomsbury

Hartley–Brewer, Elizabeth (1994) *Positive parenting: raising children with self esteem* Cedar

Kidscape leaflets on child protection, personal safety and dealing with bullying for children and young people. Contact them at 2 Grosvenor Gardens, London SW1W 0DH Tel: 020 7730 3300 and you can download some leaflets from the website www.kidscape.org.uk

Kindlon, Dan and Thompson, Michael (1999) *Raising Cain: protecting the emotional life of boys* Michael Joseph

Leach, Penelope (1997) *Getting positive about discipline* and *Why speak out about smacking* Barnardos Tel: 01268 520224

Lindon, Jennie (1996) *Growing up: from eight years to young adulthood* National Children's Bureau

Lindon, Jennie (1997) *Working with young children* Hodder and Stoughton (part three on behaviour and part four on partnership with parents)

Lindon, Jennie and Lindon, Lance (1997) *Working together for young children: a guide for managers and staff* Thomson Learning

Lindon, Jennie (1998) *Understanding child development: knowledge, theory and practice* Thomson Learning

Lindon, Jennie (1998) *Equal opportunities in practice* Hodder and Stoughton

Lindon, Jennie (1999) *Too safe for their own good? Helping children learn about risk and life skills* National Early Years Network

Lindon, Jennie and Lindon, Lance (2000) *Mastering counselling skills: information, help and advice in the caring services* Macmillan

Lindon, Jennie (2001) *Understanding children's play* Nelson Thornes

Lindon, Jennie (2002) *Child care and early education: good practice to support young children and their families* Thomson Learning

Mosley, Jenny (2001) *Working towards a whole school policy on self esteem and positive behaviour* Positive Press Tel: 01225 767157

Miller, Judy (1997) *Never too young: how young children can take responsibility and make decisions* NEYN and Save the Children

National Children's Bureau three related booklets with the title of *Towards a non-violent society – Checkpoints for Early years, Checkpoints for Schools* and *Checkpoints for Young People.* All can be downloaded free from the website www.ncb.org.uk/resources

National Children's Bureau Highlight (2000) *Bullying in schools* No 174

NCH Leaflet on Internet safety, download from www.nch.org.uk/itok/

NSPCC Information Briefing on Peer Support, download from section on the website for publications aimed at professionals. Also leaflets written for parents, children and young people, see the contact details on page 244 or download from the website www.nspcc.org.uk

Neall, Lucinda (2002) *Bringing out the best in boys: communication strategies for teachers* Hawthorn Press

Owen, Charlie; Cameron, Claire and Moss, Peter (1998) *Men as workers in services for young children: issues of a mixed gender workforce* Institute of Education

Paley, Vivian (1984) *Boys and girls: superheroes in the doll corner* University of Chicago Press – or any of Vivian Paley's books about play and how children want to talk about issues raised through play.

Peer Support Forum, 8 Wakley Street, London EC1V 7QE Tel: 020 7843 1160. A source of information about development in peer support schemes in schools and good practice in this area. Go in through the National Children's Bureau website www.ncb.org.uk and access through 'fora and councils'. The Forum has a publications list and some briefing papers that can be downloaded.

Pipher, Mary (1996) *Reviving Ophelia: saving the lives of adolescent girls* Vermilion

Pipher, Mary (1996) *The shelter of each other: rebuilding our families to enrich our lives* Vermilion

Play Safety Forum has published *Managing risk in play provision*, a balanced discussion about acceptable and unacceptable risk. Available from the Children's Play Council, Tel: 020 7843 6303 or download from the National Children's Bureau website in their free downloads section within publications www.ncb.org.uk

Roberts, Rosemary (2002) *Self esteem and early learning* Paul Chapman

Rogers, Bill (1991) *You know the fair rule: strategies for making the hard job of discipline in schools easier* Longman

Slaby, Ronald; Roedell, Wendy, Arezzo, Diana and Hendrix, Kate (1995) *Early violence prevention: tools for teachers of young children* National Association for the Education of Young Children – out of print now but worth looking for on a library shelf.

Smith, Peter K. and Thompson, David (1991) *Practical approaches to bullying* David Fulton

Stacey, Hilary and Robinson, Pat (1997) *Let's mediate: a teachers' guide to peer support and conflict resolution for all ages* Lucky Duck Publishing Tel: 0117 973 2881

Tattum, Delwyn and Herbert, Graham (1993) *Countering bullying: initiatives by schools and local authorities* Trentham Books

Think U Know campaign in Scotland to promote safe internet use by children and young people – material on the website www.thinkuknow.co.uk

Vine, Penny and Todd, Teresa (2000) *Ring of confidence: a quality circle time programme to support personal safety for the foundation stage* Positive Press Tel: 01225 719204

Webster–Stratton, Carolyn (1999) *How to promote children's social and emotional competence* Paul Chapman Publishing

Appendix 5: Useful organisations

Most of these organisations do not only deal with child protection, but take a broader agenda of the welfare of children, young people and their families. Some organisations are of relevance to the whole of the UK, whereas some are more applicable to one of the four countries that comprise the UK. The first set of organisations are of general interest.

Many organisations now have their own website and some offer a rich source of information, material that can be downloaded and sometimes direct links to other websites. If you are not yet adept at using the internet, it is well worthwhile assigning some time to learn.

Barnardos, Tanners Lane, Barkingside, Ilford, Essex 1G6 1QG. Barnardos Tel: 020 8550 8822 website www.Barnardos.org.uk
A national children's charity which runs a wide range of projects for children, young people and their families. The website has some briefing papers that can be downloaded.

British Association of Adoption and Fostering (BAAF) Skyline House, 200 Union Street, London SE1 0LX www.baaf.org.uk
An organisation that supports families who foster and adopt and provides information on the fostering service.

Children are unbeatable, 77 Holloway Road, London N7 8J6. Tel: 020 7700 0627/8 www.childrenareunbeatable.org.uk
An alliance of organisations and individuals who aim to bring children in the UK under the same legal right of protection against assault as adults. A source of information about the current legal situation around the UK.

Children's Legal Centre, University of Essex, Wivenhoe Park, Colchester, Essex CO4 3SQ Tel: 01206 873820 www.childrenslegalcentre.com
Publications and information about the legal position of children on a wide range of issues. Good for the legal situation as it affects the UK as a whole and England in particular.

Children's Residential Care Unit at the National Children's Bureau, 8 Wakley Street, London EC1V 7QE Tel: 020 7843 6091 www.ncb.org.uk
Source of information and research about looked after children and young people in residential care homes.

Department of Health – the source of information for statistics and the child protection system for England. However, the Quality Protects section of the website is a source for downloading briefing papers that are relevant for good practice across the UK www.doh.gov.uk

Early Education, 136 Cavell Street, London E1 2JA Tel: 020 7539 5400
www.early-education.org.uk
An organisation concerned with all aspects of young children's learning, promotes good practice in early years work.

Family Rights Group, 18 Ashwin Street, London E8 3DL. Tel: freephone 0800 731 1696 or general 020 7249 0008
An organisation that offers a telephone advice service for families whose children are involved with Social Services.

Forum on Children and Violence, 8 Wakley Street, London EC1V 7QE Tel: 020 7843 6309 go into the NCB website and access through 'Fora and Councils' www.ncb.org.uk
A Forum for information about violence towards children, by children themselves, and information on good practice in this area.

FORWARD Foundation for Women's Health, Research and Development 6th Floor, 50 Eastbourne Terrace, London W2 6LX Tel: 020 7725 2606
www.forward.dircon.co.uk
An organisation that supports women and communities to resist pressures for female genital mutilation. Their website gives information about FGM and there is also a short summary on the UNICEF website www.unicef.org.uk

Fostering Network, 87 Blackfriars Road London SE1 8HA
www.thefostering.net
Supporting the fostering service and foster carers.

4 Nations Child Policy Network, 8 Wakley Street, London EC1V 7QE Tel: 020 7843 6068/6063
A free network that provides updates on policy developments related to children and young people across the UK, not only about child protection. www.childpolicy.org.uk

Home-Start UK, 2 Salisbury Road, Leicester LE1 7QR. Tel: 0116 233 9955
An organisation that offers practical help for families under stress (not necessarily involving child protection concerns). Trained volunteers are

offered to families who would appreciate regular support. The address is that of the national office who will be able to give details for any local scheme.

Joseph Rowntree Foundation, The Homestead, 40 Water End, York YO30 6WP Tel: 01904 629241 website www.jrf.org.uk
A source of information and research projects relevant to children and young people. Some of their Findings series can be downloaded from the website.

Kidscape, 2 Grosvenor Gardens, London SW1W 0DH Tel: 020 7730 3300 www.kidscape.org.uk
A source of publications, information and advice on child protection, supporting personal safety and dealing with bullying for children and young people. Some of their leaflets can be downloaded from the website.

National Children's Bureau, 8 Wakley Street, London EC1V 7QE Tel: 020 7843 6000 www.ncb.org.uk
The NCB has a wide range of projects and publications relevant to children and their families. A number of departments, fora and councils are located within the NCB – see the website for full details. The NCB has a Library and Information Service Tel: 020 7843 6008

NCH – main office is at 85 Highbury Road, London N5 1UD Tel: 020 7226 2033 www.nch.org.uk
NCH is a national children's charity that undertakes projects, runs centres for children and their parents and publishes books and leaflets, some of which can be downloaded.

NSPCC (National Society for the Prevention of Cruelty to Children)
The national office is at 42 Curtain Road, London EC2A 3NH Tel: general 020 7825 2500, helpline for concerned adults or children: 08 08 800 5000 website www.nspcc.org.uk
A national organisation that works to protect children and promote their welfare. The NSPCC is the only national voluntary organisation authorised by law to take legal proceedings to protect a child from abuse. The NSPCC has local child protection teams and assessment services, a library at head office, a range of publications and training. The website offers information and material that can be downloaded, including leaflets for parents, children and young people. The section of the site for professionals has reading lists, information briefings and statistics.

Nurture Group Network UK, 24 Murray Mews, London NW1 9RJ Tel: 020 7485 2025 www.nurturegroups.org
Information about nurture groups in schools, designed to support children who struggle with mainstream classroom experience and help them back into class with their peers.

Parentline Plus, 520 Highgate Studios, 53–79 Highgate Road, London NW5 1TL Tel: 020 7284 5500, helpline: 0808 800 2222
email: centraloffice@parentlineplus.org.uk website: www.parentlineplus.org.uk. This organisation has brought together several parent and family support groups.

Save the Children, 17 Grove Lane, London SE5 8RD Tel: 020 7703 5400 www.savethechildren.org.uk
A national organisation committed to children and their welfare. Supports a wide range of projects and other units. For instance, *Save the Children Centre for Young Children's Rights*, 365 Holloway Road, London N7 6PA Tel: 020 7700 8127

Trust for the Study of Adolescence, 23 New Road, Brighton, East Sussex DN1 1W2 Tel: 01273 693311 www.tsa.uk.com
TSA aims to extend knowledge and understanding of adolescence and young adulthood. The organisation is a source of information about research projects and publications for young people and their families.

Young Carers Research Group, Department of Social Sciences, Loughborough University, Leicestershire LE11 3TU Tel: 01509 228 299
This group publishes a growing list of reports, books and booklets.

If you work in Wales

For information and statistics on child protection in Wales, access the website www.wales.gov.uk

Children in Wales (Plant yng Nghymru), 25 Windsor Place, Cardiff CF1 3BZ Tel: 02920 342434 www.childreninwales.org.uk
Works with organisations and professionals working with children and their families in Wales.

If you work in Scotland

For information, statistics on child protection in Scotland and publications that can be downloaded, access the website www.scotland.gov.uk

Children in Scotland (Clann An Alba), Princes House, 5 Shandwick Place, Edinburgh, EH2 4RG. Tel: 0131 228 8484 www.childreninscotland.org.uk Brings together statutory and voluntary organisations and professionals working with children and their families in Scotland.

Children 1st (previously the Royal Scottish Society for the Prevention of Cruelty to Children) 83 Whitehouse Loan, Edinburgh EH9 1AT Tel: 0131 446 2300 website www.children1st.org.uk

Scottish Child Law Centre, 1st Floor, Old College, South Bridge, Edinburgh EH8 9YL Tel: 0131 667 6333, in early 2003 a website was under development.
The centre can offer advice on legislation and legal practice in Scotland.

If you work in Northern Ireland

Child Care Unit, DHSSPS, Room 508A, Dundonald House, Belfast BT4 3SF Tel: 028 9052 4378 www.dhsspsni.gov.uk
Information about child care services and related issues in Northern Ireland. Some publications can be downloaded.

Childcare Northern Ireland, 216 Belmont Road, Belfast BT4 2AT Tel: 028 9065 2713 www.childcareni.org.uk
Can offer advice on the legal situation within the Province regarding childcare practice.

NIPPA – the Early Years Organisation, 6c Wildflower Way, Apollo Road, Belfast BT12 6TA Tel: 028 90 662825 www.nippa.org
NIPPA works with early years practitioners and services in Northern Ireland.

NSPPC – Northern Ireland, Jennymount Court, North Derby Street, Belfast BT15 3HN Tel: 028 9035 1135 www.nspcc.org.uk
Working to protect children and young people in Northern Ireland.

Index